Blanking

Blanking

An Annotated Archive of Projects and Thoughts on Architecture

Troy Schaum / Rosalyne Shieh

PARK BOOKS

Blanking

Rosalyne Shieh

Blank

A piece of material fashioned into an approximate shape. An element or part which can be further worked or tooled according to criteria. Stock prepared to be articulated into a range of specific forms. Blanks point to possible outcomes; their shapes embody a state of becoming.

We initially borrowed the term *blank* to think around and beyond sites and buildings deemed obsolete, in decline, or illegible. In these instances, *blank* quiets assessments that frame architecture as a solution and recognizes projects as processes in which building takes part. Blanking is about learning and figuring from what there is to what is possible. It's a way of thinking with a site, a means to direct interventions, adjustments, and additions. It is also a way of orienting ourselves in thought and work toward the continual suspension of judgment and the holding of space for drawing out and drawing into the site. *Blank* makes two provocations: to be present enough to see what is there and to be guided by your obligations.

Softness

A poet friend once said to me: "I remember being so young, when the beginning of my life was so near, it was just here, you know? Like, right behind my eyes." They described it as "that world where you can see something you are 'about' to understand." For me this resonates with an old feeling, a way of being, unspeaking—not necessarily before speech, but a way of knowing connected to observation. Being observant in this way is also being present, and it is quiet but deliberate. There is desire and expectation, there is hope, and also something like trust.

It's a way of looking associated with youth and also with vulnerability, where the possibility of understanding your environment or the people around you, of connecting with something outside yourself, is bound up with your survival. And when it happens, a sense of discernment is sometimes paired with a physical

francine j. harris

pleasure of that connection, *like when your body learns something how much of your senses come alive*, which may be expressed in a deep breath, an unwitting smile, or even a burst of laughter.

Can we choose to look this way upon our surroundings? Can hopeful, trustful looking be a way of knowing a place? And what should we look for?

Ruth Wilson Gilmore

What the world will become already exists in fragments and pieces, experiments and possibilities. We can look for fragments and pieces of the world we want, like instances where we witness softness in face of so much hardness, in face of all the glorification of harshness. Acts of care and protection are expressions of softness, but concession and certain kinds of passivity can also be. Seeing softness where it already exists is a way to begin, and it's an exercise that can be repeated until it becomes habit, until softness is at home within us. This is a way of coming to know a place that can be operative when we decide to ask: What is softness in envisioning? Seeing softness can be a precursor to envisioning softness, as we figure out what can be extended, fortified, or amended.

Instead of a total vision, let's seek glimpses of the world we want where they already exist, even if they are partial or tenuous visions. These are the pieces from which we can imagine ever-larger swaths where people can live together. Visions in place are seeded and cultivated from the ground up, and they begin with a willful hopefulness as we look into the blankness of what can be. Blanking is softness in seeing. Cultivating softness might be a method for architecture.

Attachment

Imagine architecture centered on becoming sensitive to where we are or whom we are with. Knowing a site would involve getting close to it, in the way you might become close to something or someone, like the way living beings become attached to each other, or how people or animals become attached to a place.

The example I carry is that of my great-uncle, who lived in a village of seventeen households in the countryside of southern Taiwan. Regardless of the time of day, whenever we dropped by, we'd find him sitting under the large tree that grew between the road and the gate in front of his house. The tree was old, impressive in height and girth; it rose up and fanned out into a broad canopy. Chek-kong would sit on a white plastic chair in the tree's protective range, the two of them together, like a child and grandparent. I don't remember how the information came to me, but Chek-kong's death arrived soon after news the tree had been cut down.

We can recognize love or empathy, and we might use those words to describe a relationship like this, but what is the route to arrive at and maintain such a connection between people, living beings, and the environment? Can we imagine it as an intentional process? Instead of knowing a place, can we talk about attaching to a place? For designers—those who would intervene—it may be a tool for meeting new sites, new contexts, and an aspiration for any project.

Believing is a precondition for attachment. It is true with people, and it is also true when we approach a site. We arrive in belief, knowing some things are there that we do not—cannot—yet see. We proceed with an assumption that the place has value; we pay attention, observe, listen, and ask questions. This can sustain an inquiry and drive a project; it is also a way of sustaining relationships.

The explicit task is to bring what knowledge we have to each situation but recognize that what we bring can also make it hard to see what and whom we are meeting. It can even reshape, distort, or erase. What may appear nonsensical or irrelevant is not evidence of disorder or dysfunction, instead, these are signs of things we do not yet understand. At sites or in conditions which ask for our attention, when we register emptiness or lack, it may be that we are not seeing *another state... already present.* Henri Bergson

The knowledge of place I am after is the kind that comes with attachment. Like how my great-uncle knew that tree, not what he knew *about* the tree, but the way he lived in relation to it, was sensitive to it. He was close spatially and emotionally, maybe so much so that when the tree died, his attachment to life also eroded. The relationship—between a person and a tree, alive and together in time and location, their connection a tether both fragile and life-giving—gives us something to aspire to. I hold it as a precious example of mutuality between a person and their environment.

In places where it appears there is "nothing to see," the blankness asks us to find other ways to sense those relationships, and to refrain from projecting into a perceived emptiness. The blank reminds me to hold and protect sites as not-yet-known or unknowable. This is different than empty.

Rosalyne Shieh, *Untitled (Chàp-it hūn)* (2017)

Note

Erratum

The image caption on page nine contains a misspelling; an incorrect diacritic was used. The caption should read:

Rosalyne Shieh, *Untitled (Cháp-it hūn)* (2017)

Cháp-it hūn, which translates to *Eleven parcels* or *Eleventh parcel*, is a Taiwanese place name written in Pe̍h-ōe-jī (POJ), a romanization system developed by missionaries in Southeast Asia in the 19th century. The vertical line diacritic is a tone marking not available within the font and has been drawn in manually for the purposes of this note.

Pr

In 2009, … etroit, forty miles away, was a
significar… distinct neighbor to my college
town. De… t in the architecture and urban
planning… al, I tried to sort out the ways
people v… ects, urbanists, and planners (or
anyone… ere talking, and more the chatter
that exi… or generally online. Things you
might h… offee shops, in restaurants and at
the bar… proach, assumptions, the general
attitud…

…*iction*, *blight*, *vacancy*, *emptiness*,
disapp… oregone conclusion. The story of
Detro… repeated, followed by an urgency
for it… Detroit—of unoccupied buildings
and f… the case for large-scale clearances,
even… his route would clear the land and
pave… nd re-densify for a new population,
a ge… journalist would distill these rum-
blin… is is a dereliction that spreads like
disease through a body, … n effective treatment would target
the illness by abatement and containment. As I listened to their cries, I thought we should at least ask: What ills can be brought on by a healer?

Iatrogenesis: the unintentional causation of disease or injury during the process of providing medical care

Our experience of the city contrasted with the dire proclamations. In the time we spent in northeast Detroit, the streets were mostly calm, but during the long days building the installation on Moran Street, we regularly encountered neighbors. After school and before dinner, when we were breaking and packing up, small groups of children would come around and stop outside the house. They would look on in curiosity and sometimes ask a few questions before running off. The city wasn't teeming with activity, but there was a quiet presence, a daily rhythm of living, a sense of place as it breathes and is alive in time. This would have been plain to anyone who spent even a few hours there, but the negative chatter was doing the work of interference, getting in the way of people feeling Detroit's vitality.

Blankness is establishing and allowing presence, and in that presence, sensing the aliveness of a place.

Catie Newell, *Untitled (13178 Moran Street, Detroit, MI)* (2009)

Obligations

I am haunted by my grandmother. Her life in its time and place was ordinary, yet a world apart from the one I have trained in as an architect, not only because the location is an ocean away from where I was born and raised, but because hers was a life marked by earthly survival and an early demise.

Garnette Cadogan, speaking on memory and landscape, asks us to consider: "How do we contain each other?" and reminds us that "we will never know, we will never understand… in light of that, what then are our obligations?" Under this term, *obligations*, some ideas and impulses that I had been holding on to finally found shape.

Images of her come to me wrapped in the timbre and cadence of my father's sometimes wavering voice. He was just nine years old when she died, and his stories are an amalgamation of what he experienced, what he intuited, and what he's been told. Some tales about my grandmother were repeated: she was a young bride crying inside a palanquin behind her new and strange home; she was limp with illness, pressed upright in a train packed with migrants; she craved a prized orange, but was again too sick to enjoy it when Akong brought one home after a long day on his pedicab. When I listen more deeply, I also feel a sensation of the stillness of her person as she was dying of tuberculosis: sitting upon the bed, arms folded around her knees, head down, her labored breath, a bowl at her feet. A barefoot child standing nearby, quiet in his small body.

What is the purpose of memories delivered to us across time? In one person's accounts, a chorus speaks. What might that chorus be asking of us? I've decided that the telling and retelling is a kind of insistence, an incantation that conjures my grandmother and the many voices that link me to her. *Haunting is a frightening experience. It always registers the harm inflicted or the loss sustained by a social violence done in the past or in the present.* To be haunted suggests that the ghost is near, even following you, and I think about what it means to turn around and follow her back. *Haunting, unlike trauma, is distinctive for producing a something-to-be-done.*

Avery Gordon

What started as fascination and longing becomes something more pressing as I walk alongside my grandmother's ghost while envisioning lives and places I don't yet know. *The willingness to follow ghosts, neither to memorialize nor to slay, but to follow where they lead, in the present, head turned backwards and forwards at the same time. To be haunted in the name of a will to heal is to allow the ghost to help you imagine what was lost that never even existed, really. That is its utopian grace: to encourage a steely sorrow laced with delight for what we lost that we never had; to long for the insight of that moment in which we recognize* [...] *that it could have been and can be otherwise.*

Journeying together prompts me to ask: What is a world in which she may have survived? Thrived? While I don't know for sure, I presume it would look different than one in which manufactured scarcity keeps people poor and barely able to live while resources are continually extracted. I believe it would look different than one in which self-determination is choked by societal norms, and life is a series of potential disasters beyond one's control. I envision it as a place where everyone, in their community, has access to resources for continued life and self-protection.

These imaginings reach to the edges of my vision, a place from which I don't know how to return to a daily practice. But the incommensurability of there and here feels important. Unmappable, vast, and without scale, it is an existential blankness.

I don't exactly know how to cross this divide, but some things make me feel like I'm getting a little closer. When approaching sites, the ghost of my grandmother reminds me to see who is there, what already exists, however small it is, and to listen carefully. It reminds me to wait until my understanding shifts, and then wait some more. It frames my work as doing what I can to bring about a world in which she might have survived, which can feel so ambitious and complex as to seem impossible or absurd, but also gives shape to something larger than a vocation.

Blanking is being open to haunting, to acknowledging parts of yourself that cannot be reconciled, and to always be deepening your practices of listening and observation. This may also be a practice of *withholding judgment as a tool for making later judgments more sensitive.*

Venturi, Scott Brown, Izenour

Rage

We seem to be living in a prolonged crisis punctuated by individual crises that build, one after the other. This fuels a baseline of distress in me that growls open with every piece of horrific news, particularly reports of the disregard for life, for whole categories of bodies, for entire communities. It also produces an urgency to open and extend, to take tight hold of my people and my world, their people and their worlds. And when I am overwhelmed by a sense of injustice and fear, a lack of agency, the distress overflows into anger and I look for ways to dissipate the uncomfortable emotion. I might even gather myself, identify targets, and arm myself to push back.

This progression tracks the shape of *rage*. At an extreme, rage can elicit a desire to "burn it all down," a response to destruction that only begets more. But arriving at destruction may be a simple misdirection, an undisciplined reaction to an energy untamed. Rage doesn't have to be ruinous, it may even be useful if we can harness it. I think of the question, *How do you use your rage?* Audre Lorde

Because rage is pure power in movement. I would like for us to recognize, to tune and direct this power, to understand it as a variable force. Take notice and track its intensity, sense the gathering of tension before it becomes overwhelming. Rage comes in waves; as it crests, we can identify and note the feeling, so the next time it mounts, we can try holding it at a constant intensity or sliding down with its subsidence. If we understand rage as a muscular activity, we can train ourselves to expand and contract it, explore its mobility, and stretch its range, direct its force.

And perhaps we can apply it to the urgency of that *something-to-be-done*, in response to that haunting *in the name of a will to heal.* My rage is the strength I bring with me as I follow my grandmother's ghost, which conjures lives lost, losses that were preventable and avoidable, losses that *are* preventable and avoidable. What is a world where no amount of devastation is acceptable, one without collateral damage?

Blank works against the idea that some amount of destruction is unavoidable, even necessary, by redirecting rage away from treating situations as ones to be corrected, eradicated, or expelled. It is about finding ways to move within the *brokenness*. It quiets problematization as a framework and channels force and action into creation and discernment. It is a strategy of diverting energy to honor obligations, of surviving without supplanting, of building without erasure. Fred Moten and Stefano Harney

Disarticulation

We often think of building in types—park, house, museum, theater. Each invokes an image of form and use that is certain yet indefinite. In the U.S. context, a landscape dominated by postwar suburban development, the single-family home is ubiquitous: a stand-alone building with a collection of bedrooms reflecting the structure of the nuclear family, where spatial relationships manage internal and external expectations of this social unit.

The single-family home binds form, privacy, property, and propriety into each other. Abundant, normative, and bland, it is standard architectural stock. How can we use it to imagine other ways of living? Some amount of undoing can be a useful approach.

On undoing, and how and what to work toward, I think of Eve Kosofsky Sedgwick writing about literature and queerness: *It's been a ruling intuition for me that the most productive strategy (intellectually/emotionally) might be to disarticulate them one from another, to disengage them—the bonds of blood, of law, of habitation, of privacy, of companionship and succor—from the lockstep of their unanimity in the system called "family."*

Disarticulation is a mechanism for creation, a way to work from something closed toward something else, different or even excessive. Sedgwick gives us an idea of what that thing might be when she describes *one of the things that "queer" can refer to: the open mesh of possibilities, gaps, overlaps, dissonances and resonances, lapses and excesses of meaning when the constituent elements of anyone's gender, of anyone's sexuality aren't made (or can't be made) to signify monolithically.* The *open mesh of possibilities* is a spatial provocation; in the architecture of domestic spaces, it's a provocation for the very ordinary processes of daily living, of bodies sleeping and eating, bathing and grooming, alone and gathered, watching and being watched, lying around, just spending time, in action and at rest.

Disarticulation can liberate in as many ways as we can imagine: types into figures and forms or pure quantities. For instance, instead of a house for a family, how many beds, toilets, and bathing areas are there, and how far apart are they? What is the total volume of storage and how is it distributed? What are the areas of conditioned space, unconditioned space, and outdoor space; what is their ratio and distance? How many lines are there in and out, and what is the distribution of points or zones of access? We can think of these elements separately and how they work together and scale in supporting a range of bodily and social requirements, their selection and interplay open to variation and chance, based on specific needs, wants, or aversions.

This idea partly retraces Archizoom's *No Stop City* (1968), where architecture as quantity is taken to an extreme; plans are abstract field distributions of atomized parts—structural grids, partitions, bathrooms, furniture—famously made on a typewriter, and resembling diagrams of geographical strata or the interior of animal cells. Refuting architecture as a "functional figuration of society," they declared: "The only possible utopia is quantitative."

The project is thrilling as a polemic; what remains useful is the method of creating artifacts from existing ones to propose architectures that radically exceed models we have. When engaging architectural type, I'm interested in taking things apart in a manner that may transform existing models to end up with more than what we started with: more difference, more positions, more meanings, more possibilities, more ways of being together and alone, with more ways in and more ways out.

Blanking is an undoing and remaking in which types are not ideals or places to end up, but instead supply a formal-conceptual stock with which to work, places to begin—blanks, if you will. Blanking takes building as something created by moving against dissatisfaction in pursuit of something more.

Language

Though I wasn't born there, when we talk about going to Taiwan, we describe it as a return: *Lí kám bat tńg--khì?* (Have you ever gone back?)

Tńg--khì orients me toward a place that is elsewhere and suggests a shared identity across there and here. The question is a gesture of inclusion; it implies a conception of self to which preceding generations are integral, and a relationship between identity and location that is at least double. *Tńg--khì* invites me to belong to a place I haven't been. The response to this question can be to reciprocate: *Iáu-bōe.* (Not yet.) Or to decline: *M̄-bat.* (Never.)

Accepting the invitation establishes consent to exchange, and to a reciprocal socialization, because belonging is not a recruitment of the foreign by the native, but something created between parties. It's not about the claims a group have on a place, but a mutual discernment that creates a sense of kinship connected to a place which is elsewhere. A model for this is a net or mesh, where the community grows not with the number of members, but with the number of connections between members.

I wonder how this might help us consider the terms of engagement in the studio or the classroom, where speaking is so much a part of the culture. Maybe language as a community practice can inform a pedagogy that supports both individual ideation and creativity, as well as movement of the group in willing and coordinated ways. This would also be relevant to professional collaboration. A spirit of invitation might lead to less analysis and judgment and more curiosity and reflection. Because the goal is not a single predetermined destination, but a healthy arrival by many to more varied destinations that fill out a greater range of potential.

Thinking about projects, words can be invitations to worlds we need. In Detroit, as a willful envisioning, we described the site and the city as "prepared" to counter the loud narratives of decline and vacancy. This led to observing, recording, and extending what we found there, to imagine intervention not as projection, but as amplification and growth of existing activities, a model for collaboration between architecture and place.

The words are purposes. / The words are maps. —Adrienne Rich

The craft of language and communication are tools for organizing and collecting ideas, following instincts and feelings, and honoring values. We can use these tools to describe or point toward something that is not yet clear. Blanking uses language to think toward visions and around ideas that feel meaningful. Blanking is speech as an invitation.

Chorus

In 2012 Troy and I went to see Robert Wilson and Philip Glass in conversation at the State Theatre in Ann Arbor. They were kicking off a national tour of *Einstein on the Beach*, which was being performed for the first time in twenty years. Onstage, they spoke about the genesis of the project and how they set the operatic form early on, which allowed each to work separately and then come together—a way of being able to create freely and meet in the work. It was an articulation of form not as container but as a structure for collaboration and cooperation.

It's an ethos that transfers to the opera itself. Four acts unfold over four and a half hours in a succession of atmospheric textures arising from the interaction between coordinated but independent elements: music, bodies in motion, words spoken and sung, lines and volumes of the set, its areas of light and darkness. Within this, Einstein—the nominal subject—appears as a recurring icon among figures who are distinct and clearly delineated, but without specific identity. Changes in movement and sound, in repetition and variation, set and shift patterns of convergence and recurrence. Transitions produce a sense of development without story, appealing to experience over linear narrative. The distance between elements produces an openness the audience is invited to inhabit. No specific demands are made for the viewer to follow or understand; Glass and Wilson explicitly invite the audience to come and go as needed.

In the creative process and the resulting work, there is a slackness between what is shared and the demands on individual attention. What does this leave room for? Maybe private thoughts, associative images, or even an unthinking presence. A measure of freedom is preserved for departing into daydream, contradictions between feelings and appearances, for communing with one's ghosts or shifting into the weight of one's obligations. Maybe openness holds space for the individual and protects their *right to complex personhood*, while facilitating a way to come together with others in a shared experience or a collective pursuit.

Avery Gordon

This openness could be a prescription for pedagogy or collaboration. It is relevant to the practice of architecture to the extent that building is a process of many conversations between different actors. In those conversations, I wonder how it is possible to draw from what we've inherited or lost, for our voices to contain a chorus when we speak, such that we can better give shape and force to our responsibilities, hopes, and imaginations. Maybe collaboration can be like music, where song and silence come together in curious ways.

Speaking about *Einstein* in 2009, Glass said: "The process was the piece... the subject was about how the piece was made."

Blanking is a strategy that became a practice. It started with finding structured ways to talk with one another, then writing together, and further transformed with assembling an exhibition to share with others, all in the pursuit of making architecture; it was always about searching for ways to contribute in a collective project without losing our individual voices or our divergent motivations. The collaborative process, as it has manifested over the course of our practice—the sorting and structuring of activities, the conversations, the ideas, and the outcomes of practicing architecture—is what we have tried to gather in this book.

Icehouse at Raven Tower (2015)

Geology

accrual
accretion
obtuse
denature
(out)growth
coax
train
structure
inflect
(re)route
mound
direct
tune
armature
aliveness
life
excess
refraction

What opens up when we take the built environment as both thing and process? It becomes obtuse, mute, inscrutable, but is slowly expressive; still, there is not much certainty about what it is expressing. The accretion of material, nested scales of time, relations of building and landscape furnish context and material for working.

Robert Rauschenberg, *The Lily White* (ca. 1950)

How do we move beyond thinking of human-made structures in opposition to natural ones?

What if we foreground the city as experience?

Isn't all architecture animal architecture?

The city is a geological formation. How do we proceed with this assumption?

If we look for structural and material patterns, how is activity and movement structured within and against these?

When we turn to smaller areas or the single lot, can we frame architecture as the construction of a site within which individual buildings appear?

Can the aim of an architectural project be to make sense of its context? Is this a way of achieving a sense of place?

When conceptualizing a building, how is its aging considered?

Quadtych (clockwise from upper left): Troy Schaum, *Jodphur Quarry* (2022); Rosalyne Shieh, *Untitled (Penghu)* (2017); Rosalyne Shieh, *Untitled (Penghu)* (2017); Anne Marie D'Arcy, *Untitled* (2016)

Troy Schaum, *Kaohsiung Silos* (2011)

Rather notice, mon cher,
that the moon is
tilted above
the point of the steeple
than that its color
is shell-pink.
Rather observe
that it is early morning
than that the sky
is smooth
as a turquoise.

—from “To a Solitary Disciple,” William Carlos Williams (1916)

Note

The city as a geological object

To think about the city as a geological object is to ask: What are its structures, what are its patterns, and what are the histories of their formation? It is a frame for seeing the stuff: hard and soft, pocketed or cavernous, stringy or brittle. A heterogeneous layering of textures, fills, and clearings. It is also a way of loving on the plastic experience of architecture, from the staid bulk of a stout corner tower to the rattling slats of a rolldown storefront, all the way down to paper and plastic discards that lurk in the dead corners of a block. It's a way of being curious about the stories and the soft bodies who have lived within it, but at a distance of several generations of material encrustation. It doesn't replace other ways of seeing—city as ruin, city as body, city as house, among others—these highlight qualities and relationships that can also be useful. It may be another frame for approaching the city (or building) with a sense of wonder, a recalibration of our responses along the axes of puzzlement and delight. Most cities in existence range in age from a few hundred to a few thousand years, and the long-temporal view of their geology is a view from afar, akin to the bird's eye... but instead of a survey at a sweeping distance, it is a survey at a sweeping timescale.

... let the soft animal of your body / love what it loves. —Mary Oliver

The city in geological view is made up of all the matter that is not currently alive, though much of it is molded to support, organize, or control that which is alive within it. The city is mountain and landscape, desert and marsh, it is plains or outcropping, it has form and texture, it changes with climate and weather. In the morning haze, amplified by steam issuing from its holds, its profile flattens against a desaturated sky in a chilly, wet calm. In the late afternoon, indirect light bathes the tops of the buildings in a neon glow, the rest of its mass drops down into a dim muddiness; in this view the surface of the street is all but indiscernible.

About Face (2012)

TS This idea of a blank, which we're exploring in the book, is something that has a certain embedded intelligence: there's a material blank built into it that you revisit again and again, and it produces innovation. But the blank also exists as a prepared site for work. And you can see a tentativeness about the question of autonomy and the way it's interpreted in our subjectivities as authors and designers. I remember in the Formalisms class you taught at Princeton, one of the first slides just said, *Whose formalism?* So you, too, have that question of autonomy, even as it starts to get interpreted through the individual author or the individual site or the individual situation. The certainty or the confidence that an autonomous project brings begins to break down or unravel in ways that produce invention.

SW I like that unraveling can be a positive thing. When you were teaching your Iconomics studio [at Rice School of Architecture], essentially the "assembly of parts," there was a sense of attention to form and how different forms live together. In your housing studios, it was how the different units fit together. In Shenandoah House and Transart, too, there is the idea of allowing multiple forms to happen at once. And yet you never lose the fact that there's a whole thing. And so there's a formal conversation going on, among the parts and the whole, but it's not a typical part-to-whole argument, which is inevitable in any building. It's a deliberate idea of how do you talk about forms coming together and creating some sort of whole that acknowledges them? I'm interested in a plural audience, and yet one that is not totally atomized as total individuals, and I think your work speaks to this notion of plurality.

TS Lars [Lerup] would often comment that my studios' work would set up a kind of autonomous system and then break it in some way, or there'd be a rupture. At some moment the projects were irreducible to the original kernel of the initial diagram. I liked that. I thought that in the space of the rupture or the break of the system was the potential to understand a voice of an author or an individual designer. What had been previously translated into a completely formal geometric, systematic, parametric logic was coming through.

SW I'm not crazy about the terms *break* or *rupture*. Because they imply that what's required for good work is some wild act that is totally illogical and totally artistic. What I prefer about what you're saying is, yes, it's a sort of authorship. It's judgment. It's a moment of saying, "Okay, I've set up a system, but the system isn't going to solve everything for me; I actually need to go in and manipulate it." So I don't see it as much as a rupture as I see it as your own directed authorship and control of moving a project where it should go.

TS And this is where it does relate to the teaching and some things we worked on together in Totalization [studio at Rice]: you have the construction of a diagram, a geometric diagram, a formal diagram, that's the kind of ideal system. And then you have the problem of the real; a line has a thickness, and a wall now has performance requirements. And in that space between that ideal and the real, maybe *break* is too pejorative of a word, but there's an opportunity for interpretation. We know from looking at my peers and looking through history that every architect or group of architects takes that opportunity differently.

One moment, it seems like an idealized thing. And then you get into it. The walls are thick in the case of Transart because of its wood construction, and it has a certain R-value for Houston's climate. And those kinds of things actually start to matter in how you understand the diagram.

SW That's absolutely true. And I like that framing of it. What often happens in school is you have some ideal, and then the act of changing and advancing that ideal into a project seems somehow to dilute it. I hear it often framed as a compromise. And I agree with you that instead, it's actually an opportunity. It's not where my own strengths lie; I didn't come with that same knowledge that you had. But I find it is a source of continual excitement if you see construction not as a compromise but as an opportunity. It's where invention *has* to happen, because you have to figure out how you're actually going take your work from A to B. And that's where you were perfect for Totalization and for saying, "This is a comprehensive studio, we have to buckle down and not put our ideas onto the back burner."

TS Speaking of ideas: when we met I was taking Peter Eisenman's studio, a seminar with Bob Somol, and your Formalisms seminar. It was 2005; *Log* 5 had come out maybe a year before. That publication had put you in the center of a conversation that I see as shifting how we thought about instrumentalizing history and context, a leveling of precedent and potentiality, something that was bringing the potential for multiple subjectivities to exist and new futures to emerge. How do you see that time and those ideas now?

SW I think you're right; it was a shift or maybe a loosening. You know that I was deeply influenced both by Peter and Rem [Koolhaas]. So, I was facing the challenge of how do you take Peter's project of formal autonomy and disciplinary knowledge—and I'm deeply invested in that; the Formalisms seminar was dependent on it—and marry that with an attention to program and new ways of living that Rem brings to practice? It was a super exciting challenge. Maybe it was inevitable to ask because a part of that shift was a hunger to produce work that would get built, a collective desire to move beyond paper architecture.

TS One of the things we've tried to do with the practice, which also might speak to that period, your *Log* 5 piece and what could be called a projective moment: there were producers—architects who we were all very excited about, who really invested in material, technological investigation, and invention in really beautiful ways. But their buildings—the overall form was a little more restrained, so that the material expression could be more present. And then we still had these more formally expressive architects, where materiality and invention were less critical. My sense was that we were in a kind of "red pill, blue pill" moment, deciding between the two modes of practice. I was never quite comfortable with making that decision, and was concerned that those two strategies might cancel each other out in some way. That's probably not the case—if you really get into it, there's a lot of material invention in a Frank Gehry project, for instance. But the idea that those two things had to operate separately is something we considered seriously then and still think about.

SW Totally. And I do think there are some people who got through that split. For example, Nader's [Tehrani] best work combines his material interest with formal, expressive invention. Though, I don't know if I would draw it so cleanly because I think it's always going to be a question of scale of project and client. For example, with your Shenandoah project, you were able to work with a client who believed in you and allowed for that productive combination of approaches. Same with Transart. Look at Johnston Marklee or Michael Maltzan, who I think are probably more comparable to the world that you're in. Although I still think you work in multiples, and they tend to work in singularities.

And how does program play into it? I'm not sure where program affects your work now, but I remember in your graduate thesis, which I advised, you were dealing with how program can catalyze form. In your practice, is it more about form and audience, and multiple audiences, and less about the program? I might be wrong, or it may be a question of the programs you've been working with. They are less visible or catalytic, it seems to me. It's not a criticism, more of a curiosity.

TS One project is very close to how I operated in my thesis. Early in our practice, we collaborated with Albert [Pope] on the Kaohsiung Pop Music Center, where program became—through a moving subject and the way we articulated the grid—a generator of these formal nodes that then were sculpted by movement. So form, the moving subject, and the program were all clearly articulated in that project. And then the way the collective program occupied what we called the "Wet Plaza," which was the old harbor, was really present.

"The program" is such a corporatization of how we inhabit buildings. Can we condense everything that we think about how we inhabit buildings into a kind of corporate unit? Rem was able to subtly critique this through exacerbation, really leaning into program. We have had a lot of opportunities to do projects that deal with more atomized moments of inhabitation. How do you inhabit an outdoor balcony at the White Oak Music Hall, so you can enjoy a break between sets with your friends or watch a performance? There are moments in Transart where you can find little spaces where the gallerist can hide away and have intimate conversations with artists. Spaces like these are much more atomized; I'm not sure they can scale up to the term "program," which seems so weighty.

SW There are two things that are interesting there. One, the Kaohsiung competition, it's funny that you bring that up, because if you remember, we [WW Architects] actually submitted a project that had parallels to yours. We were working separately, but we both ended up with projects with round buildings that were atomized in a certain way and related to one another.

TS Tank farms of Houston, sneaking into our imaginations, perhaps. [laughs]

SW Exactly. And also, if I think of White Oak, or Transart, or the Shenandoah House, program translates to inhabitation or what it means to be, spaces that you can inhabit as one or as a crowd, as opposed to program being something that's saying, "How would I rethink domesticity?" or, "How would I rethink the theater?" Rather than critiquing the idea of an institution, it seems that you are saying, "Okay, how do you actually consider the world and how we live in it?" And that comes back to the fact that you came into your academic project and your office after a lot of experience. You had very serious training as an architect before you came back into academia. And so you're knowledgeable about how things come together, whereas a lot of people teaching haven't taken the time to invest in that level of practice. Architecture is much harder than we sometimes make it out to be in academia and as historians. Realizing the challenges, but also the excitement of those challenges is something different.

Additionally, you also seem to be very affected by the question of occupying a space. What does it mean to be in a space? What does it mean to be going through a space? It is a reflection of a real desire to make work that works.

TS Work that works for individuals as well as ideas. [laughs] In response to your program question, I think there are a few approaches to answering it. Here's another: I did a whole series of studios, Friends Included, where I was investigating the influence of the internet of things. WeWork, WeLive, examining how we understand the fundamentals of domesticity. It was an opportunity to come at that question differently. Many, many, many of the assumptions we have about domesticity were built at the emergence of the Industrial Revolution, when people started moving into cities and living together in apartment blocks. But perhaps now we're at another kind of revolution—and is that pushing us to rethink some of our assumptions about privacy, domesticity, and how we live together? That pressure was something that, to link it back to that relationship between program and form that you're identifying in my thesis work, I think was certainly in my teaching. I am still searching for a commission at scale to really address this.

SW The Shenandoah House, in a way, does address it. I don't think that it's how you're pitching it. But the idea that these different blocks come together, that you look at the house as an aerial view and think, I have no idea where the kitchen is. But I haven't looked at the plans enough to think, How does that fluidity work? How does that self-similarity play out in the house's occupation?

TS That is a careful reading of the plan. It is probably the project in which we've had the most diagrammatic, programmatic control over plan-making. There's a line that follows the contour. Things like the kitchen, the primary bedroom, and the living room that are more public, closer to the views, and more exposed on the site, on the downhill side. And things that are more private end up on the uphill side. Then we have a series of roof forms that tie across that division, and we carefully paired the rooms formally. So a clear unfolding of a programmatic diagram is achieved. Not all our projects scale up, but I think that's an idea that could. I'd be curious to see how it would work out. As it is, it's only a 2,500-square-foot house.

SW Wow, that's interesting. Yet it has so many pieces of exterior wall!

TS Exactly. Which is why it is a simple synthetic stucco envelope. It is not an expensive project, as houses by architects go. But it has a certain monumental character.

SW That's a good word for it. That's always been my admiration of the original Menil Collection building: it's both monumental and intimate. That's so hard to pull off, especially on an urban site. It's a little easier to do it when you don't have neighbors nearby—you've got a lot of open space around Shenandoah—but it's still a question.

But beyond monumentality, how do works affect the city they're in? Transart is very curious to me. The facade that one always thinks is the front is actually the side, and that's a given because of the geometry of the site and where the parcel was. But I think about that, and then White Oak has a challenge in that it's essentially a building that's a little bit isolated. It doesn't have nearby neighbors, or maybe it does by now.

TS Partly because of my background in practice, our firm has been really focused on getting things built from the moment we started, in spite of all the constraints. In that environment, maybe we've had less control over some things. What I was describing as the break or the unraveling before was actually looking for those opportunities and the seams between things, rather than, say, being able to overtly do a programmatic analysis as you might at an institutional building. And the same thing's true with a project's urbanism. Both of those projects are evolving at different scales. Surpik [Angelini, director of the Transart Gallery for Art & Anthropology] has acquired the empty lot next door and wants to expand. So now it is a 100-by-100-foot property instead of a rectangle, so in four or five years there'll be another orientation to Transart. This continual expansion seems very Houston in a way, too. But you could see how the initial project emerges as much from the constraints of the city, like parking zoning, as it does from more autonomous questions of frontality or other kinds of urban legibility. Then, in White Oak Music Hall, we knew we wanted to orient the amphitheater to the bayou. And so we pushed the building as close as we could to the street, which actually was part of the engagement with the urban planning of Main Street. But that was just the beginning of a project that started with 1.5 acres, and by the time the project was built, it was on 6 acres, spanning across the bayou.

SW Oh, wow. I didn't realize that.

TS I wanted to come back to another piece of your work that I think was influential to us. I think about your writing on Chicago in "Superblockism" and "Bas-Relief Urbanism" as trying to understand a fluidity between the building, the individual author, the architect, and the idea of a collective something at an urban scale. That sensitivity is a sensitivity that, if you look at the work we did in Detroit, if you look at the work we did in Kaohsiung, if you see how we understand site and how we try to talk about site, that sensitivity is something that you helped our generation think about. What seems like a contradiction is actually a productive tool for making the city and making architecture.

SW The other piece I would point you to is my conversation with Peter on engaged autonomy in *Log* 28, the idea that something is autonomous, but it's not singular; it's engaged. What I like about how you're describing Transart and White Oak in terms of their sites is you didn't go to Houston and say, "Oh, I'm in Houston. I'll fetishize the car. I'll talk about the car in parking lots." Which I find is, at this point, a little bit tired and also a little sad to elevate, because ideally we're not elevating an oil economy. But speaking of Texas projects, I also want to talk about Marfa.

TS You and Guy [Nordenson] introduced me to Flavin and Rainer Judd in Marfa, and it has now become a long-term project to restore Donald Judd's buildings there.

SW That work in Marfa is very interesting because it at once acts as acupuncture, fixing something that's there, but it also offers a vision that starts to master plan a whole lot of separate pieces. It's also been interesting to see how you are collaborating with art practices, which actually are sympathetic to the work that you've always been doing but haven't been an overt part, unlike people who started off by doing galleries.

TS Through this work, a huge proportion of our practice has become engaged with artists and art sites in precarious locations. We have been working with Carol Bove Studio, whose work we deeply admire, along the banks of the Hudson River. We also did work with the Jodhpur Art Center in the desert in Rajasthan. So, we have a kind of technical preservation practice situated in sites that require innovative approaches to environmental adaptation. It's been interesting reflecting on problems like audience, permanence, and especially questions of autonomy translated into these charged but often remote contexts.

Speaking with Flavin about his father's work, he says he thinks his father imagined that project as just a demonstration of what one person could do in a life. I'm fascinated by authorship and what constitutes authorship. And what constitutes the power of the voice of an individual. We're always thinking about how we represent the collective, how we make an architecture for the collective, how we're part of a collective, how it's many people's projects. In this case, there's a huge collective that works. But what is the importance of an individual voice in the face of a collective, especially a collective that could be not always or only a good thing? Like how does one voice become a voice of resistance in the collective?

SW That's a very important question right now, because we recently experienced a long backlash against the individual voice in architecture. And so, under the rubric of being against star architecture—and this goes back to why I prefer authorship to *break*, because *break* sounds like it's chance, accidental, as opposed to deliberate. It is the deliberate judgment of knowing when to stop a system, how to change a system, how to modify a system, how to modify a building toward its site. That is why I keep saying we can't have every studio have collaborative work. Because you need to, as a student, develop your own voice, even if you develop respect for the fact that you're always working in a team. That is a really important message for schools right now.

TS It goes back to the potentiality and the possibility that certainly got me excited about the project of "the projective" back at Princeton. How do you make space for something new? Or the imagination of something new? And sometimes, maybe it's a Donald Judd or Theaster Gates or another voice who shows us the possibility of seeing a space differently.

SW And I don't think that always has to be so crazy that it shocks us into the new, I think we've moved beyond the idea that the new has to always be avant-garde and radical. The new can sometimes be very, very gentle, and it can range to being something more extreme.

TS I always tell my students that architecture, in general, operates in registers that are pretty subtle. Things that look on paper like they're not that bold actually, if you have a wall that tilts just four degrees, everyone's going to notice that wall, even though four degrees doesn't sound like that much on paper. That's one facet of practice that Donald Judd has helped me perceive—the subtlety of his work is powerful. Teaching that kind of restraint and understanding how the power of that kind of restraint can operate is a meaningful tool.

SW I think that you could say that, in a way, your life, as well as your buildings, have operated in the same way. In Marfa, someone could have taken that and solved one problem, but you took that and actually turned it into something completely new, partly because you are, as a person, very open to accepting ideas and situations and diving into them without being too anxious—in this case, about the fact that you were not a preservation architect. You were not the person that most people would typically say is appropriate for that task. And I think that's the way to approach practice.

TS That's been my ambition since we started Schaum/Shieh. For some reason, some see ours as a successful model [laughs], and when people ask about "how we do it," I say look across our peers and at all our practices. Everyone does it differently, on their terms, with their capabilities, with their perspectives. Everyone's different approach reflects their perspective and their positionality. I also find that learning from colleagues and peers and our collective conversation to be one of the magical things about living in a creative profession.

SW Architecture is often termed a very competitive profession and a very selfish one. It's also a fairly selfish moment in the world. But we've talked about what it means to be part of a school—you are part of a collective. It's not just the students you're teaching that inspire you. It's also the role of the school and the other people in the profession. That's a generous way of approaching the world. It's also a more productive way.

Competition, Performing Arts Center, with Albert Pope, Kaohsiung, Taiwan (2010)

Kaohsiung Maritime Cultural & Pop Music Center

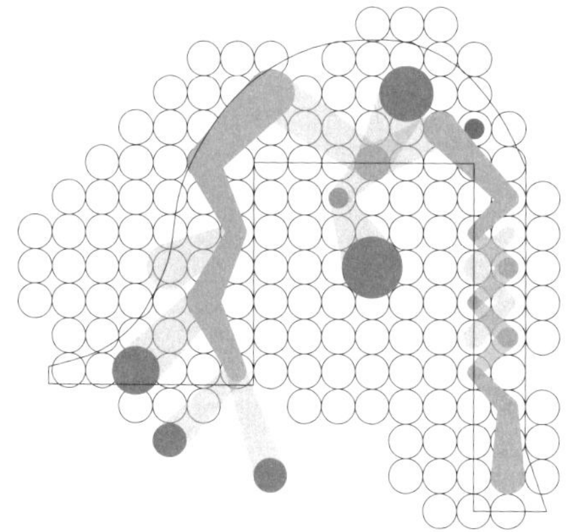

Aggregation Diagrams

A field of 50m-diameter spheres was introduced to relate scales of building, city, and landscape. This mediating diagram was a way to organize metrics and set granularity, to align movement, and make spatial relationships. It was also a generative tool for making connections between existing conditions and projected realities.

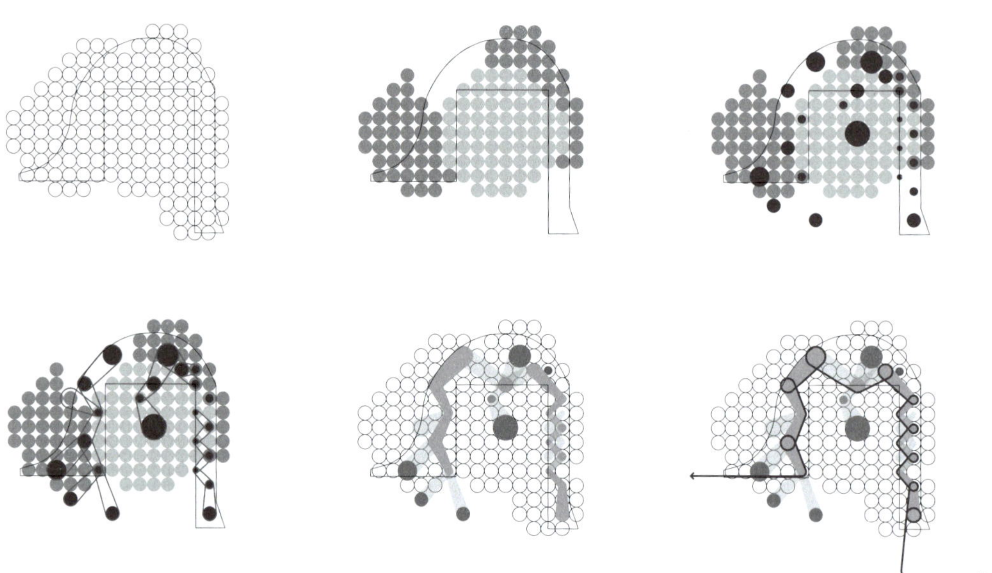

City Connection Diagrams

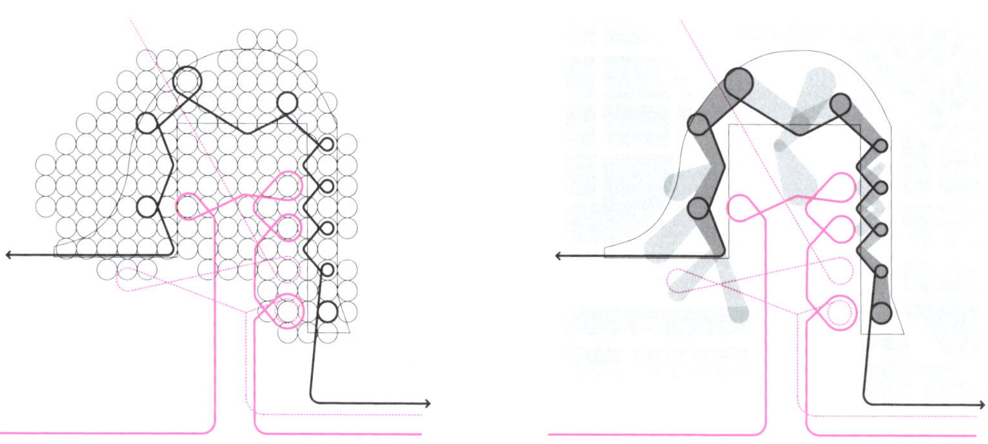

Site Plan

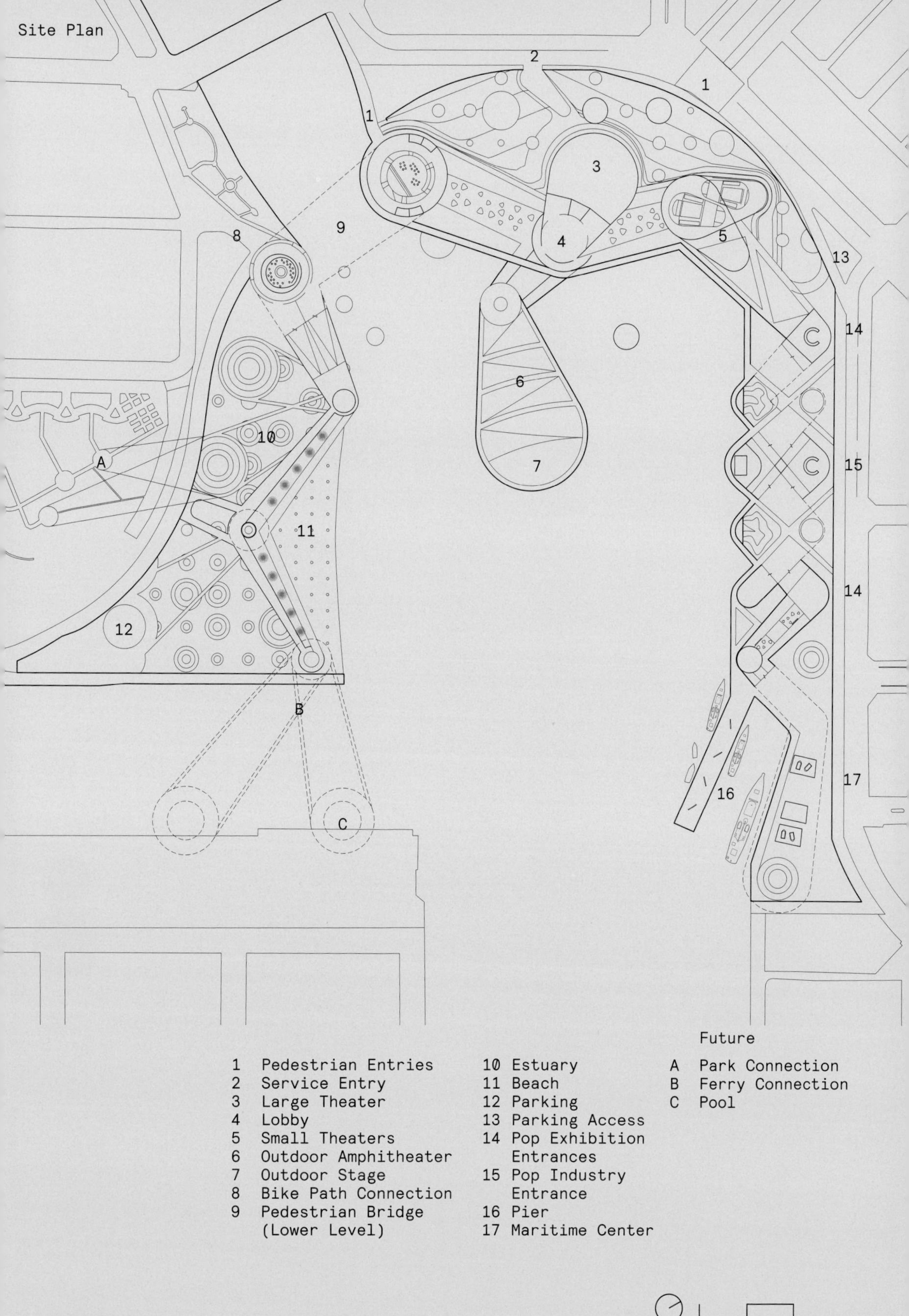

					Future
1	Pedestrian Entries	10	Estuary	A	Park Connection
2	Service Entry	11	Beach	B	Ferry Connection
3	Large Theater	12	Parking	C	Pool
4	Lobby	13	Parking Access		
5	Small Theaters	14	Pop Exhibition Entrances		
6	Outdoor Amphitheater	15	Pop Industry Entrance		
7	Outdoor Stage	16	Pier		
8	Bike Path Connection	17	Maritime Center		
9	Pedestrian Bridge (Lower Level)				

Program Loop Diagram

Study Models

Program Distribution

Program Grouped into Zones

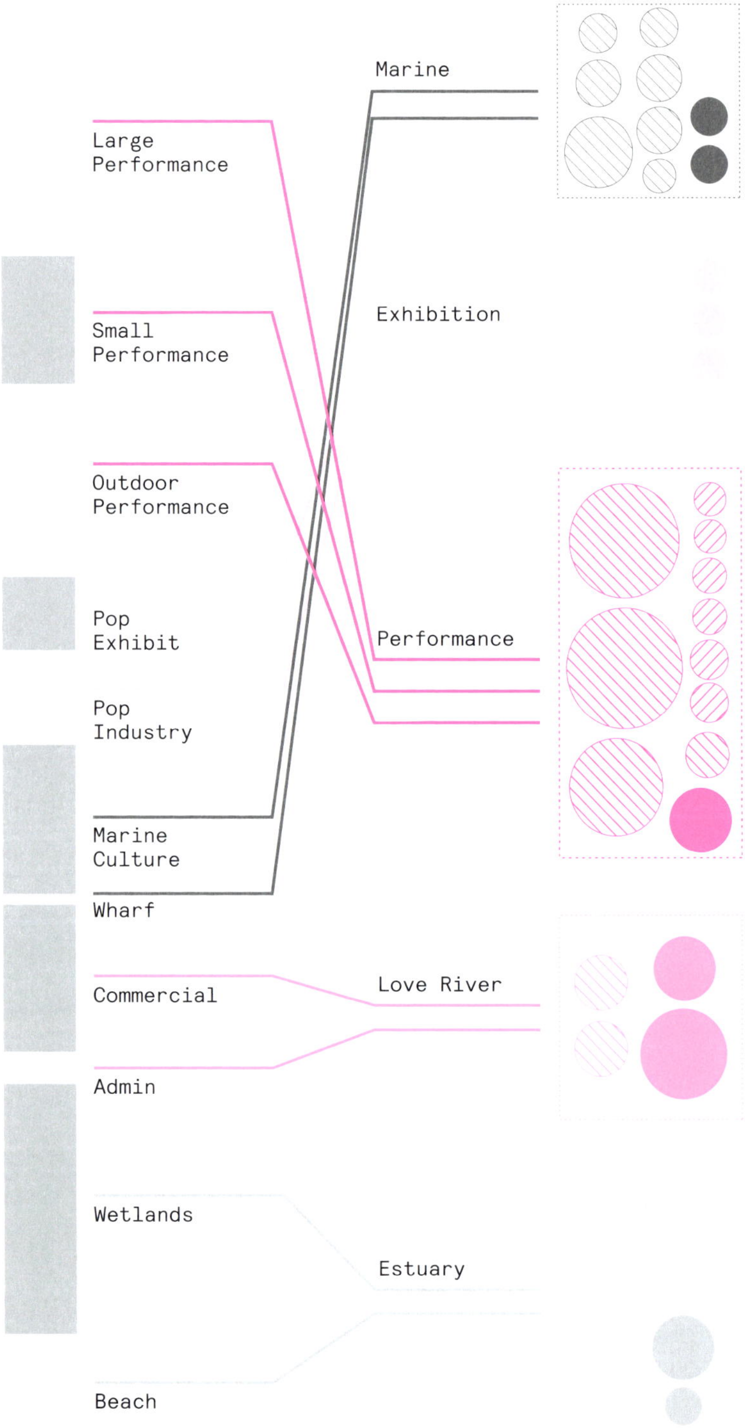

Large Performance

Small Performance

Outdoor Performance

Pop Exhibit

Pop Industry

Marine Culture

Wharf

Commercial

Admin

Wetlands

Beach

Marine

Exhibition

Performance

Love River

Estuary

0 50 100m

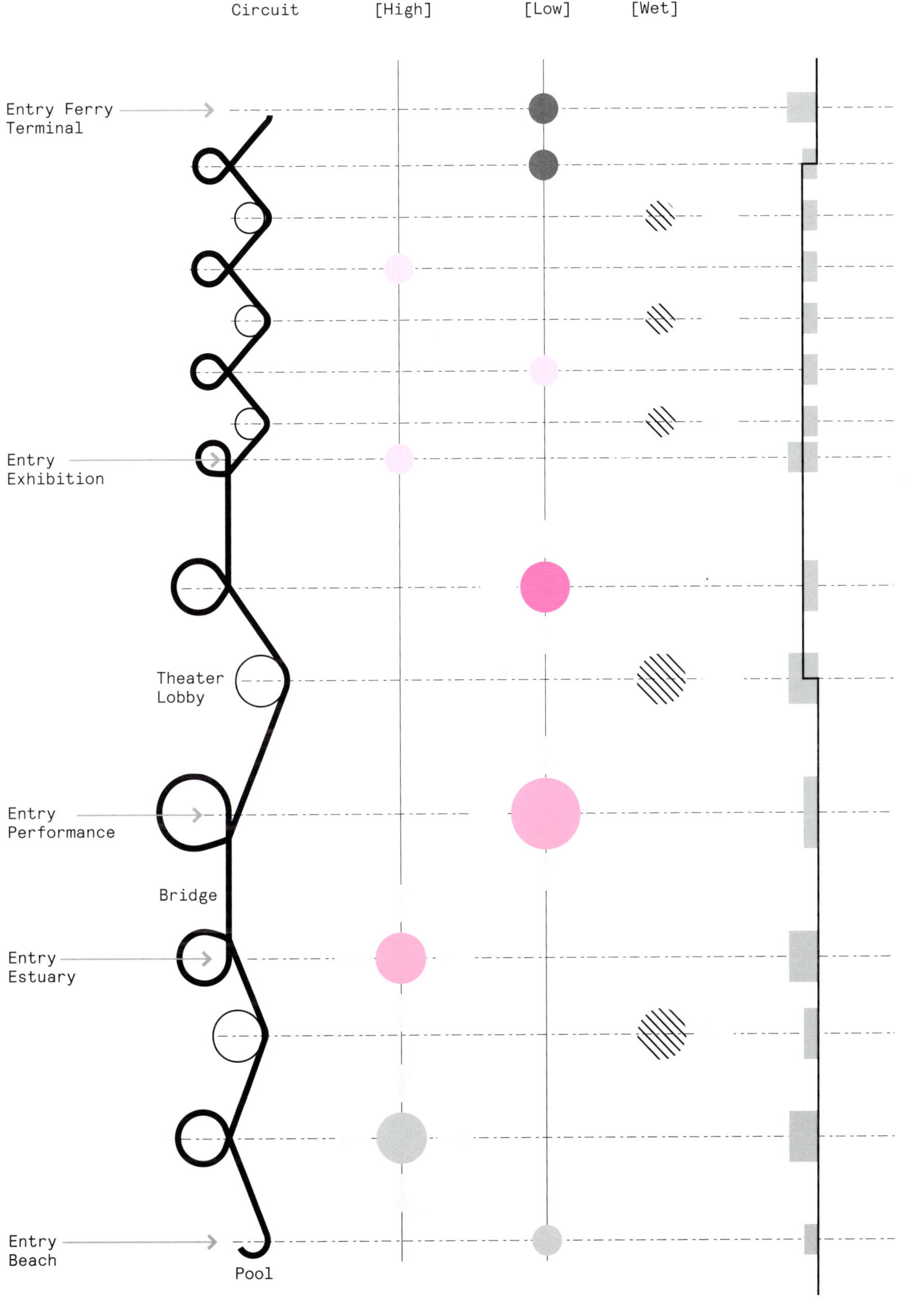
Primary
Circuit
Hubs
[High]
Hubs
[Low]
Spools
[Wet]
Entry Ferry
Terminal
Entry
Exhibition
Theater
Lobby
Entry
Performance
Bridge
Entry
Estuary
Entry
Beach
Pool
Geology

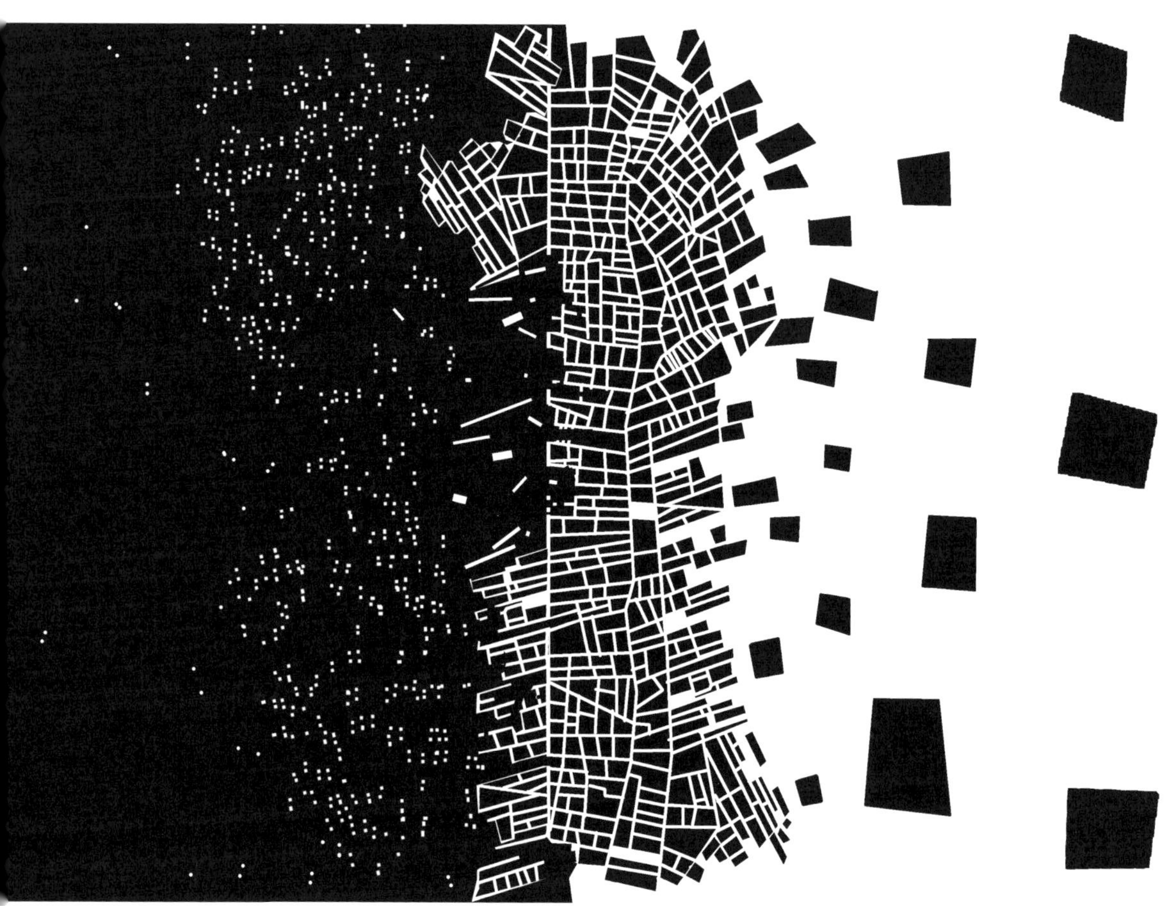

Slider Towers (2011)

By architecture of the city we mean two different things: first, the city seen as a gigantic man-made object, a work of engineering and architecture that is large and complex and growing over time; second, certain more limited but crucial aspects of the city, namely urban artifacts.

—Aldo Rossi (1966)

Note

Searching for new criteria, on Tschumi's Manhattan Transcripts

How do we grasp what is not given? The search for new criteria attempts to do this; it is one way architects attempt to liberate architecture from its rarefied discourse, from functionalism and commercialism, from complicity in systems of oppression. In his Manhattan Transcripts, Bernard Tschumi attempted to shake architecture free from the bounds of type and program, using cinema to redeploy the criteria of architecture as event, movement, and space, conscripting disciplinary tools—drawings and diagrams—to grasp directly at life beyond function, toward the poles of pleasure and violence, claiming these as rightful domains of architecture.

The aims of this project are radical, and it stirs within us a reactive impulse to evaluate, to look for outcomes. This impulse is the status quo asserting itself: its mechanism is to serve failure to expectation, to trigger disappointment. This is the system working within us to discourage radical change. It obscures the real creative outcome of the project, which is the project as method, and its redefinition of space:

> A special mode of notation—the three-square principle—underlines the deadly game of hide and seek between the suspect and the ever-changing architectural events. Photographs direct the action, plans reveal the alternatively cruel and loving architectural manifestations, diagrams indicate the movements of the main protagonists. There, attitudes, plans, notations, movements are indissolubly linked. Only together do they define the space of "The Park."

Determine the relevant criteria, get it all on the table, figure out how it can be active and present. Some will fit together quite naturally, others may not.

Tschumi's particular notation builds structures that lead outside what is currently "known" in conventional representation. With these structures, the project charts a desired outcome and offers a set of techniques and methods to get there: "They are a tool-in-the-making, a work-in-progress"—a tool for thinking about the world and, by extension, for working on the world (and an alternative to the architectural project as *proof of concept*). Not insignificantly, to the student of architecture, this project calls for the architect to define the criteria they deem important, and implies the cautionary message that we must furnish new tools, for what we do not define, name, or attempt to reach for cannot be addressed, worked on, or transformed:

Determine a notation for bringing it together; do not exclude things that do not "fit." Some examples from Tschumi are juxtaposition (Manhattan Transcripts) and superimposition (Parc de la Villette).

> It also proceeded from a need to question the modes of representation generally used by architects: plans, sections, axonometrics, perspectives. However precise and generative they have been, each implies a logical reduction of architectural thought to what can be shown, at the exclusion of other concerns.

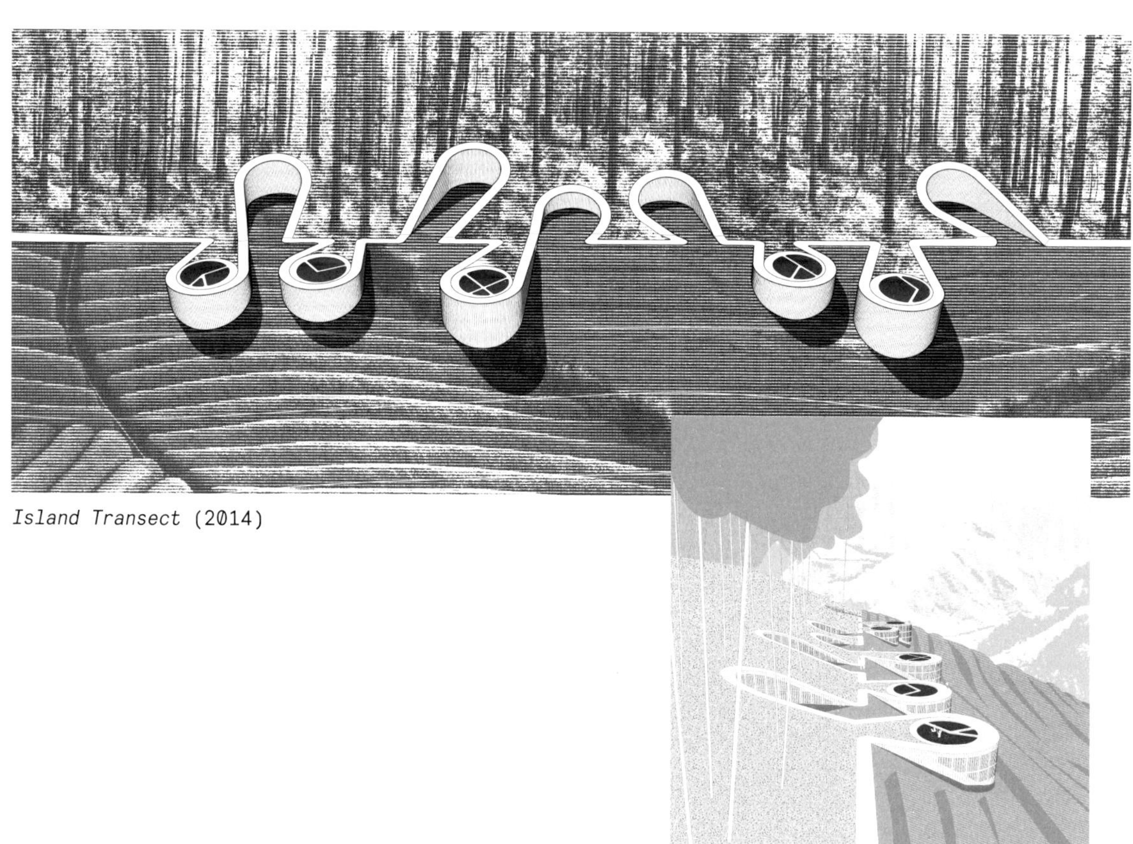

Island Transect (2014)

Note

On landscape

What is the interplay between buildings, landscape, and energy? In our projects, it can emerge as a line of movement along the interface between different conditions on the site: uphill and downhill, water and land, or more subtle shifts in topography. These landscapes, all landscapes, can be considered as layered liminal spaces of shear. Evidence of shear between various states creates different geomorphic conditions that permeate relationships across and beyond sites. These moments of shear are reflected in vastly different timescales and cultural orientations; they inform material forces and flows.

Anthropologist Gregory Bateson defines a "bit" of information as "a difference which makes a difference." As architects, this "bit" is what we need to inscribe on a plan and a landscape. It's crucial to decide what are the differences that make a difference. Which differences make it onto a map? Which differences do we retain as that map is projected onto a landscape?

During the drawing stage we sync the building with the near field and with deeper connections to a landscape. It is the initial means to test the relationship between architecture and site, a process of recognizing and visualizing both invisible and apparent elements—existing and planned—and figuring out how the various pieces and forces may or may not influence and organize the others. Differences between unlike things may blur; we also look for the surprising moments when seemingly alike things differentiate. How does this edge that interfaces with these states reorganize how architecture understands responsive and dynamic spaces? How does this model of shear create a new framework for imagining a creative force in the construction of built environments?

Private Residence & Writers' Retreat, Lexington, VA (2023)

Shenandoah House

Plan

The house was designed for programmatic indeterminacy: a private residence to start; in the future it will host a residency for 2–3 writers at a time.

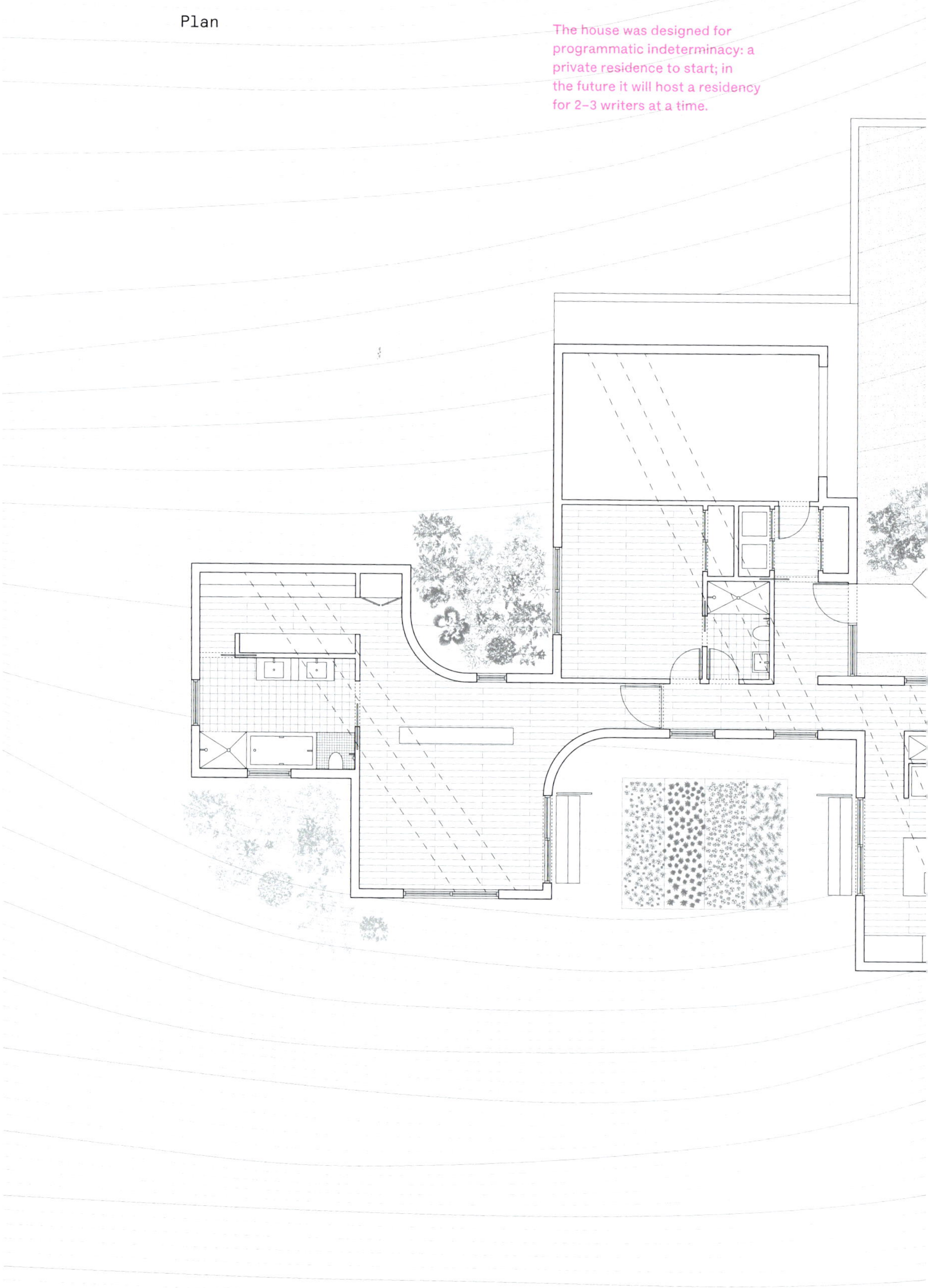

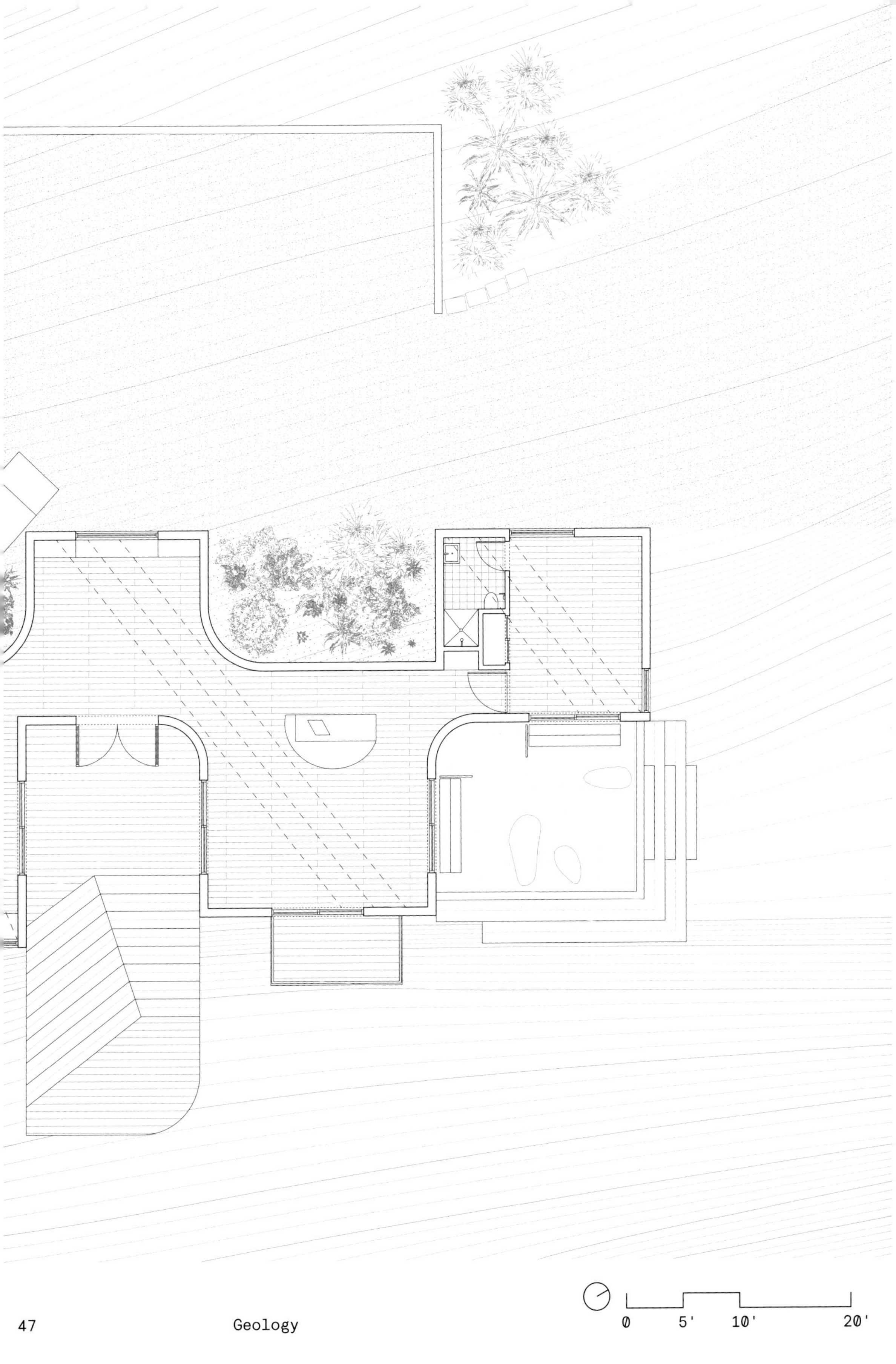
0
5'
10'
20'

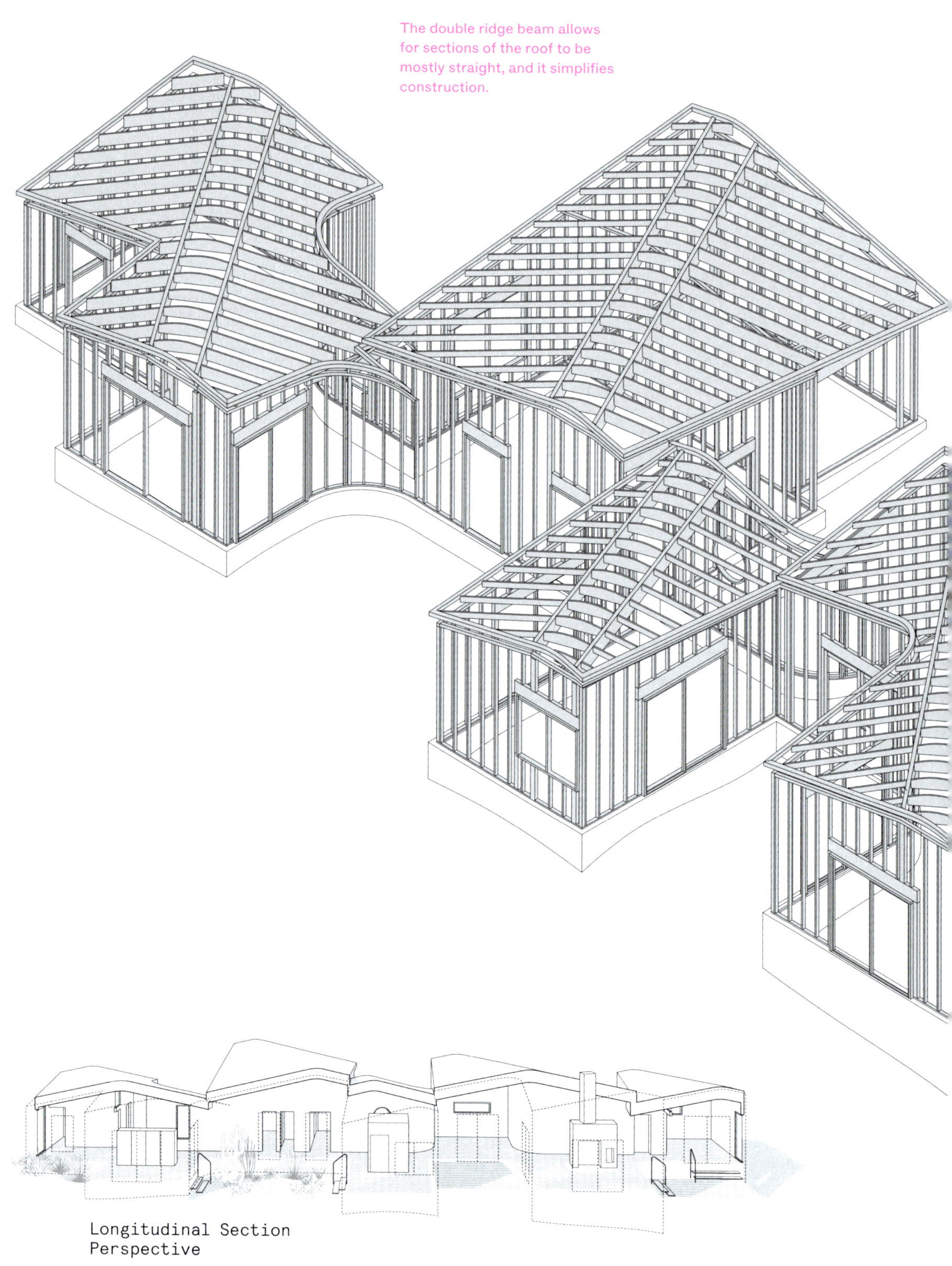

Longitudinal Section
Perspective

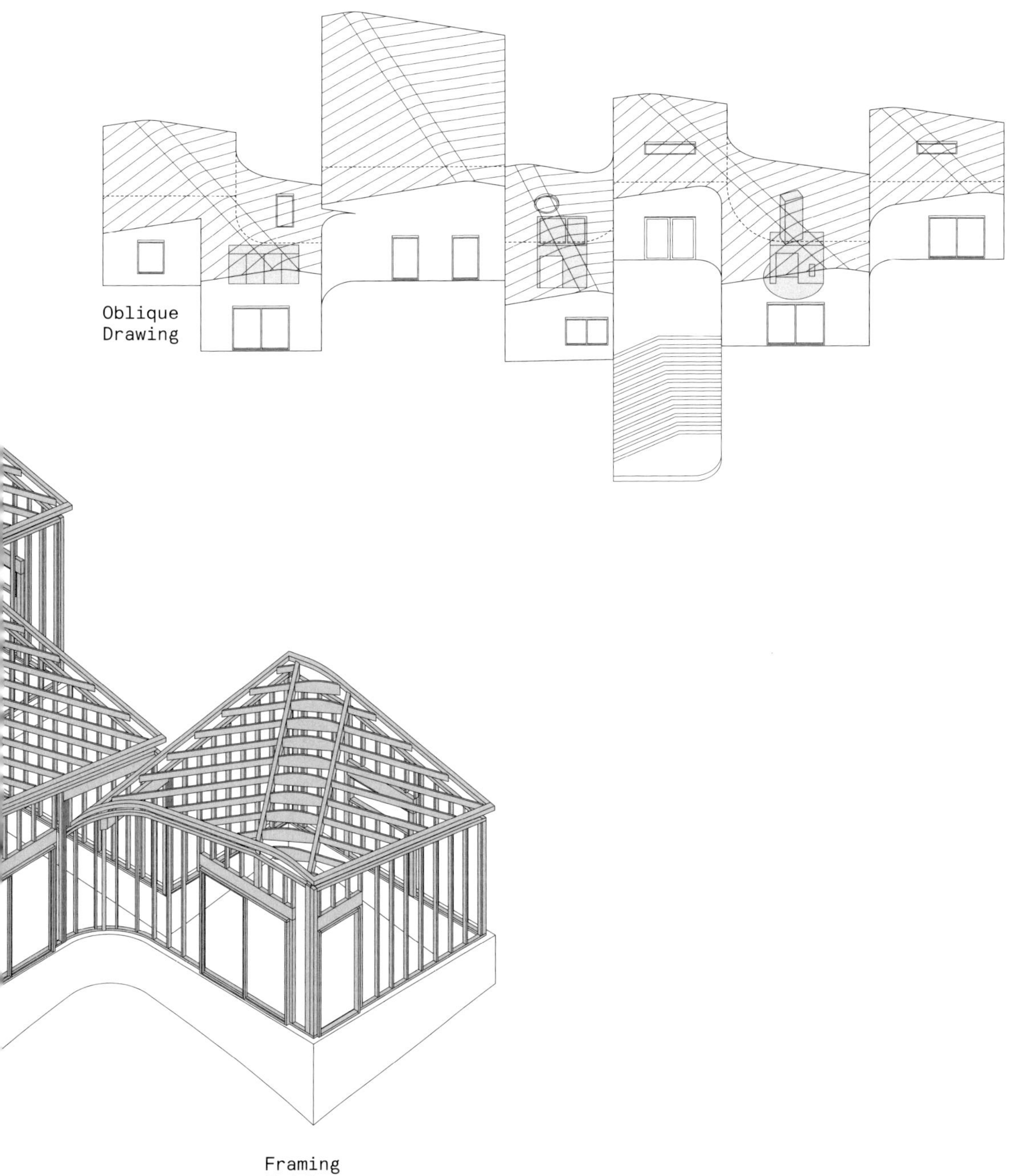

Oblique Drawing

Framing Model

This is an adaptive re-use and preservation project in Houston. These projects often engage gas stations, laundromats, and other buildings that recur in the exurban fabric.

Troy Schaum, *Site Visit (Houston, TX)* (2020)

Before practicing meditation, we see that mountains are mountains.
When we start to practice, we see that mountains are no longer mountains.
After practicing a while, we see that mountains are again mountains.

—Thích Nhất Hạnh

1. Take something small and make it big.

2. Take a thing that is usually hard and make it soft.

3. Take a thing that is usually monolithic and make it from parts.

After completing the above, spend some time describing each process or resulting object in words.

For consideration:

Environment, cities, aliveness

Taipei Performing Arts Center (2008)

Kōbō Abe,
The Woman in the Dunes
(1962)

Roland Barthes,
Empire of Signs
(1970)

Wendell Berry,
Life Is a Miracle
(2000)

Mark Dorrian,
"The Way the World Sees London"
(2008)

Charles and Ray Eames,
Blacktop, a story of the washing of a school play yard
(1952)

Aldo Leopold,
"Thinking Like a Mountain"
(1949)

Lucrecia Martel,
La ciénaga
(2001)

Aldo Rossi,
The Architecture of the City
(1982)

Robert Smithson,
"A Tour of the Monuments of Passaic, New Jersey"
(1967)

Virginia Woolf,
"Street Haunting: A London Adventure"
(1930)

Urbox (2015)

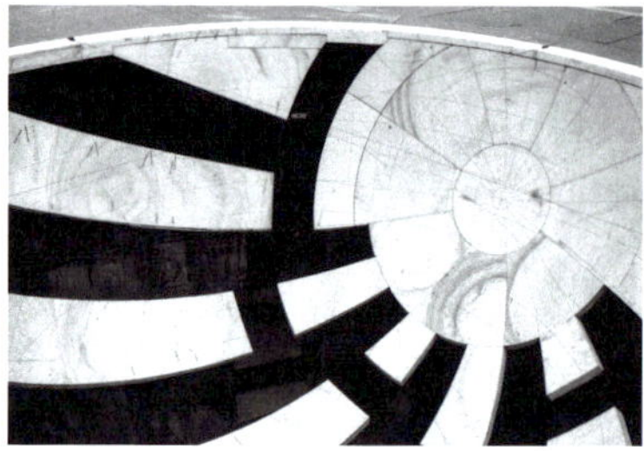

Troy Schaum, *Jai Prakash* (2004)

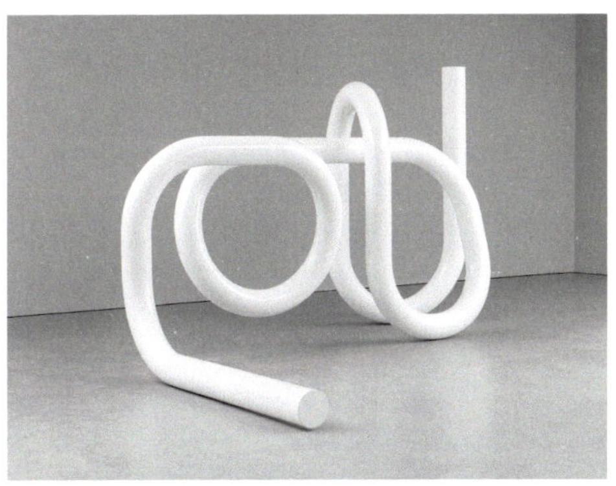

Carol Bove, *From the Sun to Zurich* (2016)

Rosalyne Shieh, *Untitled (Penghu)* (2017)

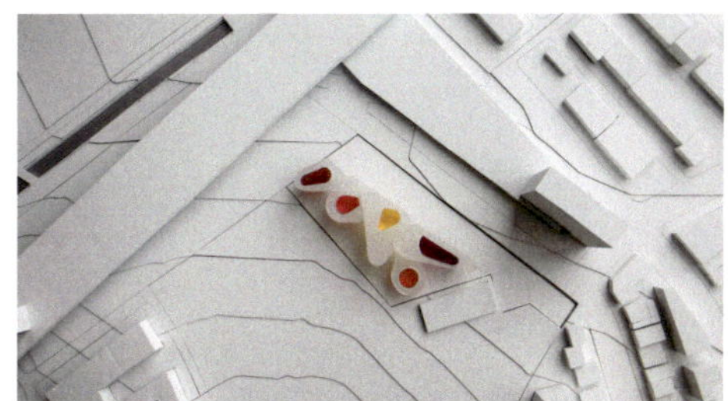

Taichung City Cultural Center (2013)

Void

stretch
thickness
thicken
cluster
alignment
field
group
hang together
sit
tap
crust
disappear
snap
drop-off
glimpse
rise
leak
haze

How might we see the spaces left by restraint? Instead of seeing a hole, note a space of non-action. You may see more if you stop looking for something. In the postindustrial city, by adjusting the gaze from active to passive, what is already at work may be revealed.

Catie Newell, *Untitled (Detroit, MI)* (2009)

[E]verything starts with a revolution. There is an existing thing against which discontent is felt. This discontent hardens, and at some point, intuitively a new image is conceived. This image is not an isolated thing, concerned purely with the plastic arts, but a sort of social-plastic entity; that is, it conceives a new way of life, a new sort of technology and a new image all in one, but in a rather vague sort of way [...] Architecture as something form-giving is involved in this business. It cannot be separated from "process"; form transforms "process" by taking part in it.

—Peter Smithson (1957)

We talk about master plans and master planning. What changes if we consider minor plans and minor planning?

Can we imagine a transformation that doesn't supplant what is already there?

Might we look at the ways people have altered their environments (particularly in those described as "dis-invested" and "de-industrialized") not as expressions of trauma, but as strategies of survival, maintenance, and community care?

When we recognize small-scale environmental adjustments, such as urban gardening, making place-based art, reclamation of material from uninhabited properties, and selective demolition of property (by fire or otherwise), as valid tactics for adaptation, can we then imagine a broader urban transformation happening in a bottom-up manner?

What happens when we think of building as collaborating with what is already there, the efforts already underway, by those already present?

What spatial order, material logics, and attitudes are emerging from the hands of many small, individual interventions? What if no intervention is too small to be counted?

In place of proposals, claims, and offerings, can we reframe a project as a set of questions? What is discovered in this process, and how might we then adjust our expectations? Can the conclusion of the project be a revised set of questions?

What is architecture as epistemology? How does it inform architecture as intervention?

Catie Newell, *Untitled (Detroit, MI)* (2009)

This is an attempt to create an image through grouping of elements that is a reflection of growth and decay in our life process—a metabolic process. This is to conceive a form in relationship to an ever-changing whole and its parts. This is an attempt to express the energy and sweat of millions of people in Tokyo, of the breath of life and the poetry of living.

—Fumihiko Maki (1964)

We regularly use massing models, solid/void figure–ground diagrams, and measured plan drawings to depict cities as collections of buildings of varying shapes and sizes organized along streets or around collective urban spaces. The clarity of these modes is a result of selection: legible images of the city are produced by extracting and isolating formal relationships. The result is especially useful for highlighting and understanding how building types, in aggregate, constitute urban form. But it doesn't necessarily follow that formal logics documented in the existing city should be extended or replicated in proposed alterations or new designs, especially where social and economic conditions have changed.

Rafael Moneo has said that using the compositional logic of the old or existing city "to structure the new forms, [provides] them with formal consistency, but no more than that." Still, as a place to start, such an exercise is not without value—sometimes for what it doesn't give you.

As we encountered in Detroit, the effectiveness of drawings that foregrounded mass, material, space, and circulation was diminished, the results illegible, especially without being able to assume occupancy and fully operational municipal maintenance. Where needs have changed, sites may be well served by an architectural response we cannot see in formal structure. Instead, the work of architecture could be used to imaginatively meet the conditions of place in ways that physically support those who make their lives there. Community members, architects, urbanists, and planners working in these sites actively bring a fuller picture to the process, so we are not suggesting that revising architectural drawing is necessary to create meaningful work, only that, as architects, we are curious about the potential of architectural drawings as deep repositories and generative instruments for recording existing realities and working toward new ones. How can drawings account for the site as it actually functions, or doesn't? How much can drawings hold—might they account for the site as it is lived?

Design Research & Speculative Urbanism, Detroit, MI (2017)

Sponge Urbanism

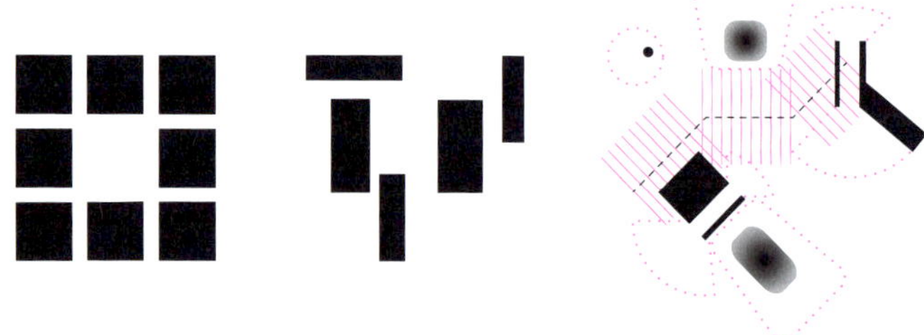

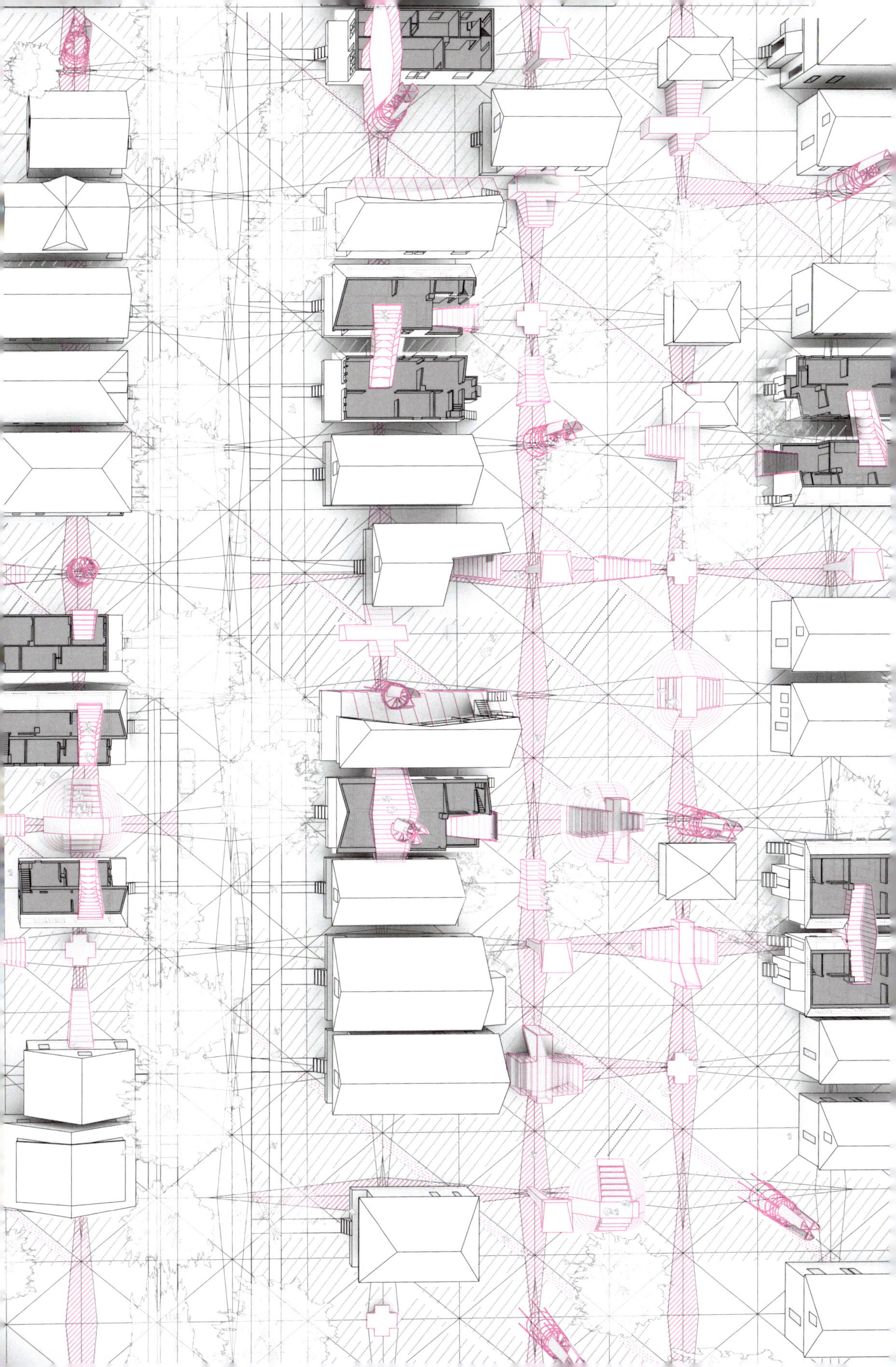

Field Vectors

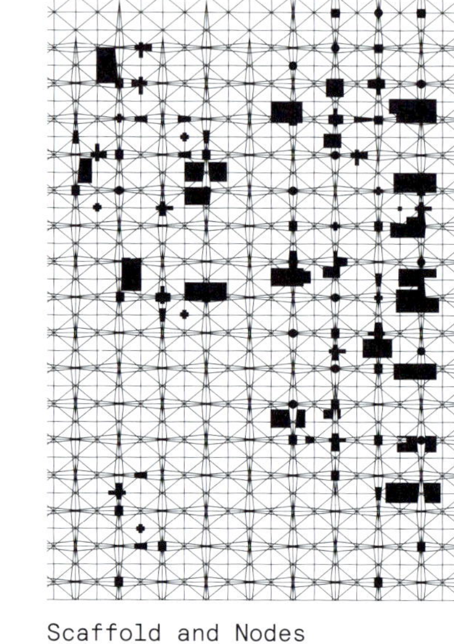
Scaffold and Nodes

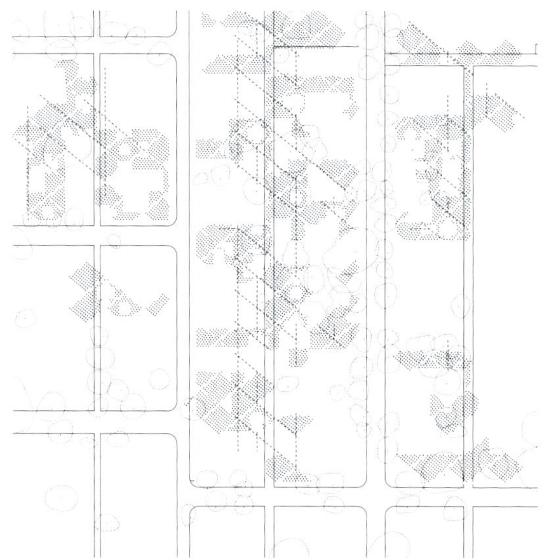
Infrastructure and Surfaces

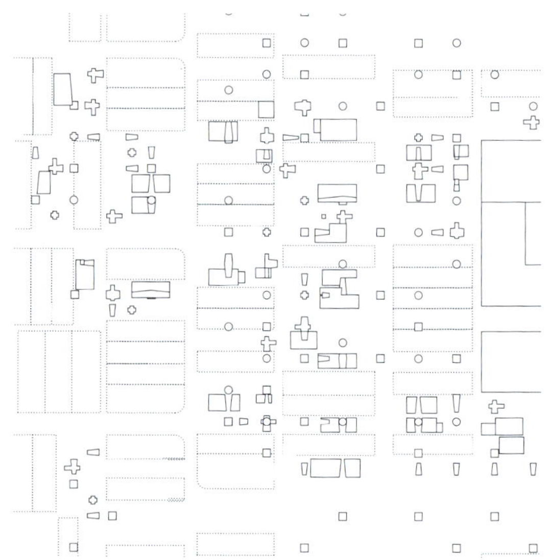
Ownership

Field vectors set our design; scaffolds and nodes helped us place programmatic structures; infrastructure and surfaces documented existing and projected power and water sources; ownership mapped occupation and vacancy.

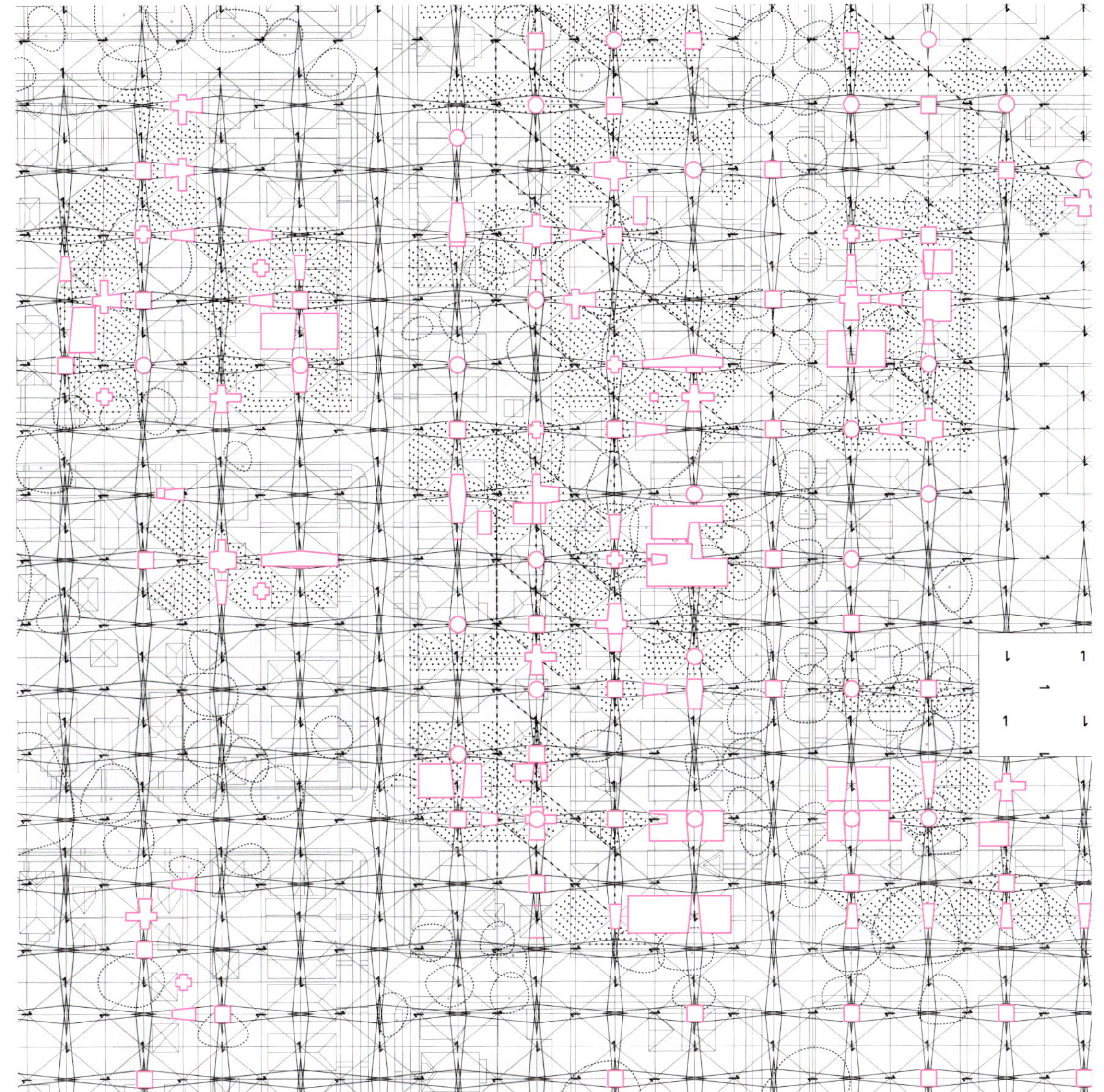

Sponge Urbanism

Insertions and interventions operate like points within a field. Some are spatial and channel environmental forces like wind or precipitation and tie into infrastructural lines; each organizes a space larger than its footprint in a way that changes over time and through different seasons.

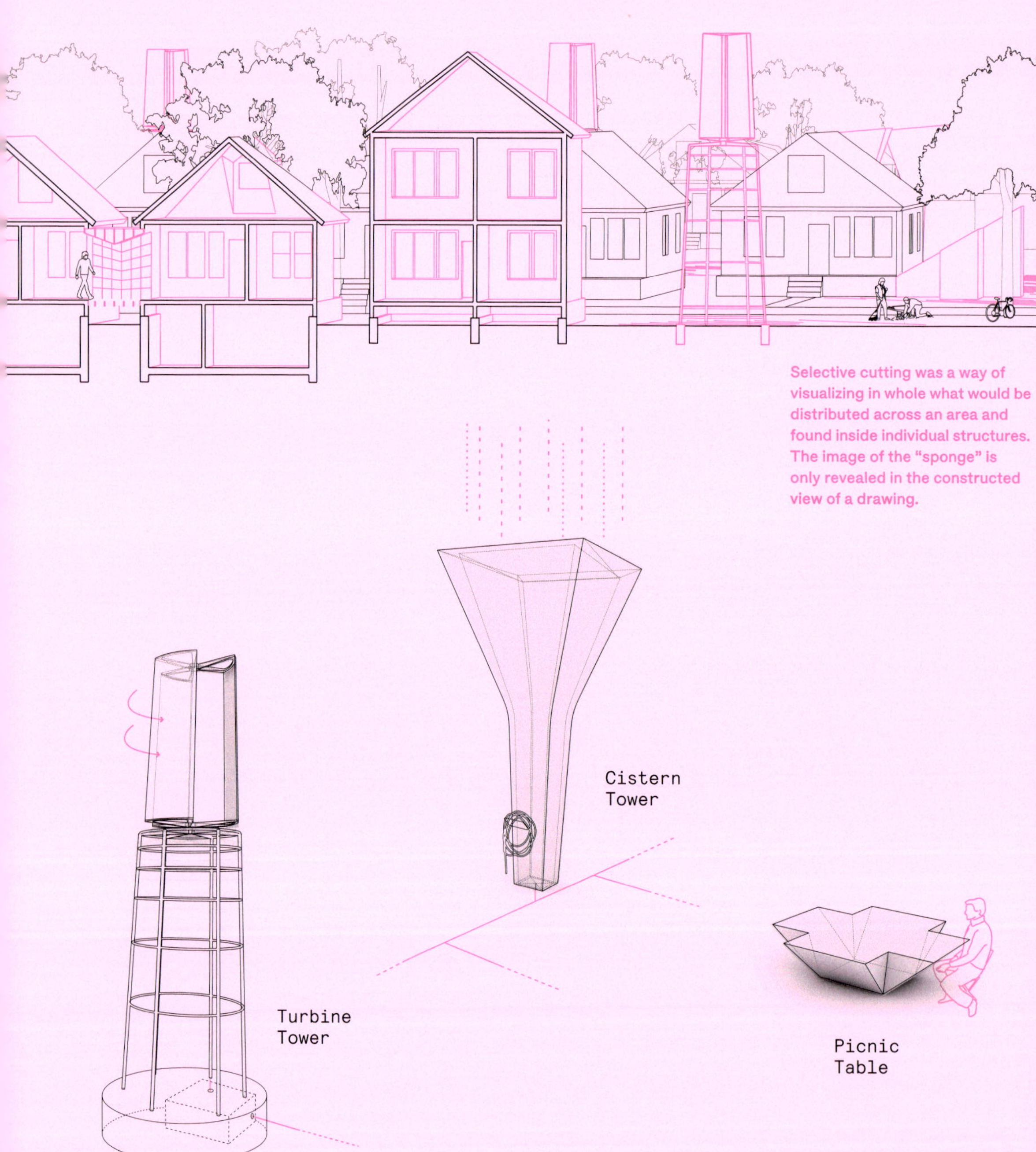

Selective cutting was a way of visualizing in whole what would be distributed across an area and found inside individual structures. The image of the “sponge” is only revealed in the constructed view of a drawing.

The individual forms are specific, but the relation between them is less so. You can add or remove one, and the field could grow or shrink over time. There would be change, but it would be incremental.

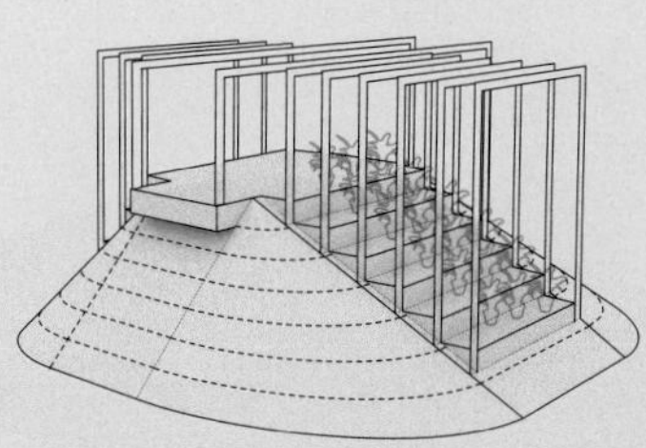

Greenhouse
Mound

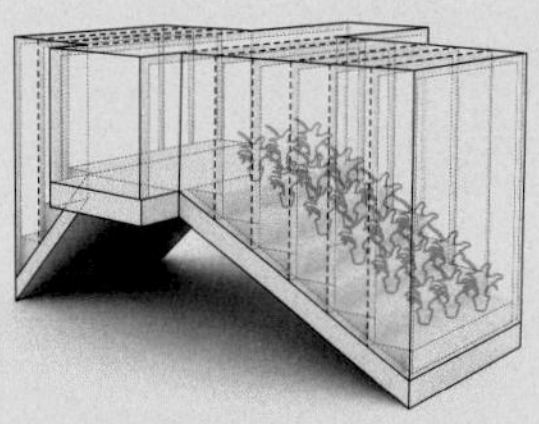

Greenhouse
Bridge

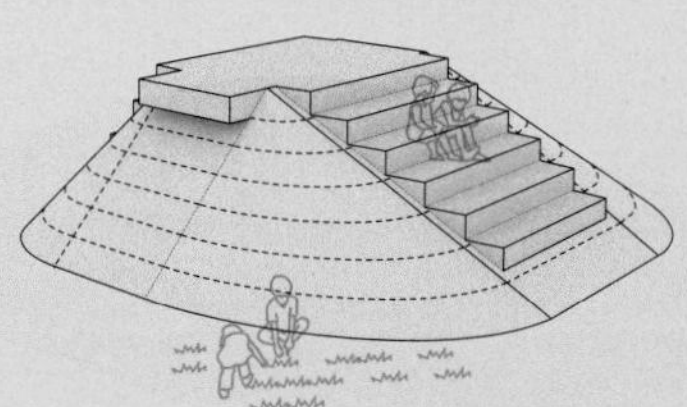

Activity
Mound

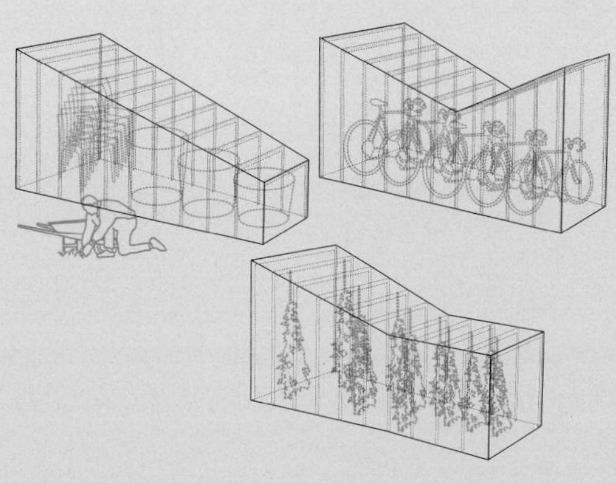

Multipurpose
Sheds

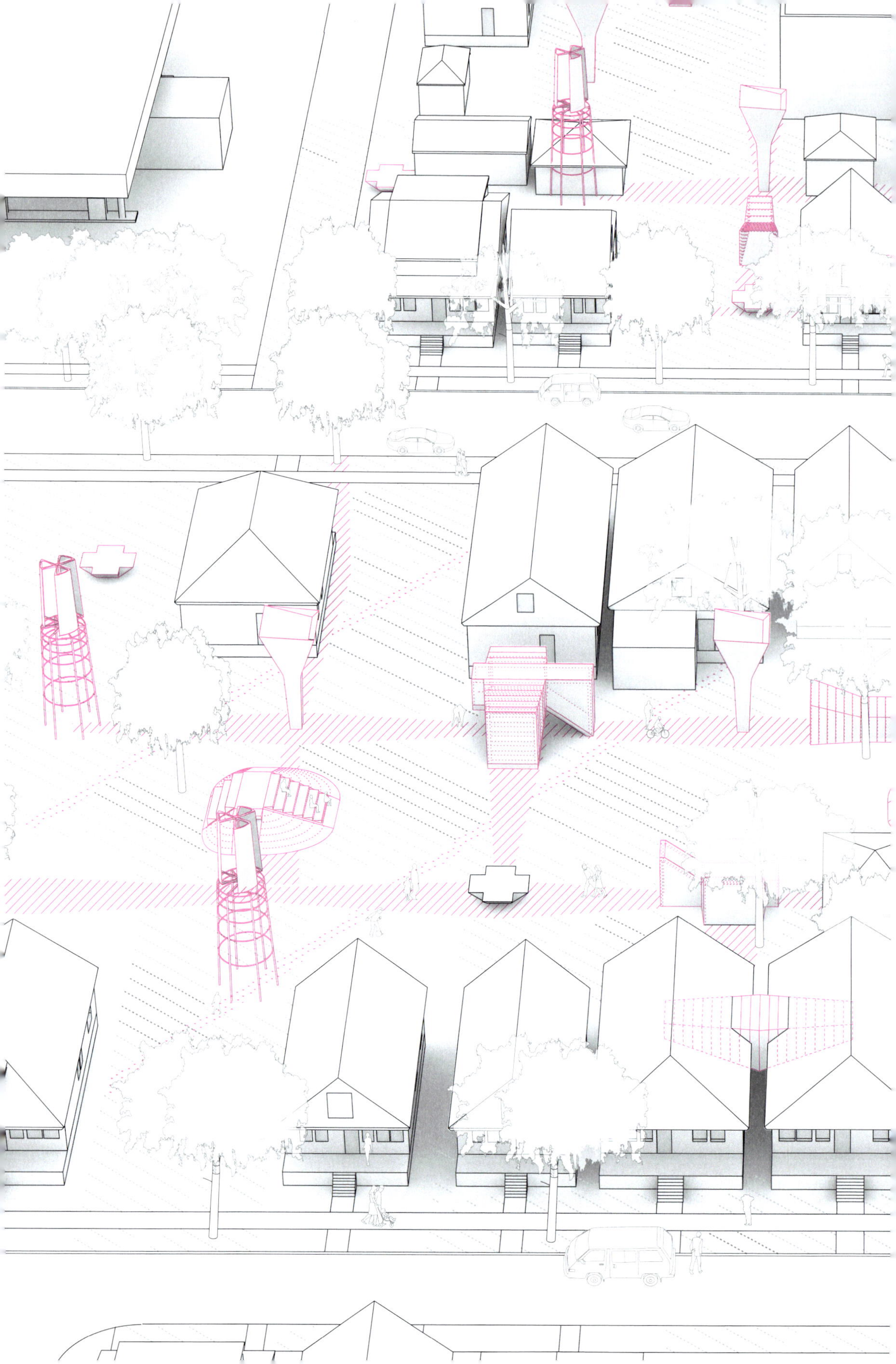

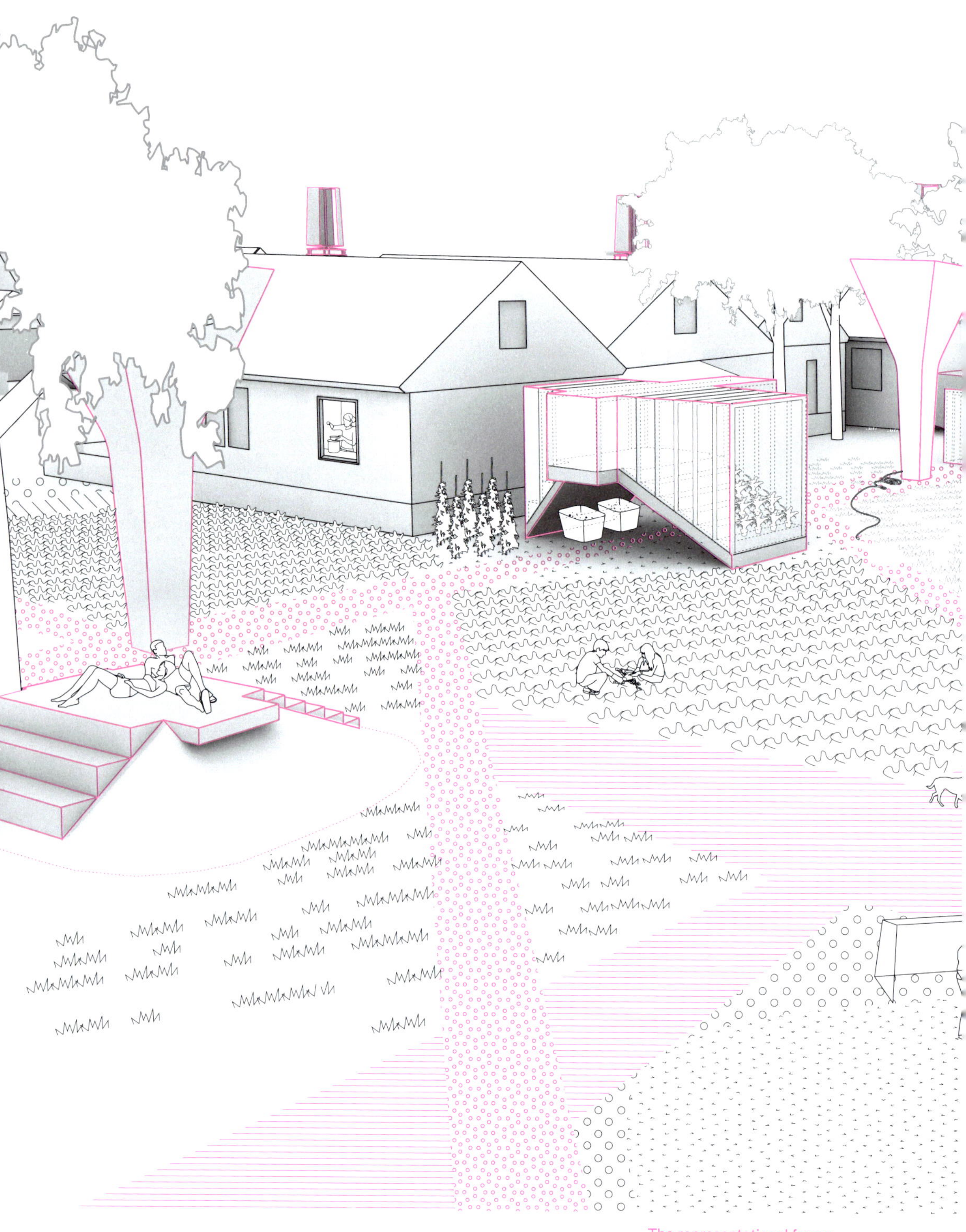

The representational frame—the plan, the cutaway, the perspective—may have formally dominated our exploration more than if the project were carried out on the ground.

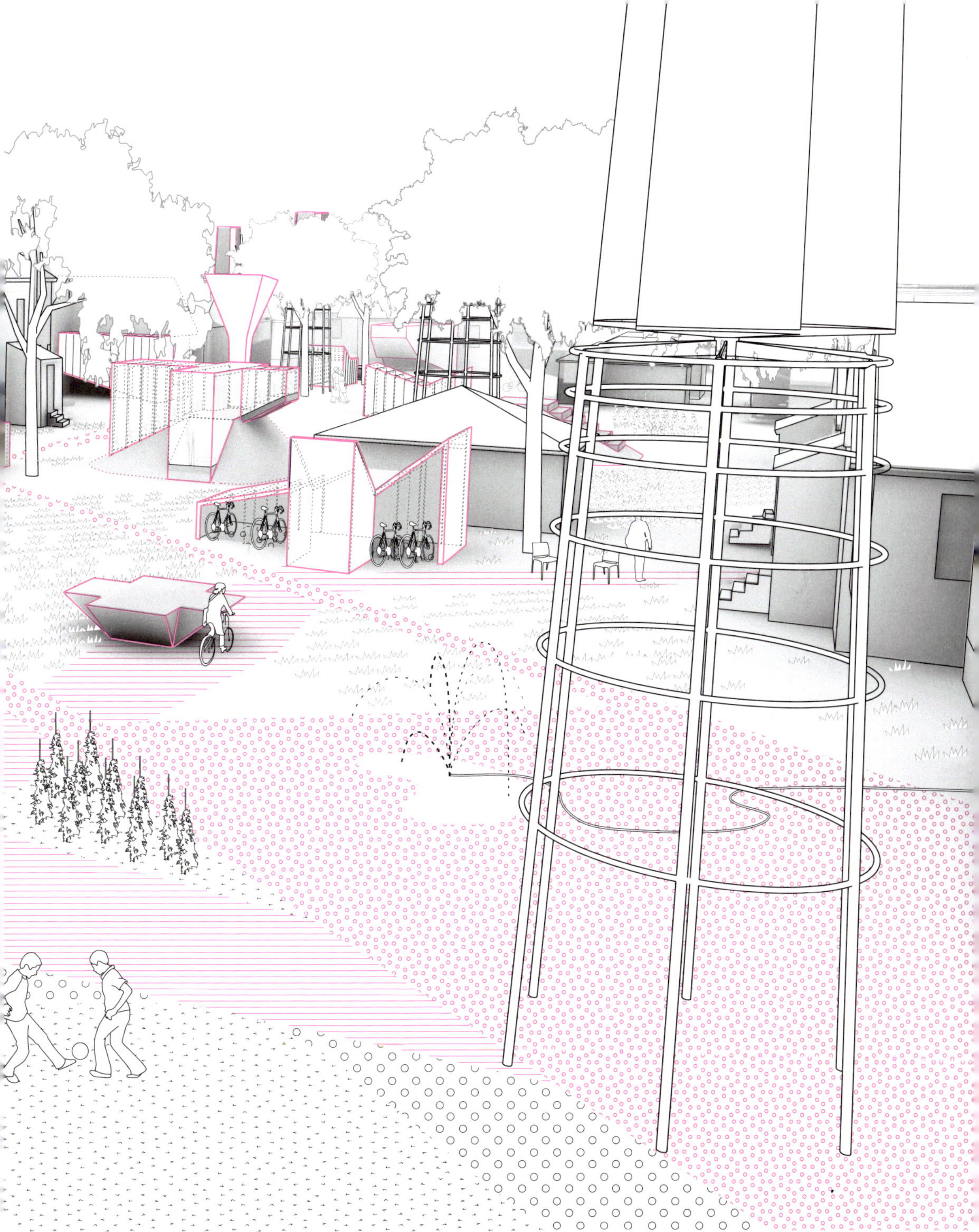

All the pieces fit within an extended framework that was built off existing infrastructure. The individual pieces are small, but the project uses the tools of architecture to ask how a larger change or order might arise from the hands of many individual interventions.

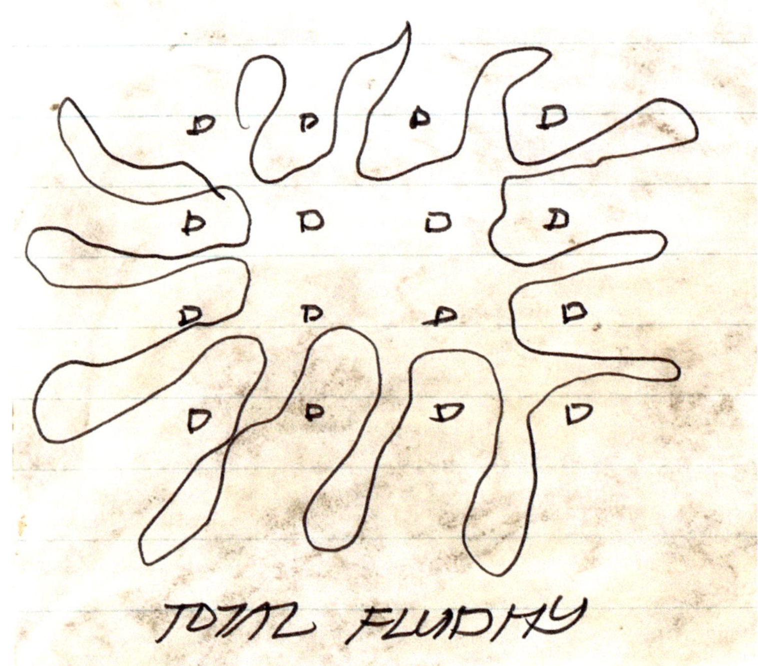

John Hejduk, detail of *The Nine Square Problem: conceptual drawings with notes* (1963–85)

We can begin by doing small things at the local level, like planting community gardens or looking out for our neighbors. That is how change takes place in living systems: not from above but from within, from many local actions occurring simultaneously.

—Grace Lee Boggs

When we think about what it means to "improve" a city, how do we think about the space between Boggs's work and life in place, and the contemporary practices of urban design and master planning?

Note

On binaries and beauty

What are binaries good for? Binaries are tools. Binaries are problematics: "a theoretical starting point that is at once perplexing and productive." We use such pairs to think through things. For example, John Hejduk set up the formal-conceptual problematics of fluidity/containment and center/periphery within the terms of a nine-square grid in his canonical pedagogical exercise.

It's important to understand that binaries do not reflect a preexisting reality, to not mistake their simplicity and clarity for essence. Rather, structural pairs—from binary oppositions to diptychs—can be used tactically to set a direction or inscribe a value system within which to work.

An example: At a conference at the Yale School of Architecture in 2016, Elaine Scarry spoke about beauty. Citing examples from the history of literature, Scarry said that beauty, as "the perceptual event that happens to the perceiver," is a life pact. When a perceiver is confronted with an object of beauty, she experiences a heightened sense; time is marked. It's not dissimilar from encountering an infant or a beautiful landscape—the experience may incite feelings of protectiveness or a desire to care for or take care of something, somebody, or a place.

In the Q&A after, Scarry was asked what she thought of "ugly." She answered that ugliness is not the opposite of beauty; injury is the opposite of beauty. Injury is harm, destruction, and disregard; it is denying access to self-protection. This definition sends us back to beauty's meaning; as an opposite of injury, it becomes that which is life-affirming, life-sustaining, and nourishing. This is clarifying, and leads us to ask: How do we seek, fortify, and construct this kind of beauty?

Aerial view of the northeast side of Detroit, MI

The conception of a void arises [...] when consciousness, lagging behind itself, remains attached to the recollection of an old state when another state is already present.

—Henri Bergson (1922)

Sponge Urbanism

The 2010 U.S. Census Report documented 713,777 residents in Detroit, charting a precipitous 25 percent drop (from 951,270 in 2000) over ten years, measuring less than half its peak population of 1.8 million in 1950.

Situated within the Rust Belt, Detroit is America's most infamous "shrinking" city. In March 2010, Mayor Dave Bing announced his intent to "right-size" Detroit through a combined strategy of large-scale demolition, population redistribution, and targeted rehabilitation; under his plan, ten thousand derelict houses would be demolished within three years. Rightfully alarming, one community member called it a "kinder, gentler" Trail of Tears for Detroit. Swaths of the city would be razed to make room for fields and farmland, and residents would be relocated to strengthen "more viable" neighborhoods. Enacting this plan would break the infrastructural and spatial continuity of the city with large open areas, making remaining neighborhoods less inter-accessible and more policeable—a spatial transformation with grave social consequences.

The specifics of the plan remain vague, but taken at face value, the vision projected is top-down and retrograde: a tabula rasa approach based on an ideal notion of the city that tacitly presumes that urbanism requires density, and that the basic unit of density is built form. Under this logic, open lots and unoccupied buildings can be seen only as emblems of loss in an attritive slide toward porosity. Yet this perspective condemns us to the limitations of prejudgment: seeing only what is missing prevents us from seeing what is already there.

Perhaps we can learn to recognize cities like Detroit as infrastructurally connected and prepared sites rather than remnants of entropic urban dysfunction. As an attempt to think through this conceptual reorientation we propose an architectural thought experiment sited within an existing neighborhood on Detroit's northeast side, a formal and programmatic extrapolation of the insertions and constructions long made by residents in response to the city's changing conditions. By testing these transformations at the smallest unit of occupation—the single lot—we investigate a strategy for bringing about a multidirectional order that emerges from within.

Sponge Urbanism imagines Detroit's neighborhoods as a porous framework within which infill and blankness, form and space, the material and the immaterial simultaneously produce the city. This methodology facilitates the transition from a condition where unoccupied parcels are seen as voids between buildings to one where the city is a thick, horizontally extended substrate within which islands of built form are suspended. In this future state, the infrastructure-rich plots and structures of Detroit can be conceptualized as variegated surfaces with a range of potential activities and uses. To accommodate this heterarchical view of urban space, we propose an alternative to the platted street grid. At present, the existing grid forms rectilinear blocks that are massed at the perimeter to reinforce the lines of the streets. Sponge Urbanism transforms these blocks into a distributed and multidirectional system that emerges bottom-up from numerous local insertions, constructions and realignments.

Voids to fields

Fields lend an unprecedented legibility to the shrinking city. Where a compositional representation of the city would relegate vacant lots as omissions in a preexisting fabric, a mapping of available infrastructural amenities across open lots might recast these same spaces toward a potential future. Such a representation produces an understanding of the postindustrial city as extensive and continuous, thus reintegrating the false dialectic of solid/void, built/unbuilt, and density/decline that has simplistically plagued our understanding of "shrinking cities." Describing Detroit as a field may help us to release ourselves from a corrective model of progress and recast what were previously seen as spaces of absence as material full of potential.

We were compelled and helped by Albert Pope's theorization of open space and the exurban city in "The Primacy of Space" (*Ladders*, 1996).

Representations both make visible what exists and project new possibilities across fields of difference. The process is one of working from effects or relationships toward the objects and material conditions that produce them. The basic premise of Sponge Urbanism is that of *radical inclusion*—we are not limited solely to the performative, symbolic, semantic, or compositional. Instead, we seek to develop a generative diagram that operates simultaneously among all of these registers with a mixture of established and inventive representational approaches.

In this project, formal and informal criteria meet in a master diagram that serves as an open repository for drawings of, into, and out of the site. We begin by projecting a field of multiple, divergent, local vectors onto a plan of the existing neighborhood. These multidirectional vectors suggest scalar and perceptual relationships that relate to yet supersede the existing geometry of the neighborhood. The diagram is scaled to a grain slightly larger than existing lot widths to project the eventual lower density of built form, while the vectors follow the existing grid and add a projected rotational overlay. This overlay becomes a scaffold of field orientations that directs the placement of nodes, attractors, or points of programmatic intensity. The points guide interventions of construction, incision, or alteration. Energy resources are located at points where environmental forces are highly concentrated and distributed along existing utility lines. Productive landscapes are defined along water lines that straddle cisterns supplied by rainwater and snowmelt. Wind towers take advantage of the newly open landscape and low building heights to collect energy and tie into remaining fragments of the municipal grid.

In response to the proliferation of unoccupied property, some Detroit residents combined empty and occupied lots into larger parcels. Interboro Partners coined the terms "blots" and "blotting" (2006) to describe the process and a design protocol that was useful to us and others.

The master diagram assumes that the current occupancy rate of 50 percent of structures (by the primarily Bengali immigrant community) is to be maintained. We propose that the other 50 percent of unoccupied homes and lots be divided into smaller units or grouped into larger parcels to accommodate a broad mix of landscape and built uses that might support this community and those directly adjacent to it.

Typological interventions

Sleeves, mounds, sheds, and towers make up a catalogue of formal interventions that include alteration to existing structures, redistribution and sculpting of the ground, insertion of objects, and the point collection and distribution of resources. A field-like, multidirectional organization can grow from these parts and emerge from within the neighborhood through the new local relationships they engender. Voids become spaces of occupation and activity as well as shared open areas.

As a formal object that directs an effect or use, each of the interventions defines a type. The qualities associated with each type range from spatial to programmatic and utilitarian to aesthetic. Each type organizes a territory larger than its material limits: inhabitable sleeves redirect light through existing houses; raked seating creates an indoor theater space looking onto an outdoor stage; hose lengths sweep out productive zones along water supply lines radiating from cisterns; bike and tool sheds provide storage and composting centers keyed to catchments of gardens and residences; windmills are placed according to wind patterns and reinforce or replace municipal utilities. Surfaces are created and considered as part of the logic of building-scale structures and infrastructural lines.

Adapted from "Sponge Urbanism" by Troy Schaum and Rosalyne Shieh (2017)

Installation in an Existing House, Detroit, MI (2010)

13178 Moran Street

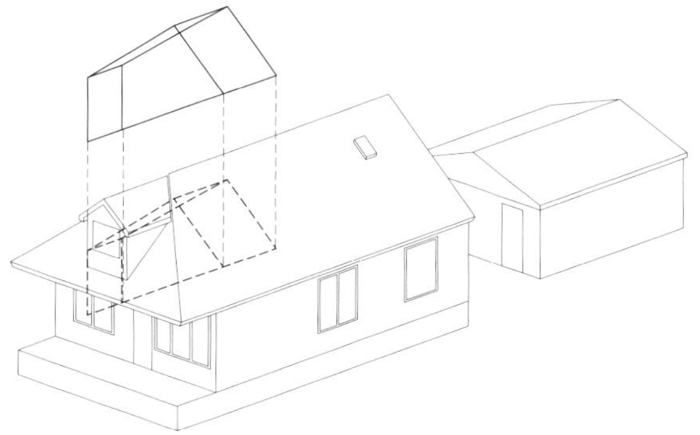

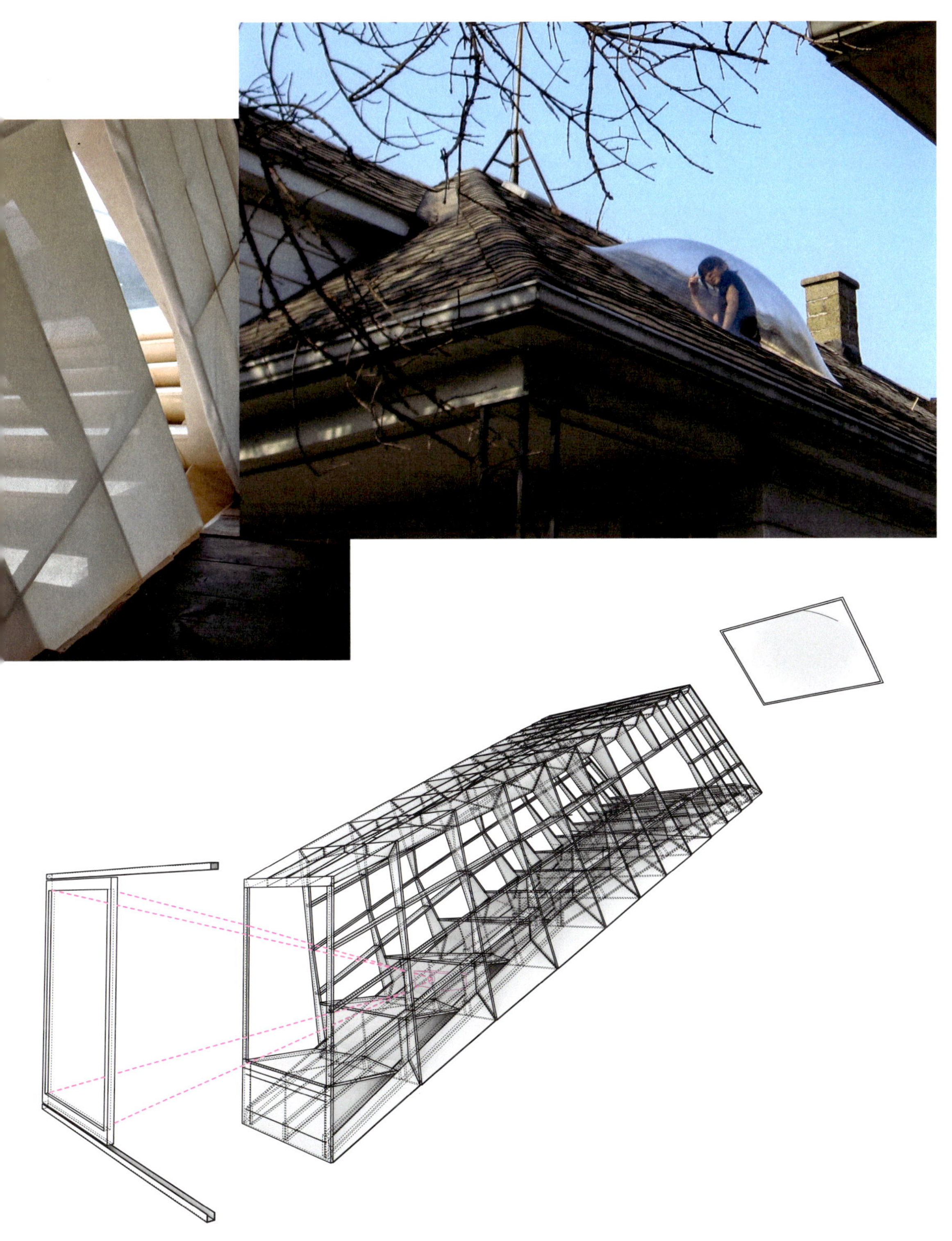

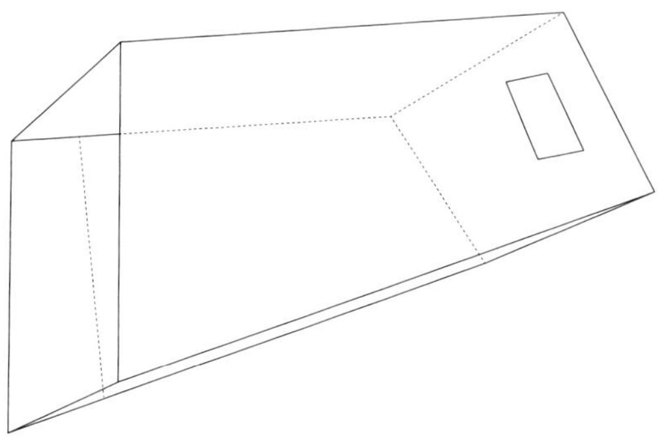

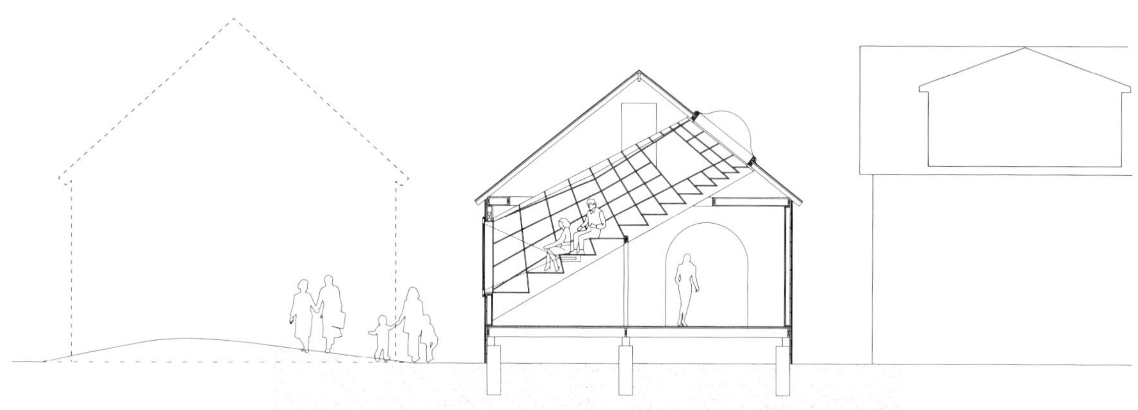

Transverse
Section

0 5' 10' 20'

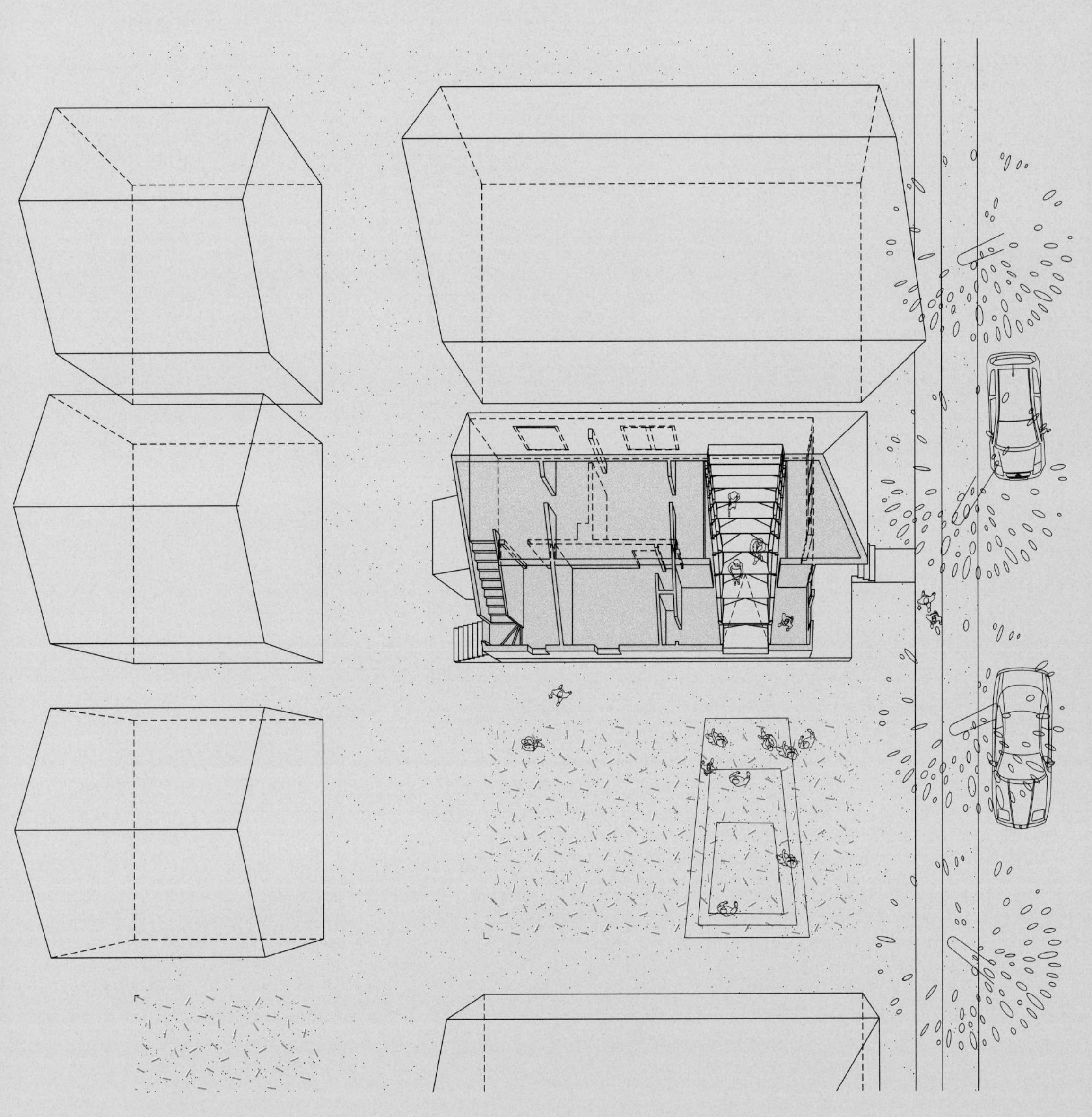

Top: Frank Gohlke, *Landscape (K-mart), St. Paul, Minnesota* (1974)
Bottom: Marco Torres/Houston Press, *Untitled* (2016)

[T]raditional fiction and documentary films [...] generally point the camera toward the subject. [...] [Masao Adachi] proposes a very simple gesture: to turn the camera around 180 degrees. It suggests that our existence is shaped by the world we live in.

—Eric Baudelaire (2017)

On photography and new landscapes

Parking lots, pavement, buildings loosely strewn, almost incidental in their relationship to each other... wires, poles, paint on asphalt. Space here is vast, loose, leaky even.

This photograph was included in an exhibit at the Los Angeles County Museum of Art in 2009 called *New Topographics*. It was a restaging of a show from 1975 at the George Eastman House, a museum of photography in Rochester, NY. At that time—35 years prior—the exhibition represented a break in the genre of landscape photography, which before had been dominated by representations of nature. You could describe it this way: the camera had been rotated, turned, or its lens retrained upon a subject formerly left out of the frame to include the human-made landscape in all its banal reality.

The photos in this show captivated me for many reasons, but mostly because they were familiar. In them I recognized the American suburban landscape I grew up in: one of highways, freeways, and half-mile-square blocks, tract housing enclaves, empty sidewalks, cement curbs everywhere. These photos also offered a way of thinking about space, site, landscape, and building... these were landscapes, but these were cities, too.

A favorite photo of White Oak Music Hall shows it during construction in the deep of night. Maybe first you see the vast darkness of space that engulfs the main building, but then a sort of mutual condition emerges, between the structure and the leaky, diffuse unevenness around it. Poles, wires, signs, and the sheets of material propped near the entrance. It feels like the detritus, all those loose pieces, are hanging in a kind of suspension, and then you can see in the distance the shed with arches, quiet and dark...

Rosalyne Shieh, *Untitled (Kaohsiung)* (2018)

We look backward at history and tradition to go forward; we can also look downward to go upward. And withholding judgment may be used as a tool to make later judgment more sensitive. This is a way of learning from everything.

—Robert Venturi, Denise Scott Brown, and Steven Izenour (1972)

Take a walk around a neighborhood or urban area you are familiar with. Take photographs that capture buildings as subjects, with the single constraint that the building being represented cannot be in the frame.

Spend at least 1 hour to make at least 20 captures.

Print and review your pictures on a table. Arrange and make groupings as you see fit. Make a selection of 5–8 to share with others in a gallery or salon format.

For consideration:
Drawing, space, community, art

Stan Allen,
"Diagrams Matter"
(1998)

Grace Lee Boggs,
Living for Change
(1998)

Patricio Guzmán,
Nostalgia de la luz
(2010)

Marlen Haushofer,
The Wall (1963)

The Heidelberg Project
(1986-)

George Lipsitz,
How Racism Takes Place
(2011)

Albert Pope,
Ladders (1996)

Power House Productions
(2009-)

Harry Smith,
Early Abstractions
(1946-57)

Étienne-Jules Marey, from *Du mouvement dans les fonctions de la vie*, fig. 18 (1868)

Troy Schaum, *White Oak Music Hall Amphitheater* (2016)

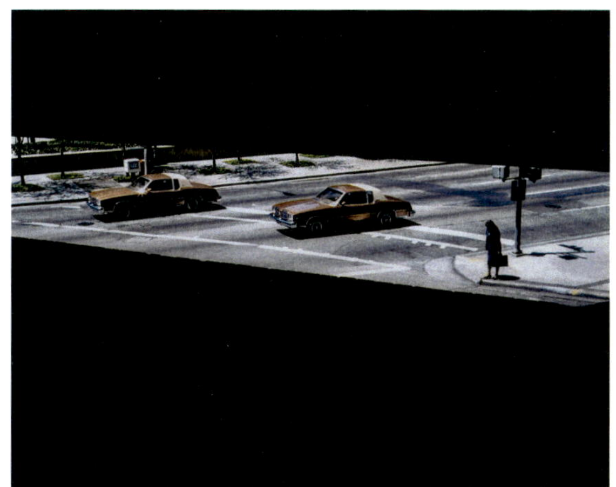

Wim Wenders's photos of Houston have helped us see the city's particular beauty, whether through the slot of a parking garage or the particular slant of a lofted view.

Wim Wenders, *Two Cars and a Woman Waiting* (1983)

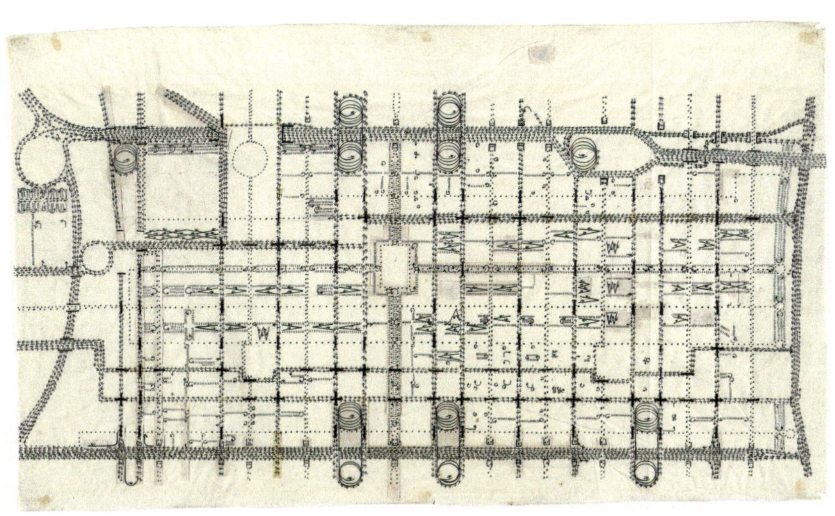

Louis I. Kahn, *Traffic Study Project* (1952)

Wally Santana/Associated Press, *"Taiwan lawmakers brawl over trade agreement with China"* (2010)

A cheap formal analysis can interpret this pileup as an expression of struggle, of effort and agony, but without further information, individual motivations—which may diverge wildly (say, toward resistance or destruction)—cannot be discerned.

Joe Deal, *Untitled View (Albuquerque)* (1974)

We can see what's happening in the moment: people, running across the open space, in lines waiting to get in, standing together, talking. The ground is the picture plane in this point of view, upon which figures are unevenly distributed but ordered. You can trace lines and identify directional clumps as legible elements.

Unknown, *Eiffel Tower, Top-Down View* (n.d.)

The tower is the subject of the photo even though it's not in the photo. What's foregrounded is not the city as artifact, but its activity, a moment in its life or process. How does building organize or make possible such processes?

Wim Wenders, *Drive-In, Marfa, Texas* (1983)

Platform

extend
prepare
encounter
gather
orient
address
sense
appear
clearing
stage
perform
witness
presence
arrive
hold
close
sit with
collect

Might all places be understood as a stage for the incidental? Any space can become a place to reveal or conceal, regardless of shape. Become attuned to the simplest encounters. Become sensitive to the mere possibility of an encounter.

Christian Unverzagt, *Untitled (13178 Moran Street)* (2010)

Within a scene, figures or characters appear. They may be nearby, interact with, or relate to each other. They may appear among others as individuals or in groups. What is a space for a group to appear before itself?

How do we support a general sense of belonging to all those who show up? Can we provide many ways to enter and make leaving easy?

How do we build a connection between the inner life of conscious beings, their social relations, and stuff (cities and buildings as physical things)?

Can we build a place that extends what already exists as well as make something new? Can it both support those already there and all who will arrive in a manner that feels okay to everyone?

Buildings bombard us in their realization (electrical panels, aluminum storefronts, mastic, silicone, drywall), and at the same time, they are also something else. Are they sites or parts of sites? Sites as scenes, frames for encounters, seats of a collective?

How is naming and distinguishing these terms useful: scene, group, community, and collective?

How do we recognize the fragments of a better, different world—perhaps one of community care and mutuality in place—that already exist? What are ways architecture can support, assemble, or augment?

What if we foreground the city as an experience and prioritize the balm it provides its collective inhabitants, instead of something to be understood? How would we describe it? What art can guide us?

Peter Molick, *Raven Tower* (2016)

The original Raven Tower was built overlooking downtown and Interstate 45 as a "conversation piece" by the owner of the metal shop on the ground floor. A giant plastic rooster weather vane was blown off during Hurricane Ike. In an attempt to inhabit the site, we cut holes in the metal shop siding, opening it to the surrounding bayou. We brought a couple of Columbia faculty to the top on a particularly active night after White Oak opened; I don't think they knew what to say.

At stake is the notion of the city as a public sphere, in which all city residents can make political and spatial claims of citizenship and have a right to city life and livelihoods.

—Kian Goh, Anastasia Loukaitou-Sideris, and Vinit Mukhija (2022)

Note

"Houston has no zoning"

You often hear people say: "Houston has no zoning." That's technically true—Houston has no use-zoning under its development code. This fact is enough to turn our architect and urbanist minds toward imagining: What might happen if life across ages and vocations were simultaneously conducted, all of it threaded within a dense and supportive architectural fabric? Old people, young people, people of all races and cultures, in cafés, hardware stores, greengrocers, offices, playgrounds, on buses and bikes. Pedestrians and strollers, doctors and corner stores, dogs on leashes, people chasing hats. We can scale up from this fine-grain to the hulking mass of a large city, sliding from the register of the individual to the collective, a single life to the multitude. At the street level, Jane Jacobs's loving portrait of Boston's North End is conjured, as is Richard Scarry's multispecies busy city (one fondly recalled from intro urbanism courses, the other from childhood libraries). Both images bask us in the glow of the city as a hive of activity and a collective body harboring a place-based sense of togetherness, of social connection, even interdependence... all within arm's reach of the project of urban public space, a place where all people mix freely and belong equally.

Houston is and has many things, but it is not exactly *that*. America's long history of policing black bodies and criminalizing homelessness continues apace in Texas's largest city, making the sort of harmonious visions described above a product of privileged experience or complete delusion. For Houston, in place of zoning, other protocols exist to restrict or control use, form, and who lives where, such as neighborhood-based private deed restrictions and historic districts. So although the statement "Houston has no zoning" is true, Houston is as segregated as any U.S. city in terms of use and type, as well as race, class, and wealth.

We still want to make physical places that are inclusive and free. How do we work on that within the urban reality of Houston? In Houston, it is less a question of the classic street section and more a consideration of the loose, collective mass of parking lots, islands and curbs, isolated patches of green, walkways, awnings, and building fronts. These are the dominant elements of strip mall urbanism, and collectively they are underconsidered sites for publicness. What positive or poetic visions can we have for these liminal spaces? Especially where they meet buildings and projects, these are sites that can be designed as openings onto a collective city. Can we direct our attention toward ways these spaces might be designed beyond functionally funneling people into retail boxes? How they can be supportive of bodies of different needs and abilities, of various vulnerabilities, of life in all its dimensions? Might they also link together into larger areas for rest, gathering, or passive togetherness, sites of ecological and urban systems brought together on principles of mutuality?

We want our work to contribute to the city as a public sphere, and remind ourselves to disengage the received image of that (e.g., plazas, squares, courts, and their associations with ideas of fora and agorae) from the reality of it (exurban landscapes), and actively look for it in all the spaces we actually have.

Amphitheater & Multi-Stage Music Hall, Houston, TX (2016)

White Oak Music Hall

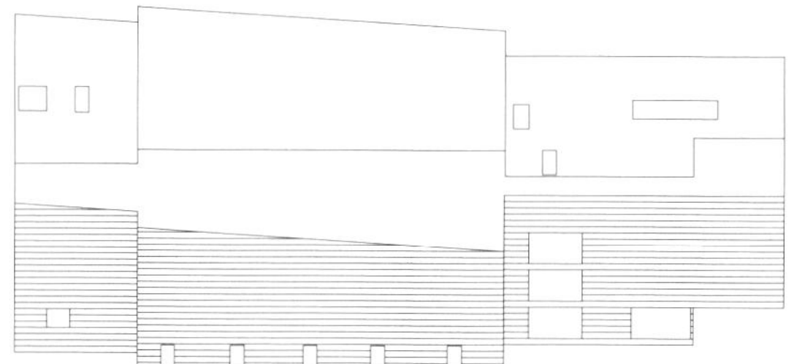

WHITE
OAK
MUSIC
HALL
North ST 400

WH
OA
M
H
FDC

Elevations

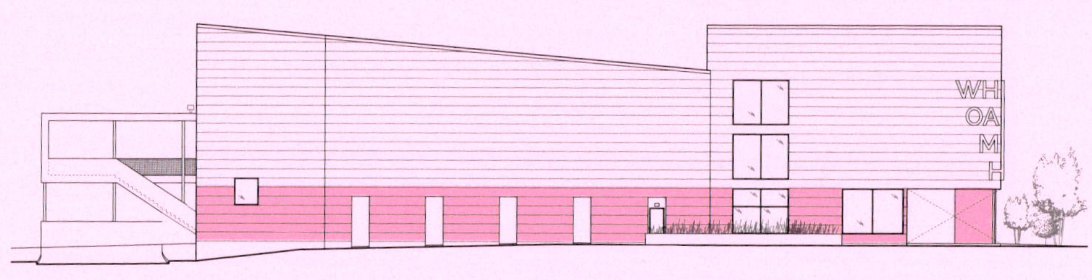

North

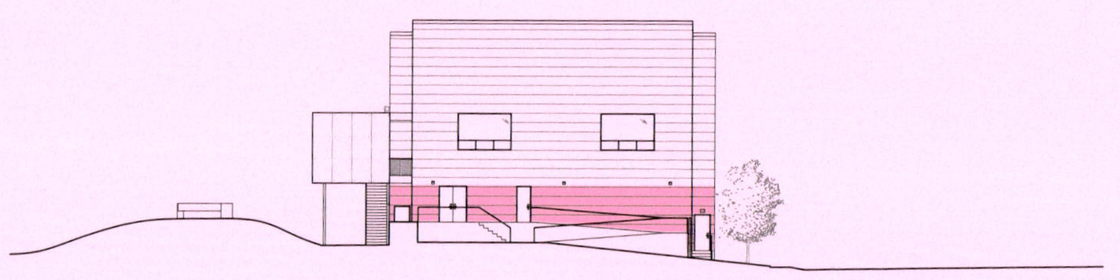

East

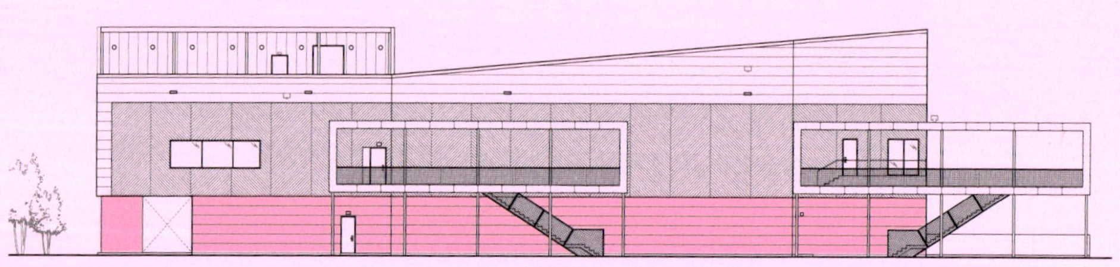

South

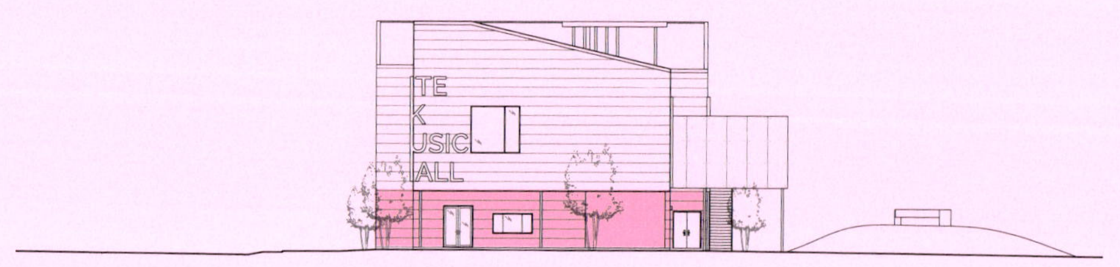

West

Sections

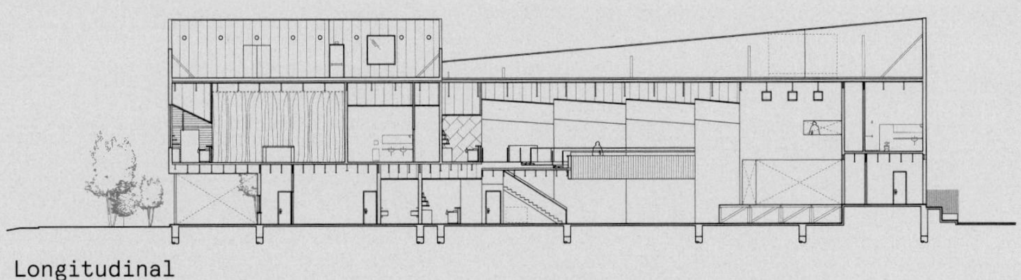

Longitudinal

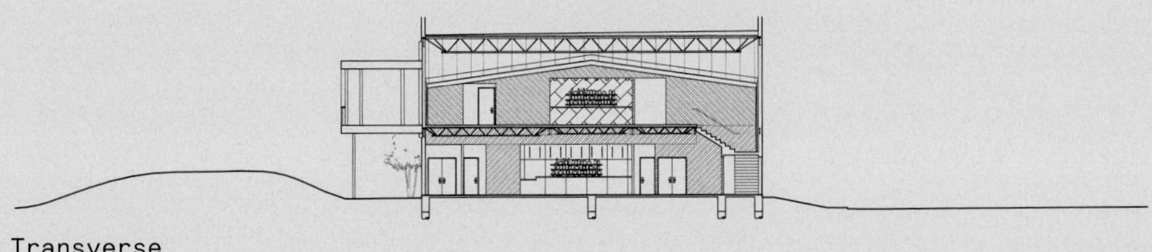

Transverse

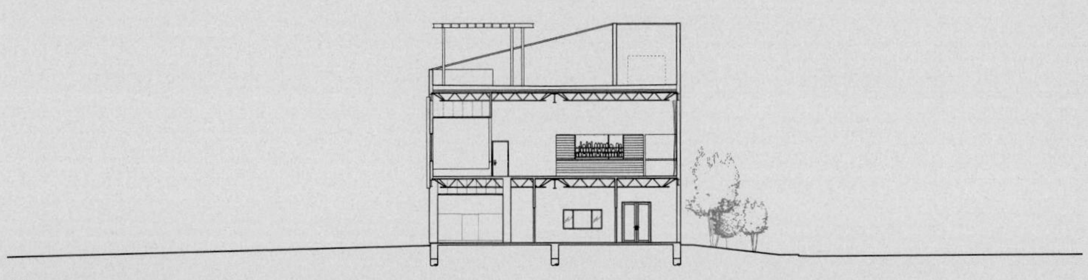

Transverse

0 10' 20'

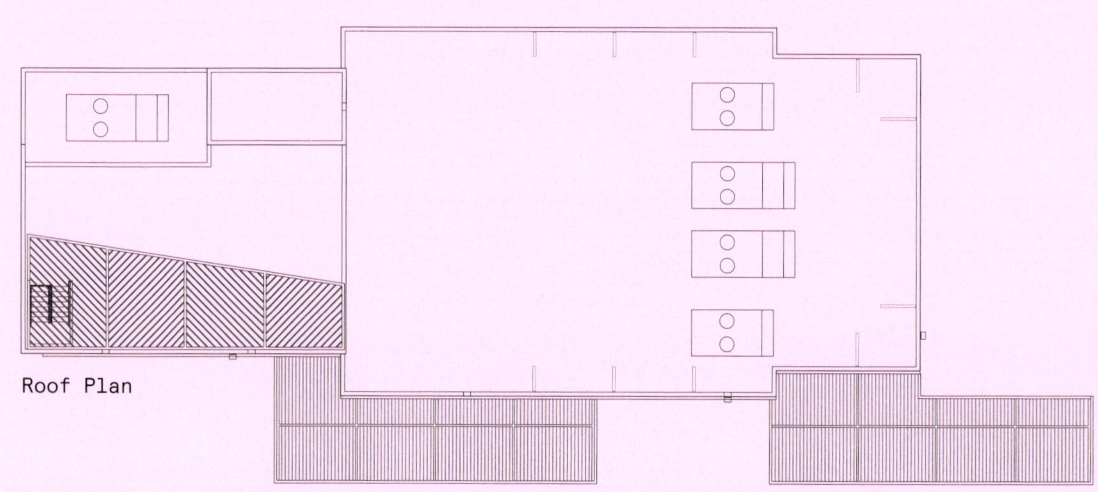

Roof Plan

Roof Terrace Plan

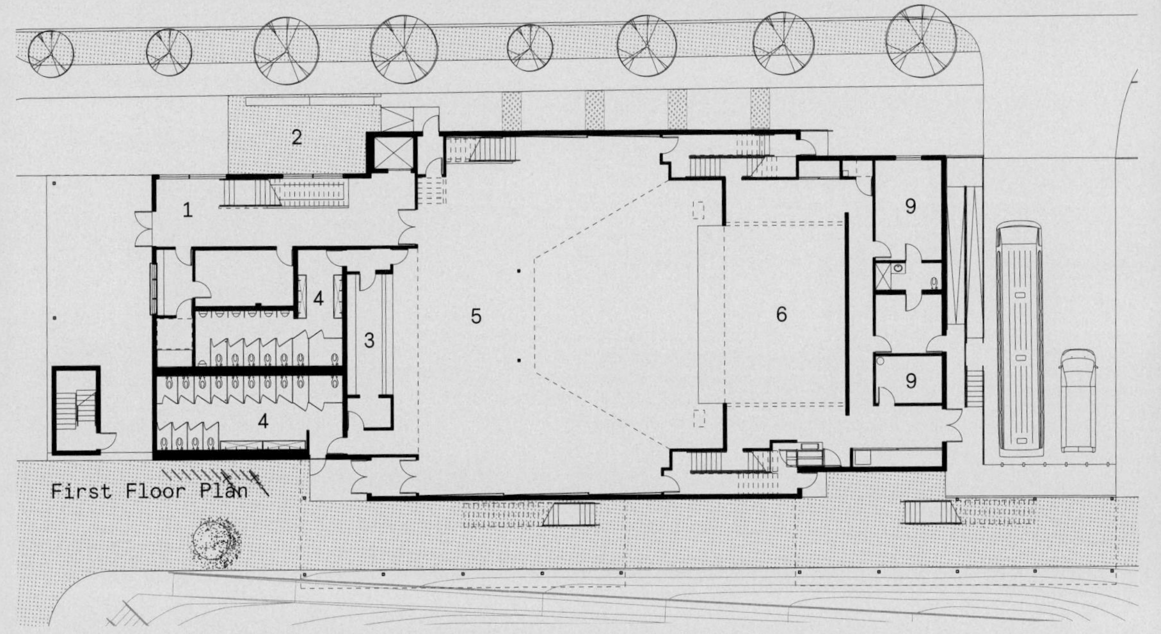

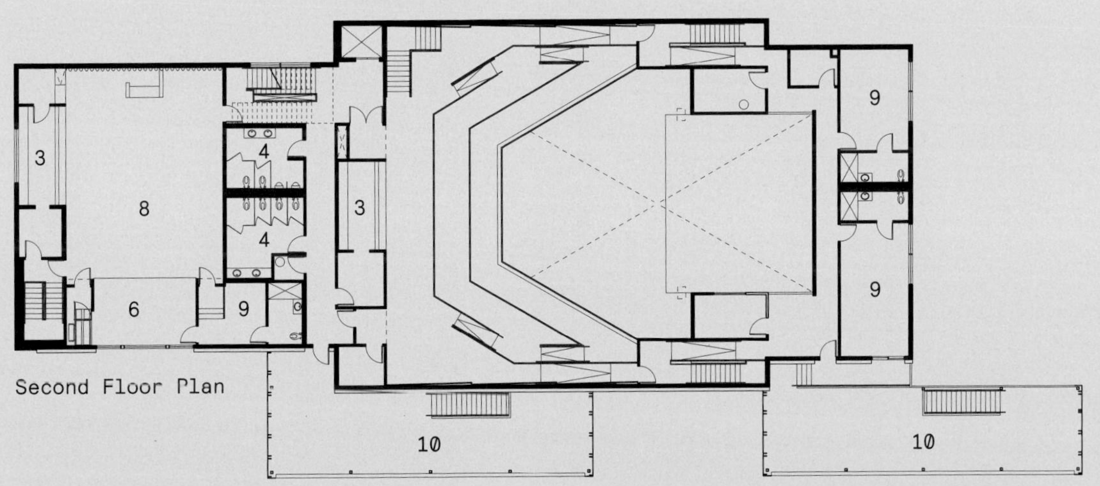

1 Lobby
2 Outdoor Patio
3 Bar
4 Restrooms
5 Main Venue
6 Performance Area
7 Roof Viewing Terrace
8 Small Venue
9 Dressing Room
10 Balcony

0 10' 20'

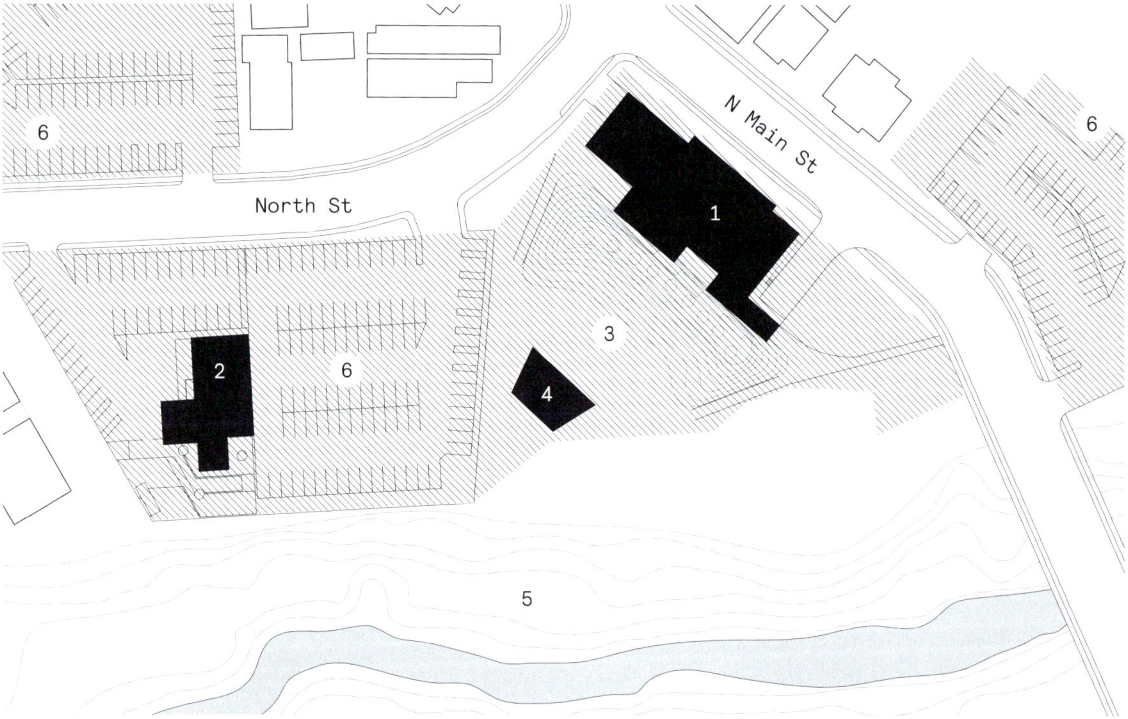

The site is in a former light-industrial zone on the Little White Oak Bayou, which is kind of like a muddy river. Interstate 45 is to the west of the site, and downtown Houston is a few miles south of it. Places like WOMH are becoming more connected through growing transportation networks: Houston's hike and bike trail runs through the bayou and a light-rail station is accessible in a ten-minute walk.

The entire project is a loose assemblage of landscape, buildings, outdoor structures, parking lots, and adapted existing structures. Together, these form an open campus feathered into the existing neighborhood.

1 White Oak Music Hall
2 Raven Tower Icehouse
3 Amphitheater (White Oak Lawn)
4 Outdoor Stage
5 Little White Oak Bayou
6 Parking

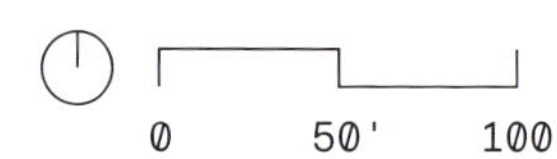

Wood slats tune the room for unamplified human voice and acoustic sets.

WH
OA
M
H

WOMH's neon was an afterthought. The sign is a throwback to neons and has become an icon of the neighborhood. A perhaps too on-the-nose lesson from Robert and Denise!

Troy Schaum, *Arare-Koboshi at Katsura Imperial Villa* (2024)

RS I was thinking back to one of the first times we hung out. We had just met, and you invited me to come with you to dinner at a colleague's house. I was new to MIT, still commuting from New York. I wasn't familiar with the area and didn't have many friends up here, so when I accepted your invitation, I realized I would be going along for the ride. I have a very impressionistic memory of that night, but not because the memory is hazy, more because I never knew exactly what was coming next. Walking, walking, some talking, more walking. Maybe there was some time we spent in a T station waiting for a train that never came, only to leave and continue walking. At some point, I gave up on extracting an overarching plan from you, and started to see marks we could hit, with time and the route between being elastic, adjusting block by block. We saw faces we recognized, sometimes stopping to chat, others you waved at and called to across the street. At some point, someone happened to be going to the same dinner and we became three. As three, we arrived to a dinner where everyone was already seated and smiling. I remember some faces and gestures, but no names. And then later, close to midnight, I gave you a hug and stepped into a car, leaving you at the side of the road, smiling and waving as you prepared to embark on your night of walking across the city back to your bed. Were we in Dorchester?

GC Yes, in Dorchester.

RS Pretty far. You were going to walk all the way across Boston to Cambridge. I think what struck me about that night was the continuum of the experience. The continuum and the intimacy of it. There was a kind of continuous energy that seemed to keep the city open. I think of it maybe as psychogeography in reverse—if we understand psychogeography as an uncovering of a personal geography of place, what I experienced that night with you was a creative creation of place, a kind of forging, a fashioning. Maybe it was alchemical. I'd love to hear you talk about the elements of that evening, which have to do with the city and place and people and relationships, about a spatial or social practice.

GC Impressionistic is a good way to describe the evening, because I walk with a desire for my movements to be more art than science. But I recognize that the art of walking dovetails with a more scientific and rationalistic approach to cities, one interested in collecting data or carefully mapping contours and analyzing forms or features or cultures. Too often it's done from a distance, with a focus on the aggregate or the abstract, two groupings that you have to be careful about because of how much they get away from the deep specificity and particularity of place. Abstraction pulls many things together to have some generalized observation, and with the aggregate, whether it be quantitative studies or qualitative analysis, many features and behaviors and stories are at risk of being hidden in the cracks, crevices, and interstices.

My main problem with abstraction and aggregation is they encourage an approach to the city that's about mastery—a means to master the city, a means to create the grounds for control or dominance. I'm interested in continuing to see the city not as something to control but as a messy and often inchoate, deeply improvisational, surprising, unpredictable, ever-evolving organism. How do we embrace or even rush headlong into the city as an often mysterious entity, and how might we have a richer understanding of the city, but also of ourselves, if we loosen our grip for mastery, step back from that desire? I know the desire to control can feel insatiable, especially for those in the academy or the city-focused professions (architecture, urban design, city planning) whose projects are finding ways to make them move in directions they envision as "best" for the city (or for their own purposes). Maybe that movement is motivated by goodness, but it may also be inspired by making a profit or making change or opposing change—there are so many motivations for asserting control over the city.

By contrast, sometimes beginning with no sense of control or mission allows me to make myself the target of the unexpected, allows me to have surprising encounters with people and places and the ubiquitous nonhuman life around us. Rather than enter with an agenda, I try to see what makes the strongest claims on my imagination and my emotions as I move through the world. What lays claim to my senses? The smells that hit me, whether a magnolia bloom or diesel exhaust, the sounds that arrest my attention or soothe it along, the textures of the places I sit and lean against and walk upon. What directed my movements that evening? We've been calling it impressionistic, but maybe it's more a pointillistic sensibility—filling in things little by little by little in an unsystematic way that invites further exploration and encounters.

RS So you're constructing images, to extend the metaphor.

GC Yes, and I'm often putting them in conversation with other images, ideas, scenes, and characters that occupy room in my imagination. Literature, especially literature on cities, already inhabits a lot of that space. For example, Calvino's *Invisible Cities*—remember the city of Esmeralda, in which people don't take the same route between any two places? They move with a wonderful sense of discovery and adventure because of their zigzagging routes. I often think of myself as one of Esmeralda's residents, creating a zigzag route in the city. Another work that frequently comes to mind is China Miéville's sci-fi fantasy/social novel *The City & the City*, in which two cities occupy the same geographic space but "unsee" each other. I find this—being blind to the existence of those right before us—too symptomatic of modern life; we are in the same physical space, but we unsee each other because we've been trained from very early to not see the other person, the other neighborhood, the other city. My walks are, in part, a pursuit of routes to undermine my bad training.

Here's an example: I find that landscape sometimes resists me, only to (re)discover that my body craves a grid. I suspect that my love of New York and my decades-long socialization within it, shaped by my wanderings and explorations there, have soldered a grid map to my imagination and bequeathed me a strong attachment to the city form. I have to rip myself apart from that longing, and unfetter the grid from my sensibilities, to appreciate places like Boston, with its many cul-de-sacs and different urban formations. I walk, then, not merely to discover what's out there: I aim to discover what's in me and what in me resists what's around me. The hope is to be more generous and more accommodating. I hope for a more capacious view and understanding of the city, but also a richer engagement with it. Moving through the city at walking pace, around three miles an hour, encourages movement at human pace—humane pace?—and fosters the ability to construct—à la Kevin Lynch—images of the city.

RS I had that experience with the grid too. I encountered Manhattan as a grown person in my twenties and it was an illumination, right? You're like, "Wow, this makes so much sense!" And then I remember traveling to Prague and going on a city tour and saying something to the tour guide about how confused I was about how the city was laid out, and him saying something back to me along the lines of, "It makes total sense to me." And I thought, Oh, maybe I am projecting something and I thought that I was so rational. I had a moment where I realized my own naivete or my own ignorance or my own, I don't know, maybe it was an American moment.

GC Or a moment of seeking control, or of categorical understanding.

RS Right. That's interesting because I think your way of walking and experiencing the city shifts us out of the oppositional relationship between self and city or between planner and city or between architect and space or place. I think a lot about binaries as a way for us to organize the world, but they also limit our understanding of the world. With you, there seems to be some project other than mastery and binaries. Maybe it's of self-realization, of fashioning a way of being in the world that gives meaning to the creative practice? I know it encompasses writing and walking and teaching and talking and relating and building relationships, but I'm not sure how to define it. I remember a lecture in which you said, "What is important is not so much the symbolic as the social."

GC Walking is a social act. You step out to write a story with your footfalls as you encounter others. That precedes—and trumps—any symbolic weight we put on its shoulders. To walk is to recognize how much the assembly of humanity and other living things are bursting with wisdom, are bursting with lessons for the self, are crucial to how we construct the self—sometimes with their help, sometimes in opposition to them.

It makes me think of Wordsworth in *The Prelude*, walking through London, talking about "all the specimens of man": "Through all the colours which the sun bestows, And every character of form and face..." He talks about Russians and Swedish and French and Spanish and Moors and Native Americans and Malays and Chinese. How intoxicating and beguiling to observe a city's variety across a broad geographic range. And across generations, too: children at play with wondrous abandon; teens promenading at the mall with their best disaffected-cool style; young couples exchanging delicious whispers; the bemused old man running to keep up with an eager granddaughter; strangers complaining about slow train service and outdoing each other with memories of unreliable transportation. All this is beautiful to regard, and it leaves me a happy eavesdropper. It shouldn't surprise you, then, to hear that the richest emotion that emerges from my walking is gratitude: gratitude for who I encounter, gratitude for what I encounter, gratitude for reminders of our possibilities and finitude. Gratitude invites generosity, invites recognition, invites acknowledgment, invites devotion, imbues us with a sense of responsibility. And this is why as I walk I ask, What does it mean to move through the world with gratitude?

It's about a self that's poised to give, rather than the flâneur whose sensibility is to notice and come back with some lesson or pronouncement. It's not a reporter's sensibility, although I spend considerable time looking around, speaking to strangers, and recording impressions and observations and exchanges. The question that chases me as a walker, as a writer, as someone thinking about urban design and urban planning and architecture, is: What do we owe each other? The heart of much of what I'm interested in—pluralism, governance, the accessibility and openness of our public spaces, racial justice, inequality, the climate crisis—takes its beat from the questions, What kind of claims do we have on each other? What claims do the living have on us? But, a caution: We ought to approach people without condescension, without saying, "Oh, I know what you need," or even, "I'm here to help." Because as well-intentioned as those statements may be, they come with a dose of arrogance, an inability to listen. The basic task is to look around and see resplendence or lack and seek what it asks of us, invites out of us.

RS This seems to tie back to another thing I remember about our walks—that first one and the many we've taken since. It's so far from the flâneur's disconnected looking and observation—you are building and maintaining and cultivating relationships. The saying hello, the recognizing people who you've seen on other walks, the walking to a colleague's house, bringing another colleague along... Walking and relating and encountering and engaging are actually all one in your practice. I keep going back to that word *practice*, your building of the social through space. But you're also a writer. So how does writing fit into that practice?

GC Writing is thinking that's unsatisfied with mere noticing. My writing practice shapes my thinking, and often the thinking is produced during walking or through walking or sometimes for walking. To walk is to think, not merely of myself, but of others, whether it be neighbors or those wild turkeys that show up around Cambridge like sidewalk gangsters. My interest in thinking of others is one of the reasons I'm uncomfortable with the flâneur tradition, where a lone person walks through the city like an aloof scout. And yet, I'm never sure what I truly think until I write. *Solvitur ambulando*, they say: "It is solved by walking." True enough, but even more: It is solved by writing.

Writing is, crucially, witness. As walking is an attempt to cultivate the habit of witness, of bearing witness, my writing—informed by my walking—also becomes a habit, a practice, of witness. Whether it be in a notebook or on my phone, I'm jotting things down as I walk, and later when I'm at a desk—or at my favorite place to scribble and compose, a kitchen counter—I write to make sense of my observations and thoughts. Maybe the words are just for me, or for a larger audience, anything from a letter to an essay, but I have to write to speak to and about experiences lived in the open.

A walk is an act of sharing, of recognizing that most spaces outside our homes are shared spaces. I want the opportunity to be in people's lives and have them in mine. I want a chance to see as much of this resplendent world as I can, and to respond to appropriately. So, I walk. And write.

Pen to paper, fingers to keyboard, feet to ground are varied and interrelated forms to produce and process thought, to witness, to share. The walking—in its shape, rhythm, observations, mood—informs the writing. The writing—with me as a stand-in for the reader, as the reader's advocate—informs the walking. But writing allows me to do things that walking can't, such as the freedom of a do-over, the forgiveness of a revision. The sharing that's possible with words goes far beyond the reach of my legs, and the walker in me wishes it were possible to transcend geography and time in ways my writing can. Writing doesn't always go three miles per hour, but that's part of its attraction and power—the ability to build the social through space. And time.

RS I want to come back to the city as the site of walking. What you've been describing is possible to see or experience in cities. Those sites and experiences would be accessed differently in a suburban or rural environment. The city offers something specific, certain things and not others. Why do you choose to walk in cities?

GC I absolutely love the city. Part of this is an accident of biography; I've always lived in fascinating cities. I was born and raised in Kingston, Jamaica. Then I moved to New Orleans, which I left for a megacity, New York City, which was followed by Charlottesville. By the time I got to Charlottesville, I was in my forties, after decades of being habituated to cities. In cities I had formed my thinking, my habits, my sensibility, my passions, my desires. Cities were ingrained in me by then, their DNA running through my bloodstream. Charlottesville forced me to also consider what it meant to connect to landscape; in turn the need to understand the varied meanings of cities and landscapes made me walk with more zeal and studiousness in cities. In Cambridge, where I live now, and in nearby Boston and Somerville, I constantly walk to put myself in the crosshairs of histories, memories, and sensibilities. The cities keep repaying my efforts and show me how to ask new questions—or old questions with renewed attention.

What draws me to walking—or, rather, what walking draws out of me—happens in a more abundant and concentrated way in cities. One clear answer to "Why cities?" is their abundance. I love the rural, and I like the suburbs... As a side note, I think American suburbs are more complicated and enriching than many have given them credit for. For all the flaws of the suburbs, and despite their historical tendency to retreat or withdraw or disengage from difference, they are also places of abundance. Despite the history of their formation, and although they boast repeated, homogeneous forms of architecture, suburbs contain a "hidden abundance"—fifteen houses might look exactly the same from the street, but you just need to open the garage doors to see how diverse interests and passions and beliefs are. One person's garage has loads of train sets because they're an obsessive hobbyist, while their neighbor is an avid collector of early 20th-century tools, and the next house has a bunch of dads practicing as if they are about to start the next popular punk band. And there's the neighbor whose garage I most want to hang out in, the editor with a garage overflowing with thousands of books, spanning scores of genres, cultures, generations. The suburbs are places of abundance, but that "many-ness" feels more private, more hidden, more removed from me. In the city, that abundance, that multiplicity, is way more in the open.

Cities by their nature are places that people gravitate toward, coming from many, many other places through migration and movement. The city is a place of refuge, a place of hope, a mecca, a promised land; city life, with its economic, social, cultural, and religious mix and aspirations, offers a vibrancy that is as remarkable as it's inexhaustible. The many different experiences and communities and strata in cities (though that's rapidly changing because of how expensive cities have become) make walking in them feel like being in an endless classroom. Different social and cultural formations create an abundance, and they lay bare so many more claimants before you, allow so many more forms of witness because of the very publicness of cities, which in turn allows a place to ask much more of you. Add to that the anonymity that one can have, which allows levels of observation that one can't necessarily have in the suburb or in the rural without inviting or arousing suspicion. All of that makes a city enriching and full of surprise, a place of spectacle, a site of serendipity. For me, it's a walker's paradise.

RS Our conversation has been about a creative practice constructed through walking and connection. And a part of that practice has to do with people, and with the relationships we have to place. We are both here, and have become friends, as two people at a specific place—educators and colleagues at a university. What role do students and education play in all of this? Does teaching become a way for you to explore certain things or to practice your gratitude or to remind yourself to bear witness?

GC Teaching is an invitation to gratitude: you get the privilege of learning from and alongside students, staff, and colleagues; you get paid to share your curiosities and passions; your other creative practices—walking and writing, in my case—are informed by the conversations you have daily with the many communities and disciplines you're fortunate to inhabit or overlap with. In all this, teaching is also a reminder to bear witness.

I invite my students to see how design, urban planning, walking, and writing can mediate experience, and how experience becomes a way of measuring life. We often speak about teaching people to read like a writer, but I also fundamentally want my students to read like a walker. What does it mean to read like a walker? In some sense I'm reading the streets and I'm reading myself, but I'm also allowing experience to loop into how I read. This reading informs how I see places, and it fosters patience and sustains attention. If I'm fortunate, I make better sense of what I see and encounter; when I don't, I more thoughtfully live with ambiguity or confusion. Part of my role as an educator is to communicate this. More important is this reminder: To read like a walker is to recognize how literature is not like life. Narrative, with its neat arcs and order and control, is unlike life with its unpredictability, injustice, loose ends, and confusions. Therefore, I read the streets to see within writing the resonances of experience, but also how writing reaches its limit in the presence of the multitudinous complexity of experience.

With walking, one could say, "Oh, it's a design practice," or "It's a creative practice." But more than anything else, it's a hermeneutical practice, because it asks basic questions about how to discover, interpret, act, or be silent and express awe in the presence of mystery. My teaching is an extension of this practice, and often its precursor. How do you understand yourself? How do you interpret the self, whether it be yourself or other selves? How do you understand and engage with the world in its variety and complexity? This understanding will then inform behavior, inform practice, and inform the necessary questions that we have missed or taught ourselves to unsee.

Invited Competition, Cultural Institution, Houston, TX (2019)

Houston Endowment Headquarters

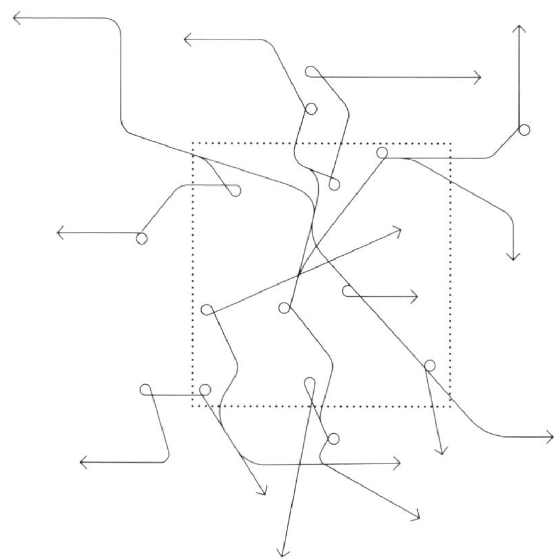

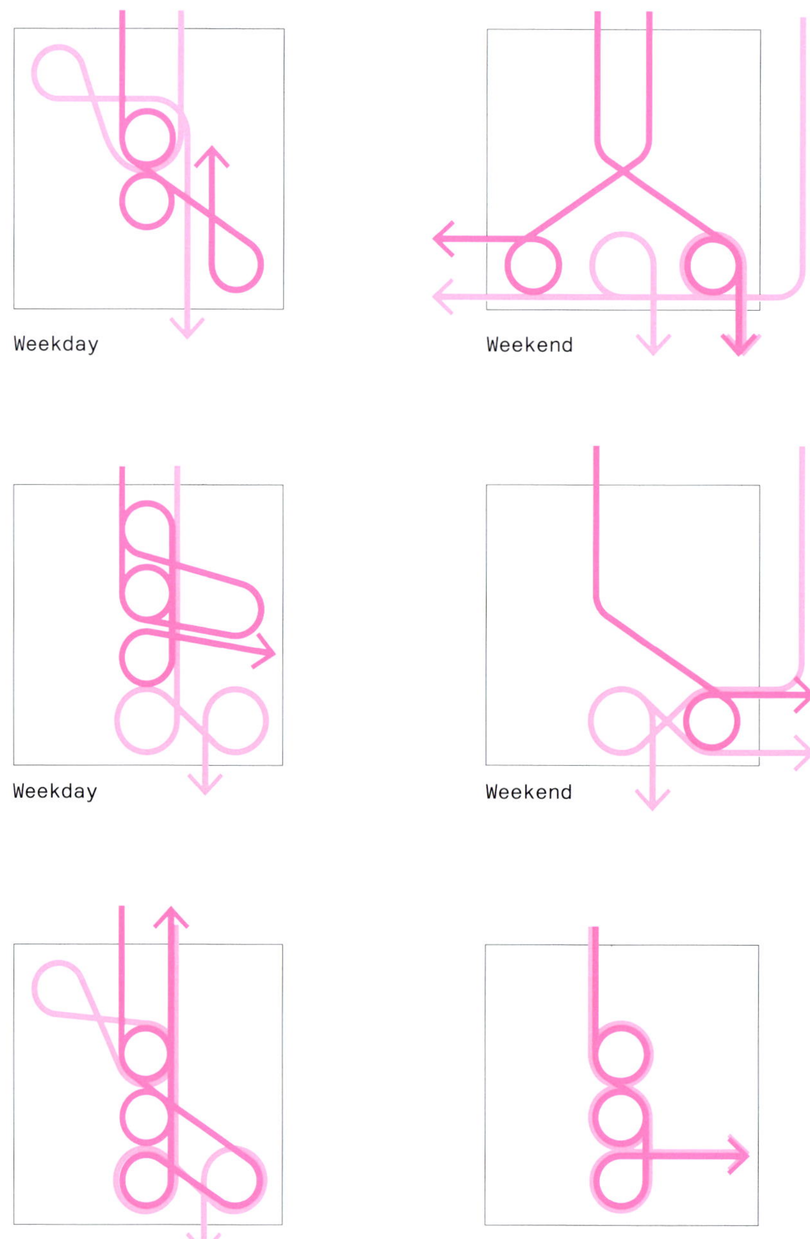
Weekday
Weekend
Weekday
Weekend
Board Meeting
Event

Houston Endowment
Program (sq ft)

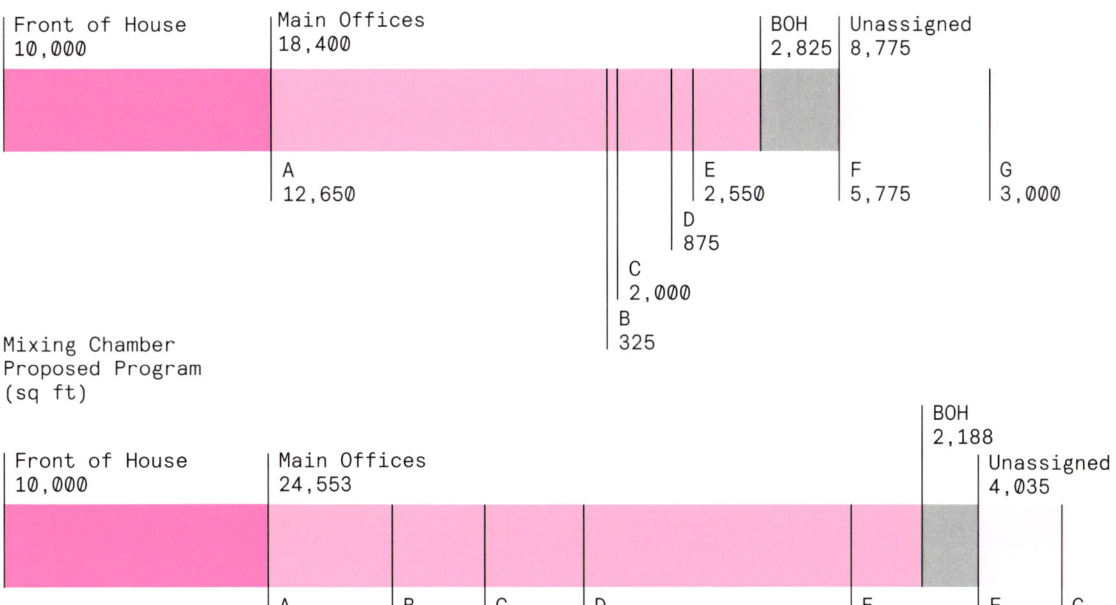

A Cellular Offices
B Open Plan Work
C Meeting Rooms
D Breakout & Collaboration
E Other Support
F Circulation / Structure
G Mechanical / Electrical

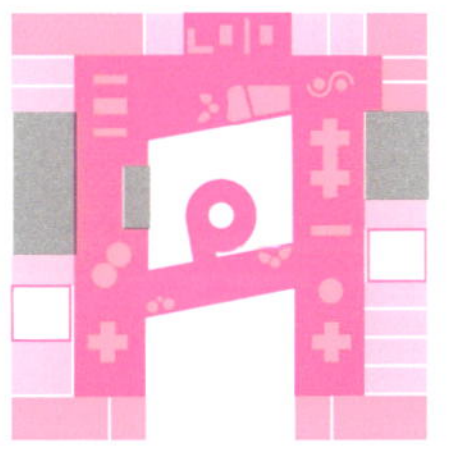

Private / Individual
Semi-Public / Group
Mixing Chamber
Exterior
Back of House

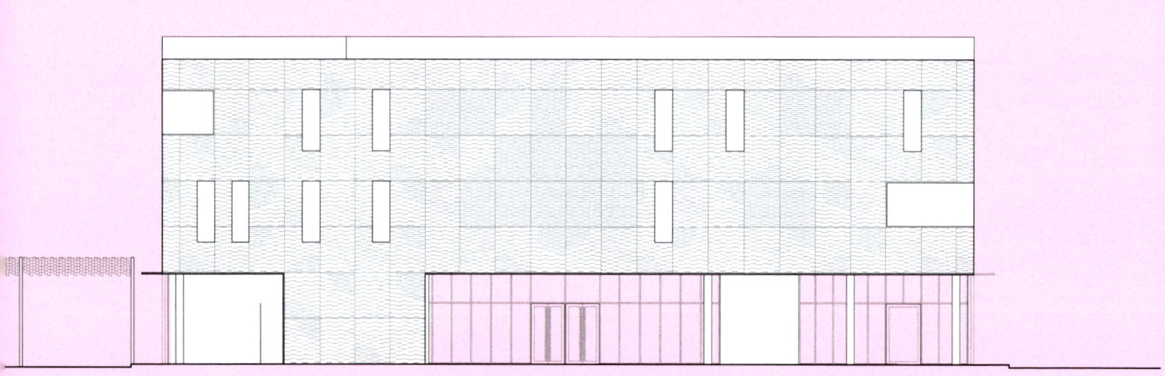

North

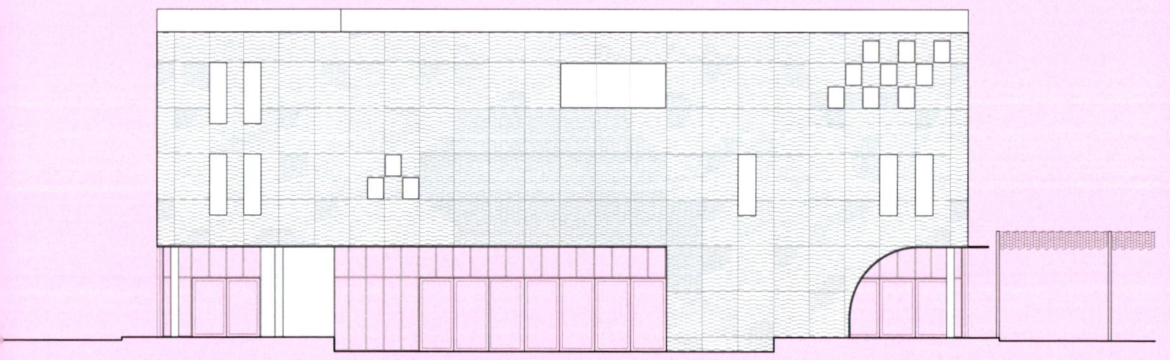

South

The logic of the terracotta facade is that it could be tuned, it was designed to be responsive to the environment, and most importantly, it was soft. Cities like Houston too often focus on their hard edges; we wanted this to feel lighter.

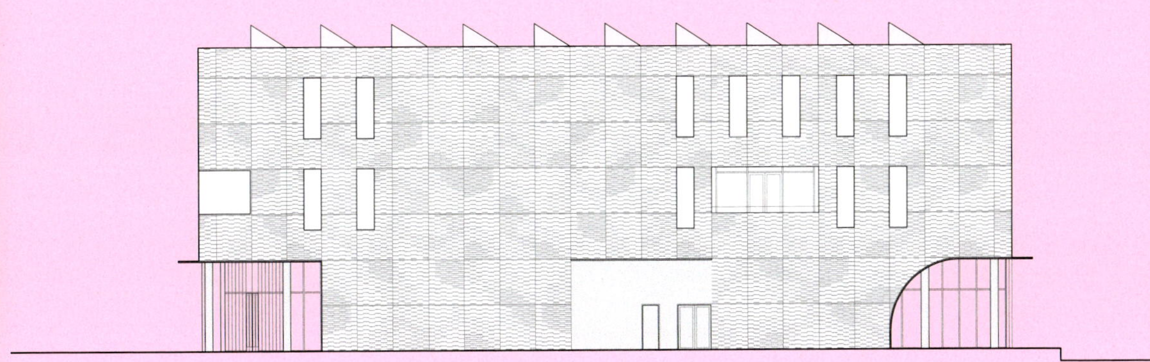

East

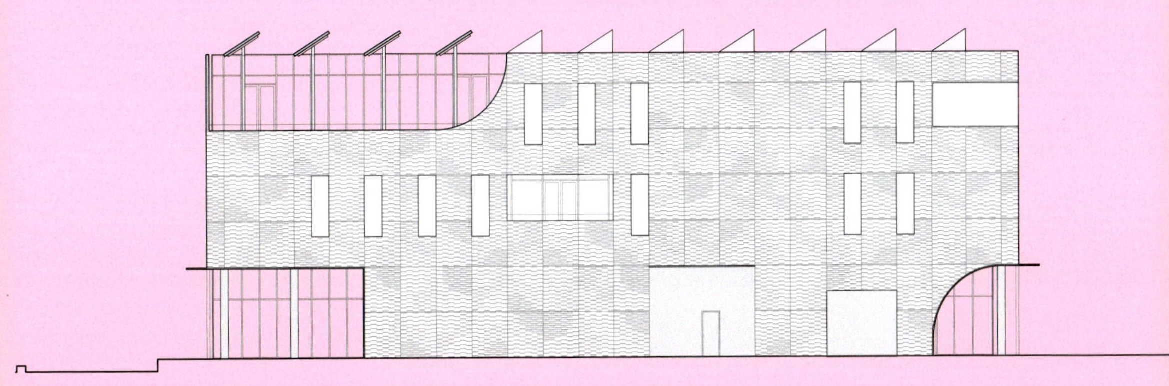

West

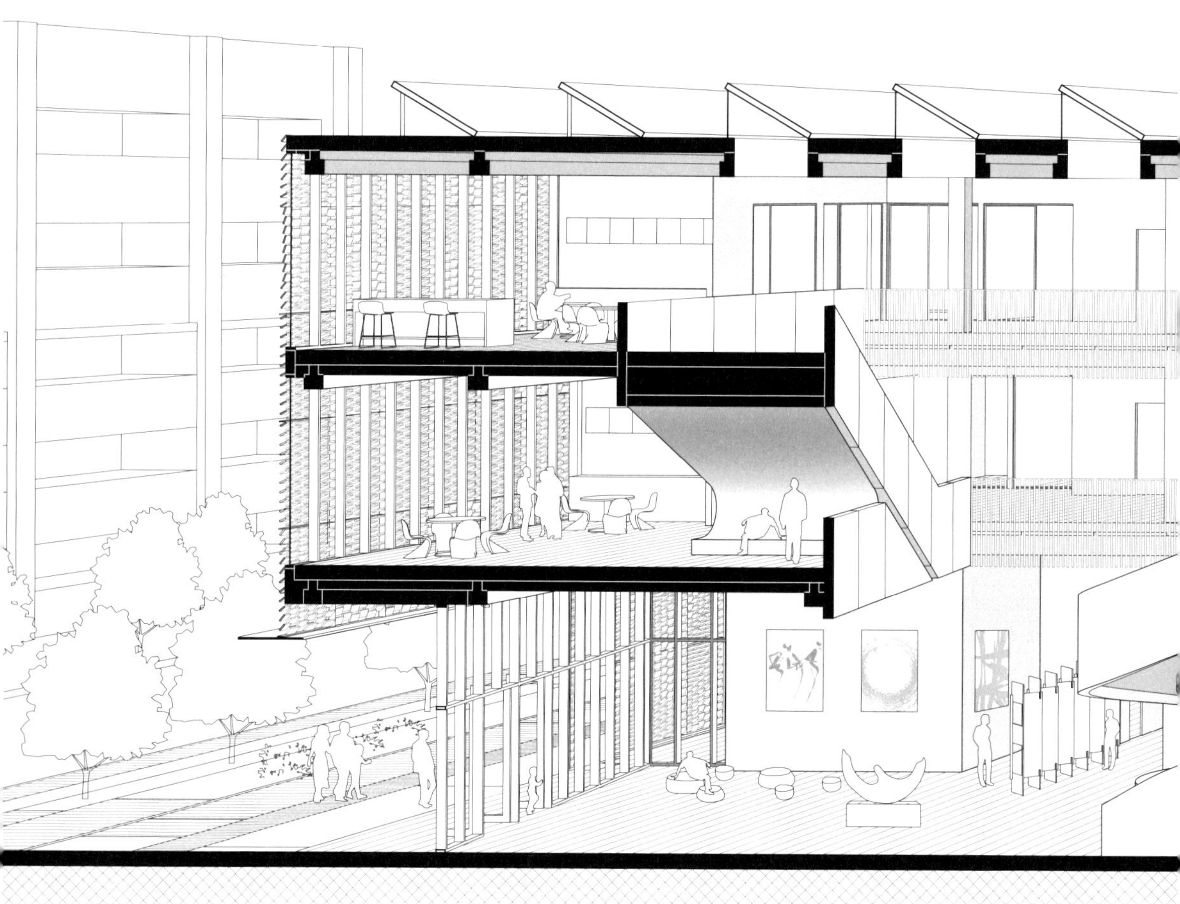

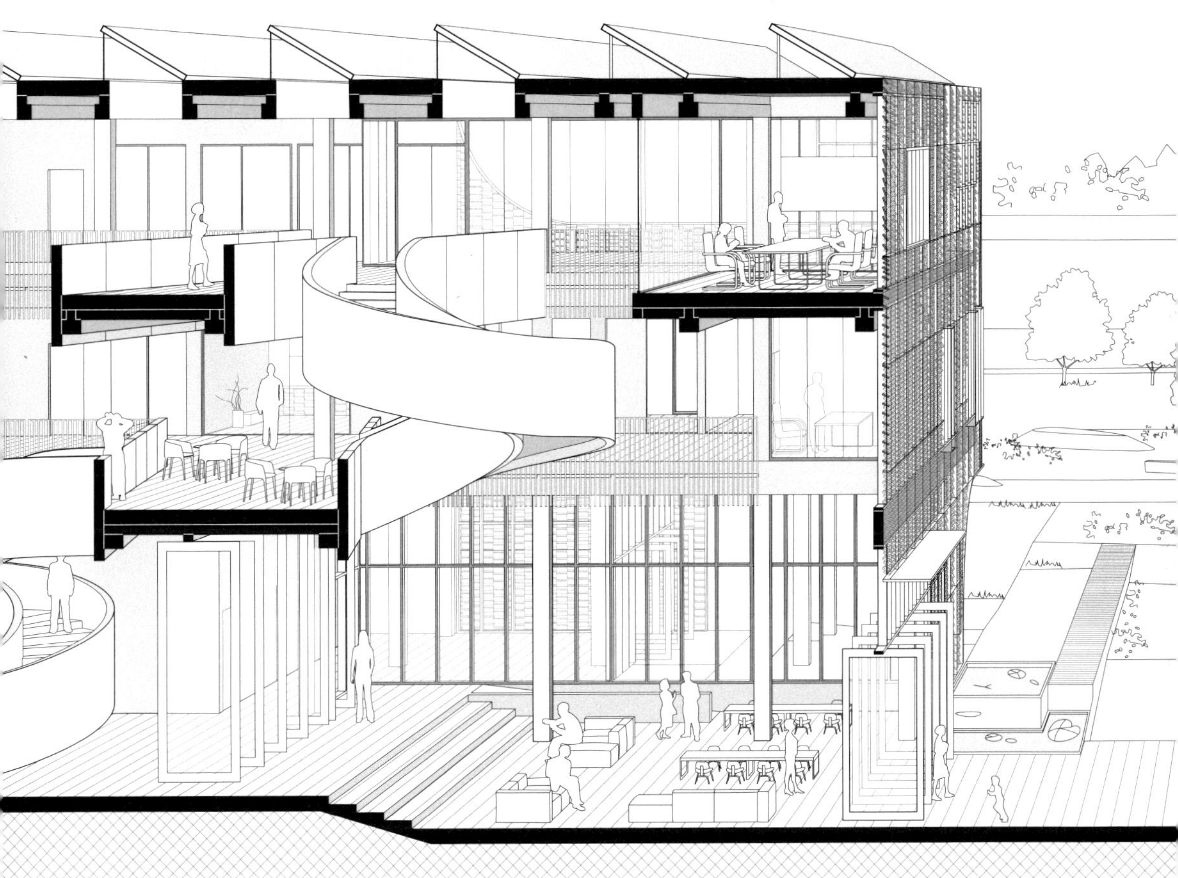

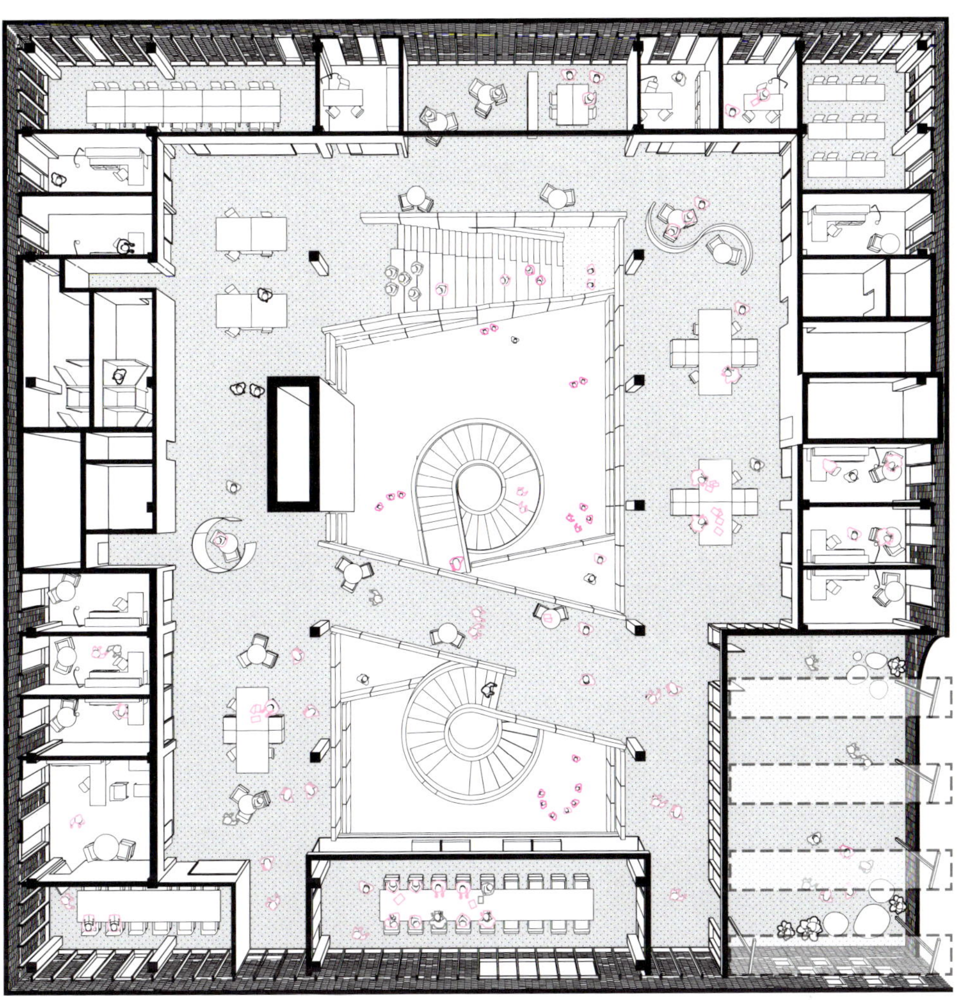

Joe Deal, *Corona del Mar* (1978)

What does nostalgia keep us from seeing? In 1992, Michael Sorkin published the edited volume *Variations on a Theme Park: The New American City and the End of Public Space*. It was widely assigned in architectural schools throughout the decade. We read it as a takedown of the suburbs, of new urbanism, of fake main streets; as an indictment encapsulating the dictum attributed to Gertrude Stein: "There is no there there." A lamentation for the loss of the public city and its colocation of the public sphere and urban space. The nostalgia was catching; by omission, it idealized a certain kind of urbanism that was by definition not to be found in the postwar U.S. cities that we knew and grew up in, validating a sneaking feeling some of us suburban kids grew up with (one exacerbated by intergenerational immigrant family dynamics) that life must be elsewhere. What it did not give us were tools for seeing the qualities of actual postwar American cities and examples of how to recognize public life specific to these spaces and communities.

This 1994 review of *Variations on a Theme Park* by Teresa Caldeira is still timely, if more apparent, thirty years on:

Three decades later, it remains a chilling analysis. Beyond the shock of Caldeira's declaration, the idea that sociality and space are intertwined and analyzed as such is critical to the continued project of preserving and building the public sphere in our cities, especially as conditions continue to change in challenging ways.

> Throughout the book, we sense a nostalgia for another type of city and urbanism: the modern city of movement and heterogeneous crowds, of cars and anonymous citizens strolling in all directions, intersecting one another. The fact that new elite urban forms—theme parks, shopping malls, under- and overbridges, exopolis, and suburbia—negate the model of the modern and relatively democratic public life does not mean that public life has disappeared. It continues to exist, although in a much more segregated, enclosed, and controlled way. What is rapidly disappearing is the fiction of an equally open public space, the vital character of its urban mixtures, and a certain experience of collective life in the streets. Indeed, what is in trouble is American democracy.

Once we are given permission to look for it, we can see how public life shows up in the postwar U.S. cities we grew up in: it is in parks, it pops up on street corners or deep within neighborhood tracts, it gathers on the edges of parking lots or at the underpass, it happens through informal economies, meetups, and swaps organized through online social networks. Without a set, shaped, designated space, public life's potential location is spread across the vast, extended city, and that is what is a bit odd about it: it is almost never as teeming or dense or busy-looking as one might expect public life to appear. The nature of space and organization in the postwar U.S. city is that these moments of publicness are often a collection of figures gathered against a vast horizontal spread of built environment, dissolving into the scale of 45 mph roads, where the city-walker cuts a lone figure against a subdivision wall.

A behind-the-scenes view of the 13th International Architecture Exhibition and the *Grounds for Detroit* installation.

Catie Newell, *Grounds for Detroit* (2012)

On Jacobs and Shakur

Writing about Greenwich Village, Jane Jacobs describes the movement and activity of the streets as a sidewalk ballet, celebrating its aliveness:

> Under the seeming disorder of the old city, wherever the old city is working successfully, is a marvelous order for maintaining the safety of the streets and the freedom of the city. It is a complex order. Its essence is intricacy of sidewalk use, bringing with it a constant succession of eyes. This order is all composed of movement and change, and although it is life, not art, we may fancifully call it the art form of the city and liken it to dance... an intricate ballet in which the individual dancers and ensembles all have distinctive parts which miraculously reinforce each other and compose an orderly whole.

It's a lovely description. What's worth thinking about is how Jacobs mentions freedom and safety in the same breath, and connects a lively quality of urban life to insular protection. In this case, protection from whom?

In her autobiography, Assata Shakur provides a contrasting contemporary account of Greenwich Village at about roughly the same time. She writes:

> Any Black woman, practically anywhere in amerika, can tell you about being approached, propositioned, and harassed by white men. Many consider all Black women potential prostitutes. In the Village, this phenomenon was ten times worse than elsewhere. It was almost impossible to go from one corner to the next without some white man hissing at you, following you, or jingling the money in his pockets.

Gratitude for Romi Morrison, who helped us see this, for being in conversation, and for leading us to Assata Shakur's biography and work.

This is the same Village told from a very different—racialized, sexualized—experience. Whose Village is the real Village? Segregation produces asymmetrical experiences of the same space. Jacobs's account betrays a sense of ownership, a positionality that excludes the views of a perceived other, the alien or outsider, the barely tolerated, thereby perpetuating that exclusion, upholding segregation. On the outside, those who do not fully belong see the situation with a different clarity, feel the force of self-protection and fear pushing them out. Their safety, even survival, may depend on it.

In the face of such hostility, Shakur gives us the expansive charge in her exhortation:

> It is our duty to fight for our freedom.
> It is our duty to win.
> We must love each other and support each other.
> We have nothing to lose but our chains.

What does it mean to shed Jacobs's principle of protectiveness, and to hear Shakur's words instead when we think about working on place, publicness, and belonging?

Troy Schaum, *Patrones y conductas by Elia Arce at Transart Gallery* (2018)

In this performance piece, Elia played the role of the building's architect, based on his observations of workers during the last month of construction. Troy watched the performance from Transart's third-floor office, and suffice to say, his behavior was faithfully represented in the piece. Perhaps he could have just floated away.

When it is said that we are too much occupied with the means of living to live, I answer that the chief worth of civilization is just that it makes the means of living more complex; that it calls for great and combined intellectual efforts, instead of simple, uncoordinated ones, in order that the crowd may be fed and clothed and housed and moved from place to place. Because more complex and intense intellectual efforts mean a fuller and richer life. They mean more life. Life is an end in itself, and the only question as to whether it is worth living is whether you have enough of it.

—Oliver Wendell Holmes Jr. (1961)

You'll need a small notebook or some way to keep a running list of notes together.

Spend a half hour to one hour each day outside walking, strolling, or at rest among strangers. It can be during your daily commute or other standard activity, or you can go outside specifically to do this exercise.

Look for signs of public life. You do not need to define it first. Respond to what you see and record observations in a descriptive manner (e.g., two people make eye contact and nod while passing on the street, on First between Main and Summer Streets).

Make a minimum of five observations each day for five days.

Find one or two partners, do this exercise concurrently and share your lists with each other at the end and discuss.

For consideration:

Positionality, togetherness, (im)possibility

Garnette Cadogan,
“Walking While Black”
(2015)

Laura Oldfield Ford,
Savage Messiah
(2011)

China Miéville,
The City & the City
(2009)

Jafar Panahi,
No Bears
(2022)

Park Chan-wook,
Thirst
(2009)

Eve Kosofsky Sedgwick,
“Queer and Now”
(1993)

Assata Shakur,
Assata
(2001)

Abderrahmane Sissako,
Timbuktu
(2014)

Haskell Wexler and
Johanna Demetrakas,
Bus Riders Union
(1999)

Arthur Leipzig, *Chalk Games* (1950)

Taichung City Cultural Center
(2013)

Eleanor Antin finds a proscenium on this travertine ledge, taking advantage of the deep drop beyond and borrowing the distant bluff as a backdrop. We admired this piece for years before realizing that it was taken at the end of the courtyard at the Salk Institute.

Eleanor Antin, *Death of Petronius* (2001)

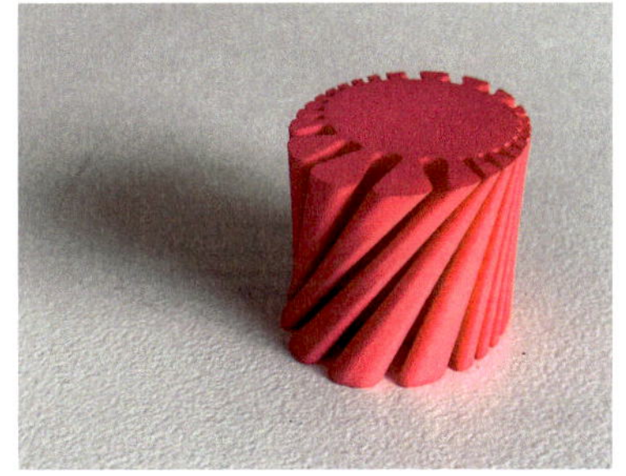

In the Round (2018)

Island Transect (2014)

Sets

forms
groups
bed
parts
likeness
discrete
pieces
things
objects
artifacts
collections
lots
open
loose
some
pile
stacks

How to be both finite and free? First identify boundaries, then explore around them. The framing of limits leads to an exploration of internal relationships. Look at how parts are constituted, and how they come together; consider adjacencies and qualities of difference, understanding they may be transient.

Roy Yoshida, *Unreasonable Lineage* (1975)

But, said Alice, the world has absolutely no sense, who's stopping us from inventing one?

—frequently misattributed to Lewis Carroll, author unknown

How do relatively compact forms, in combination, orient people or activities between them or in their vicinity?

Can we think of surfaces as a backdrop for organizing like and unlike things? In relation or completely free from each other?

How can a limited set of forms be arranged, assembled, or associated to organize a space?

What if we assign ourselves two tasks: one, employ some formal repetition for efficiency; two, create a sense of atmosphere. Can we do both?

Architecture is often made of and made up of parts. How do these parts relate to structure and material? How do they break down? Can constituent pieces be interrelated but unlike?

Both formal and material parts can be at play, sometimes simultaneously. What is the relationship of parts to building materials? Identical or constituent? Ambiguous, ambivalent, unrelated, or even suppressed?

Robert Morris, Green Gallery Exhibition, New York, Installation View: *Untitled (Table)* 1964, *Untitled (Corner Beam)* 1964, *Untitled (Floor Beam)* 1964, *Untitled (Corner Piece)* 1964, *Untitled (Cloud)* 1962. Painted plywood. Photograph by Rudy Burckhardt (1965)

The flatbed picture plane makes its symbolic allusion to hard surfaces such as tabletops, studio floors, charts, bulletin boards—any receptor surface on which objects are scattered, on which data is entered, on which information may be received, printed, impressed—whether coherently or in confusion.

—Leo Steinberg (1972)

An exercise in naming: Active Forms, Flatbeds, and Sets

An *active form* supports a specific relationship between form and function. Comportment, disposition of material, and character shape activity as well as perception. Active forms are programmatic, infrastructural, atmospheric, and representational. They do things and make things possible. But in addition to performing and enabling, the form is also assertive. Active forms are iconic—they signify function through formal gesture as well as make things physically or materially possible.

We borrow the term *flatbed* as an idea about representation and technique. In *Other Criteria*, Leo Steinberg connects Robert Rauschenberg's paintings and "combines" to the horizontal surface of the printing press—the flatbed. Both are distinct from the illusionistic, vertical, transcendental space of the canvas, which is inherently invested in the orientation of the upright body. The flatbed, like a table, is a site of exchange: "Rauschenberg's work surface stood for the mind itself—dump, reservoir, switching center..." We have been interested in experimenting with representations that mix a broad range of non-visual design criteria with the visual, and the resulting noise and reverberations that result from their overlap.

The idea of *sets* gathers together aesthetics, organization, and tectonics. Sets are composed of differentiated forms: the part is not in service of the whole, nor is it simply "one thing after another." Rather, the parts are individual and the whole is also individual. It's a quality of low resolution.

Architecture is made up of parts, and we are interested in how these parts are constituted and how they come together. Two conditions to play with: matter and material. You can take a tectonic approach (where the material is expressed, it becomes the part) or a compositional one (where material is suppressed, the figure is the part). Making these distinctions on how matter combines with space furnishes tools and informs a process.

Active form is an objective; flatbeds are a technique; and sets describe a move beyond composition and parts toward an interplay between space, material, and matter.

Gallery & Archive Building, Houston, TX (2018)

Transart Foundation for Art & Anthropology

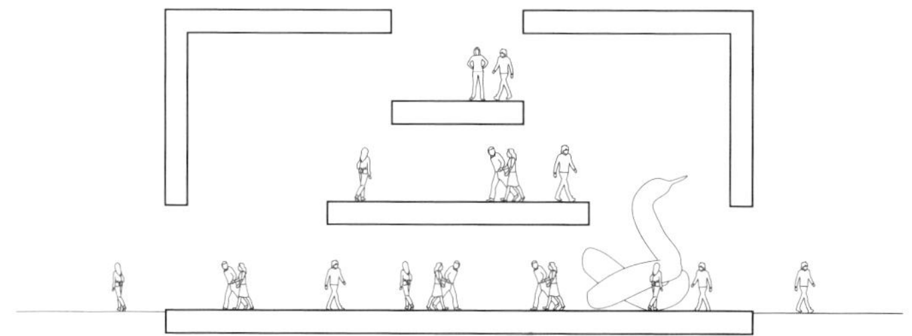

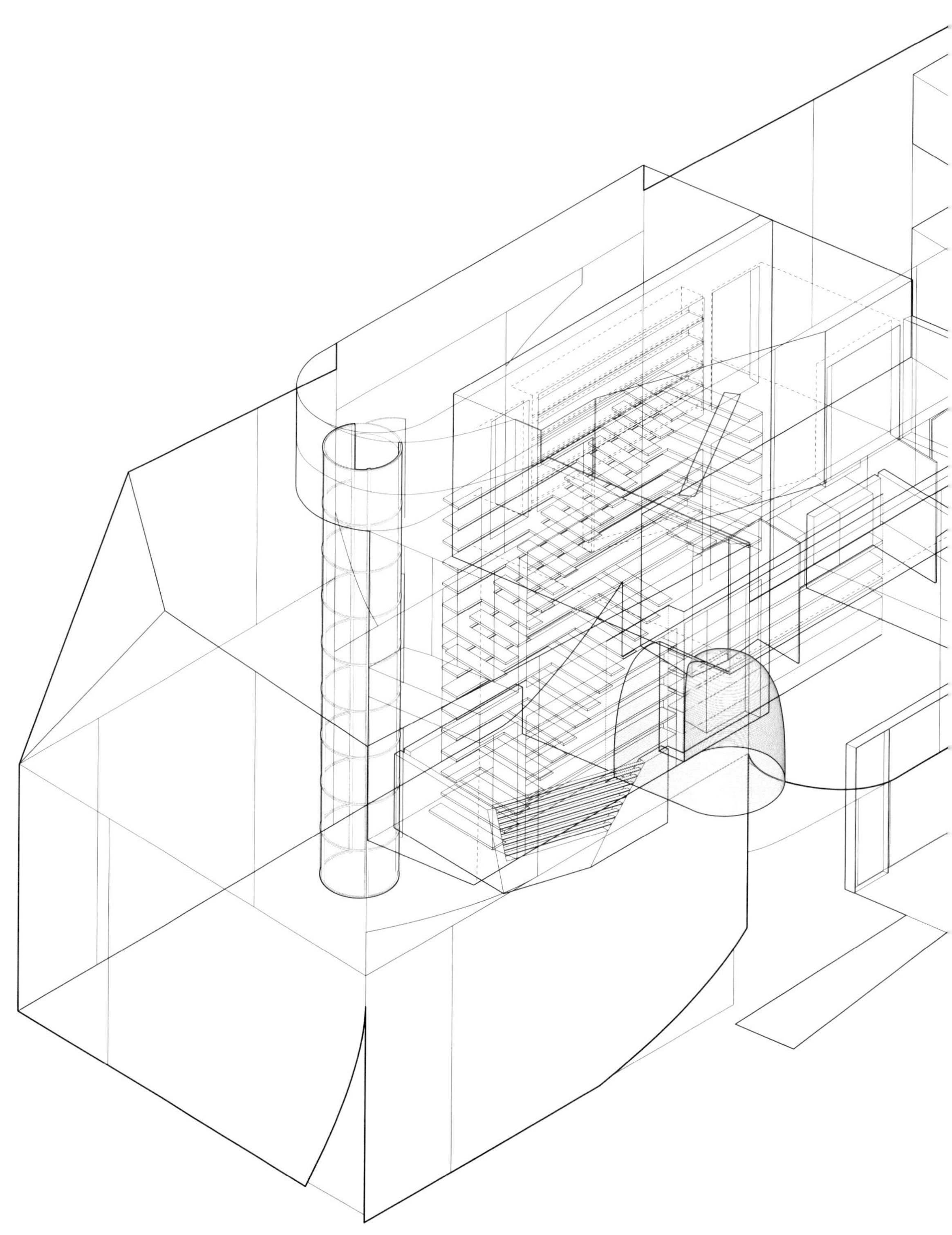

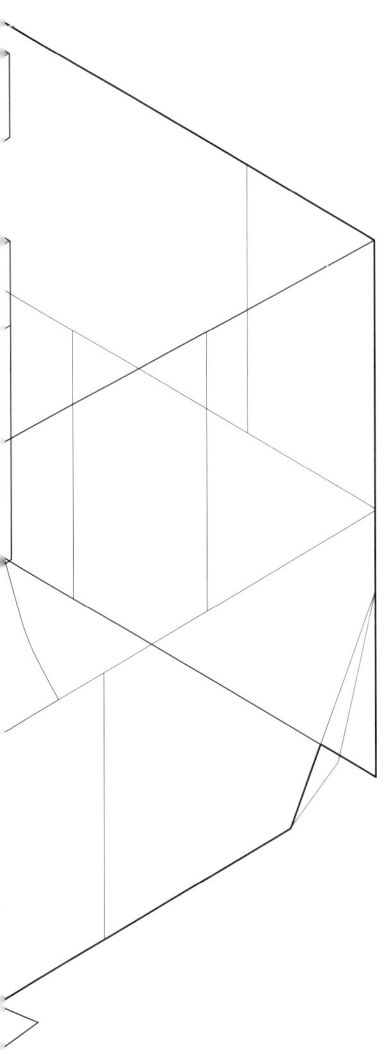

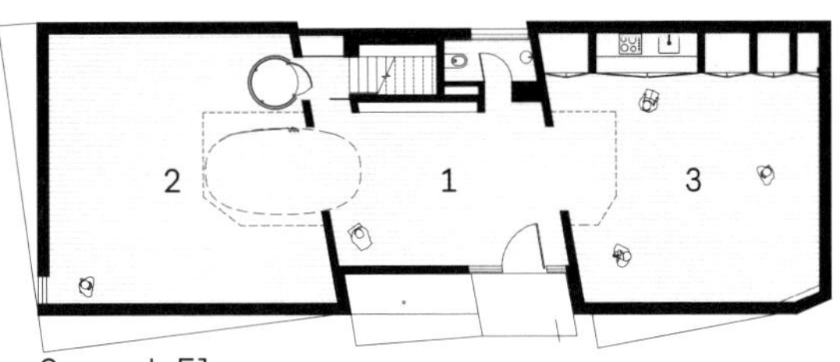

Ground Floor

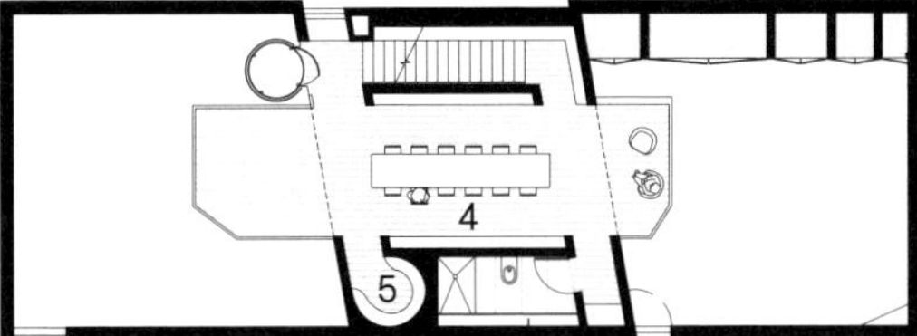

Second Floor

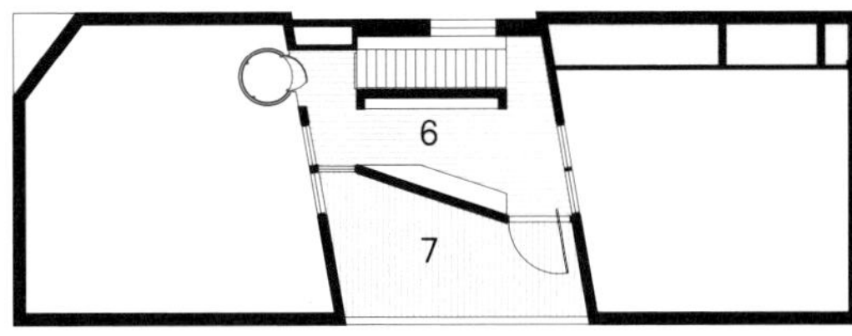

Third Floor

Ground Floor

1 Entry
2 Gallery 1
3 Gallery 2

Second Floor

4 Research Salon
5 Meeting Nook

Third Floor

6 Office
7 Roof Terrace

0 5' 10' 20'

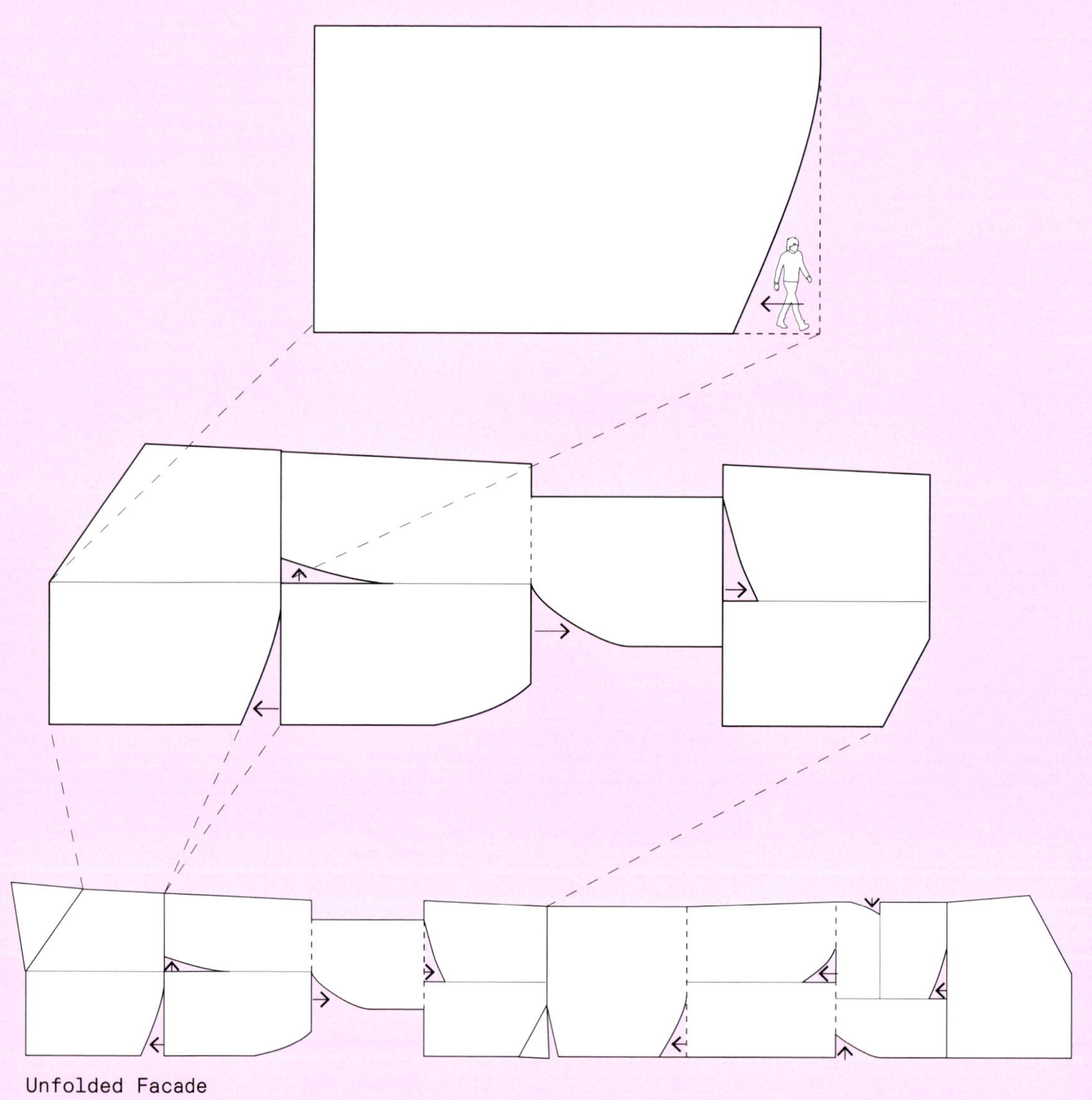
Unfolded Facade

Study Models

ASTRO

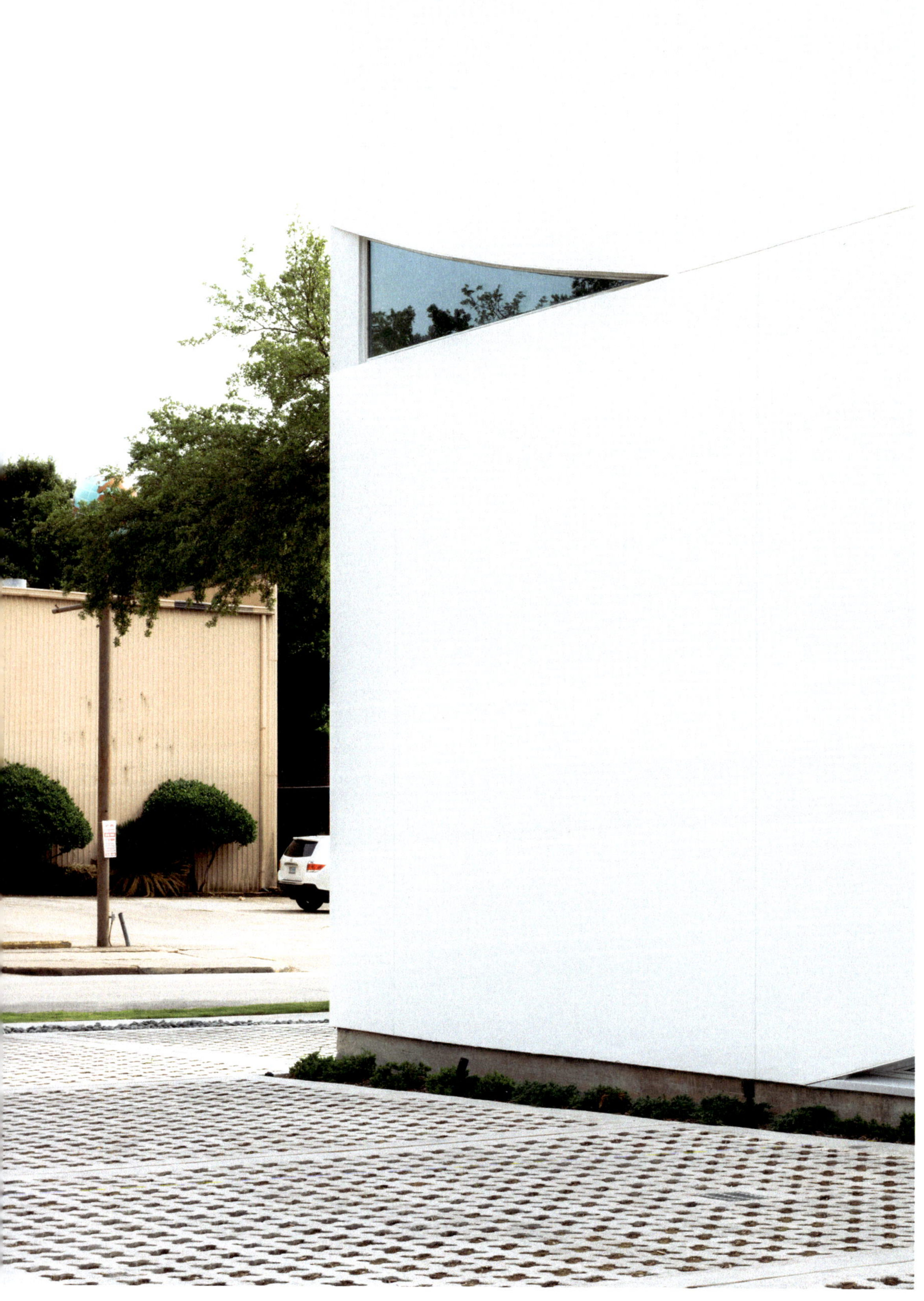

The siting is slightly back from the sidewalk and off to one side, with its entrance on the long side. It opens onto a side court that extends to the existing back building.

It's a relatively confined site—you can see where the pavers stop at the edge of the empty adjacent lot. We tried to make some small wrinkles in the fabric of the neighborhood via the project's movement, siting, and landscape.

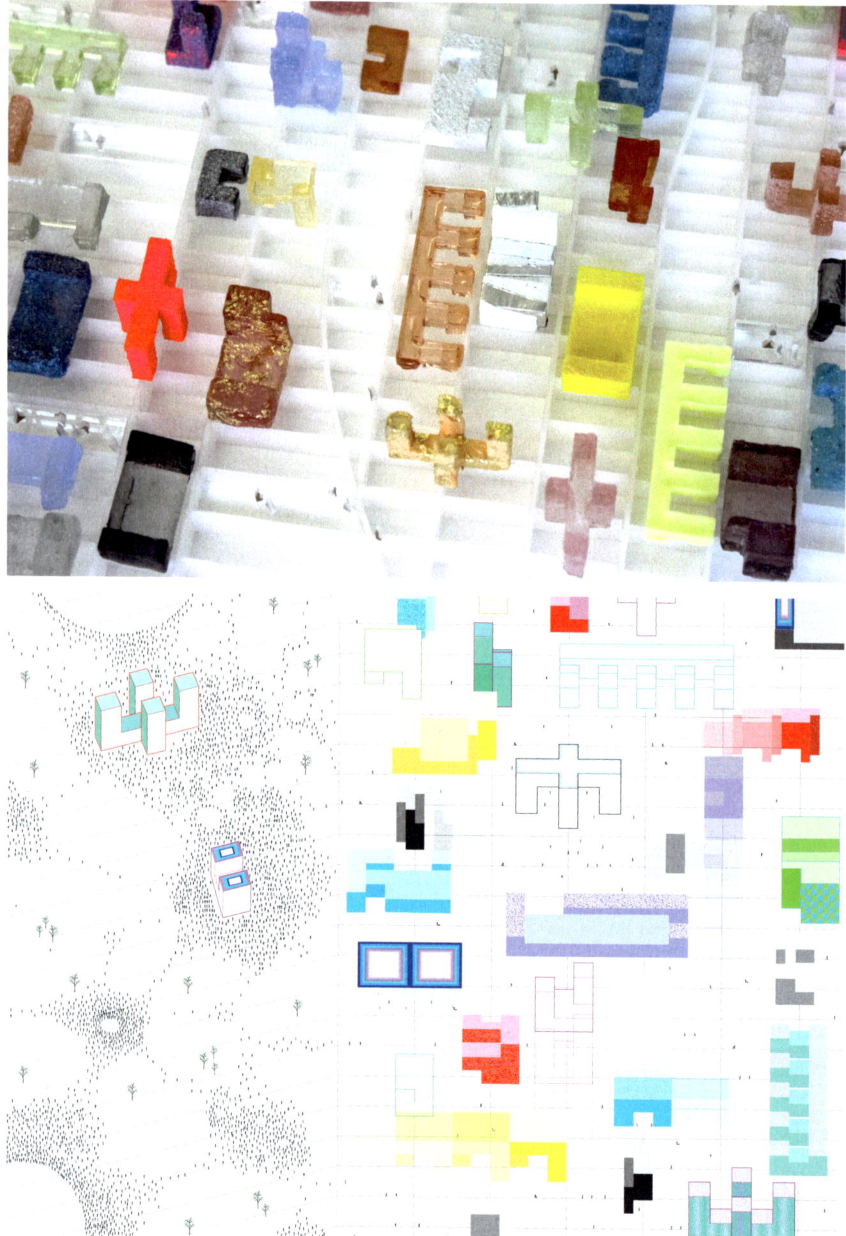

Beyond the Totems (2016)

The order is not rationalistic and underlying but is simply order, like that of continuity, one thing after another.

—Donald Judd (1964)

Iconomics search

Drawing 1

Draw a closed object with maximum 8 and minimum 5 sides.

Devise 3 operations for the object (for example: skew, rotate, scale, scale 1D, scale one face).

Impose a metric of calibration that will control the range of variations.

Map the range of variations for each calibration in 3- and 2-D matrices.

Drawing 2

Construct a 3-D matrix that integrates the 3 operations and describes their potential.

Model 1

Model composite objects combining 2, 8, and 32 of the calibrated objects.

Model 2

Construct a model that builds on what you have learned from one of the previous models. This second-generation iteration should formally and materially illustrate your conceptual agenda for the selections and assumptions you have made.

About Face

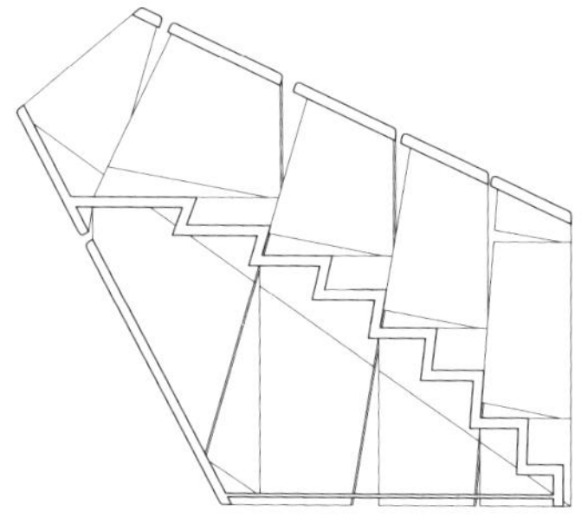

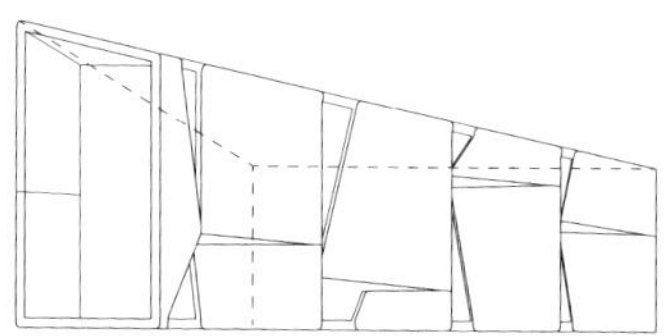

LIVING ROOM

MUD ROOM

In the end, our obsession with lightness and the economy of bio-resin turned out to be relative. Both Troy and Rosalyne sprained their backs moving our "easy-to-assemble" objects around the floor of the Arsenale.

What is the context, how is it altered or tuned between and among structures or small buildings, within or inside larger buildings?

With *Site Double* by MILLIGRAM-office in distance.

Slider Towers (2012)

...beautiful as the accidental encounter, on a dissecting table, of a sewing machine and an umbrella.

—Comte de Lautréamont (1865)

The Finite Set

Contemporary strategies of multiplicity in architecture, such as seriality, fields, tiling, tessellation, and horizontal repetition, seek to reflect and define spatial experiences in the city through visual cues and spatial constraints. They structurally organize surfaces, preempting or projecting ideal or intended movements through space and becoming actants in social life and order. Often, they are set against the traditional hierarchical orders of the city, which are structured around particular axes, blocks, or boulevards. At other times, they emerge from a specific landscape in the dispersed context of the post-metropolitan city, offering a more informal alternative to object-in-the-field strategies that dominate those urban environments.

While their formal characteristics provide important organizational cues, these multiplicities also rely on and reproduce certain understandings of social and political relations. It is important not to confuse the modular grid with the ideal of democratic equality. In their embodiment of such liberal ideals, however, these multiplicities efface differences and repeatedly propose a uniform understanding of social life without any space for radical interrogation or transformation.

The multiple and, more importantly, how it is rendered and defined as components of contemporary architectural form, critically intersects the discipline's conception of the subject and competing notions of temporality. The project of horizontal multiplicity and its association with informal, bottom-up tactics of "non-composition" has been well documented in the work, from the exploration of Mat typologies of Team X in the 1960s to more recent explorations of unstable formal installations by peers like SANAA and MOS. Rather than explore the contrast in strategy that these serial techniques provide in comparison to work that relies on the solitary object, perhaps it is more fruitful to examine the differences between these strategies of the serial. Several of these differences can be traced in parallel discourses around form in art and sculpture in the last half of the 20th century. So, in responding to the question of multiplicity, we propose a new formal mode in the spectrum between infinite seriality and the solitary object—*The Finite Set.*

What if the multiple is bounded and set within finite limits? How do the terms change? Borrowed from the mathematical, the finite set offers a different possibility for understanding the work in relation to space and time. The bounding of multiples within defined sets has the potential to imagine a difference that is not tied to even gradations of the field or progressive structures of infinite temporalities. The logic of the finite set requires editing the multiple into a limited selection. These sets can operate locally and relationally by relying on terms defined individually for each set, while maintaining their status at another scale as a bounded solitary object. In other words, these projects oscillate between global autonomy and local specificity to rupture those distinctions and allow for the emergence of new individuated and collective modes of inhabiting the relentlessly expansive city.

Rather than reducing the shared set of formal tactics to the whims of style, the finite set assumes these practices reveal a shift in the temporal and subjective attitudes in the practices that deploy it. This shift allows for techniques that implicate more contingent, local, and nuanced meanings, leaving behind the undifferentiated global mass subject inhabiting a universal temporality.

This potential to create distinct difference across a bounded field of otherwise related forms illustrates the potential of the finite formal set, in contrast to the more familiar understanding of multiplicity as unbounded and extensive seriality.

In contrasting two parallel art practices that remain critical to understanding seriality—the work of Robert Smithson and Donald Judd—we can see two distinct sensibilities regarding time. Robert Smithson has noted how time "as decay or biological evolution" may be eliminated by deploying a multiplicity of surfaces or structures. Accordingly, in Smithson's work, time is portrayed to be infinite: a theme explored repeatedly in the oozes of *Asphalt Rundown* (1969). Formal characteristics not only act as vehicles for spatial experiences or as embodiments of a flattened collectivity but also reflect a particular understanding of temporality. In this teleological conception of temporality, there is no room for last things. In fact, what is expected to arrive will differ from everything prior.

While Smithson's relationship to endless and unbounded temporalities allowed for a future defined by openness, Donald Judd's work and writing refutes the notion of endlessness and proposes a sense of time bounded by individual experiences and lifespans. This has a direct impact on his conception of form and sculpture as he describes the organization of sculpture in his work "Specific Objects"; he sees it as an act against traditional and progressive modes of composition, and instead proposes to build "one thing after another." This technique of composition pervades his work, from the simple stacks of his untitled stack works (1967), which vary in number in relationship to the boundaries of the room they are in, to his 100 untitled aluminum works in Marfa, TX (1983–86), which are carefully bounded by both by the number 100 and the site-specific installation in the old artillery sheds. In his last interview from Marfa, Judd explicitly suggests: "There is no time that goes on and on and on and is something all by itself." Formally, he materializes this perspective by producing the bounded set—a seriality that conforms to clear boundaries.

This logic of the finite set is of course not a practice strictly limited to 20th-century minimalist art. We have developed a strategy at multiple scales to grapple with various problems of formal organizations and their attendant subjective and temporal corollaries. In our scheme for Kaohsiung's Maritime Cultural & Pop Music Center design competition, we deployed a set of circles in a field bounded by the formal square shape of the historic Kaohsiung harbor area. Against the ill-defined fabric of the postindustrial context of Taiwan's old port, the finite set of circles created a relational definition of space and form that also establishes a base logic of urban form. The landscape's looping trajectories intertwined the pop music visitor with families headed to the beach and office workers on break. The same set of circles produces a multiplicity of forms and events, each within its own timescale and rhythm.

This strategy of the finite set was deployed at a radically smaller scale in our installation *About Face* as part of the Common Ground International Exhibition at the 13th Venice Biennale in 2012. Our installation reimagined a room we had built two years earlier in a single-family house in Detroit. The original room cut through and was supported by several existing walls and floors, which opened up the rooms to new exposures and relationships. In Venice, the structure had to be self-supporting and easily transportable. The self-contained logic of the project set against the deteriorating background of the Arsenale in Venice led us to deploy a set of 23 self-similar forms that could be just stable enough to support the cross-axis of the structure as it cantilevered over the gallery floor, but loose enough a configuration to unwind from top to bottom. The looseness of the relationships in the set created a movement within the form and provoked a dynamic engagement as visitors moved up, around, and through the installation, both bodily and visually.

In the commission for Houston gallery Transart, we explored the dynamic of the set at the scale of a complete building. The complex consists of four pavilions organized as distinct but connected art spaces for a private curator. The building's facade comprises 15 large panels stacked against each other, wrapping the pavilions one after another to contain a gallery, library, and meeting space. The simple program works against the typical part-by-part logic of the neighborhood of single-family homes and art institutions, including the Menil Collection and Rothko Chapel. The logic is a three-dimensional one, layered in the production process and not in a more typical hierarchy from ground to sky.

The Finite Set and the projects it embodies reframe the multiple's relationship to subjective and temporal definitions. The emergence of formal tactics, like the relational potential of the finite, can penetrate the gloss of style to recode our definitions of time and the urban subject within the projects that deploy them. Considerations of the spectrum, from multiplicity to singularity, can address which multiplicities exist and how they operate to produce new directions.

Adapted from "The Finite Set" by Troy Schaum (2015)

Proposed Installation, MoMA PS1 Young Architects Program, Long Island City, Queens, NY (2017)

Blow up the wall!

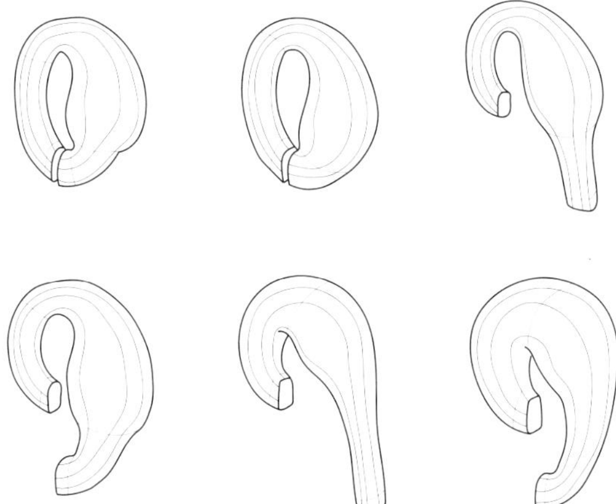

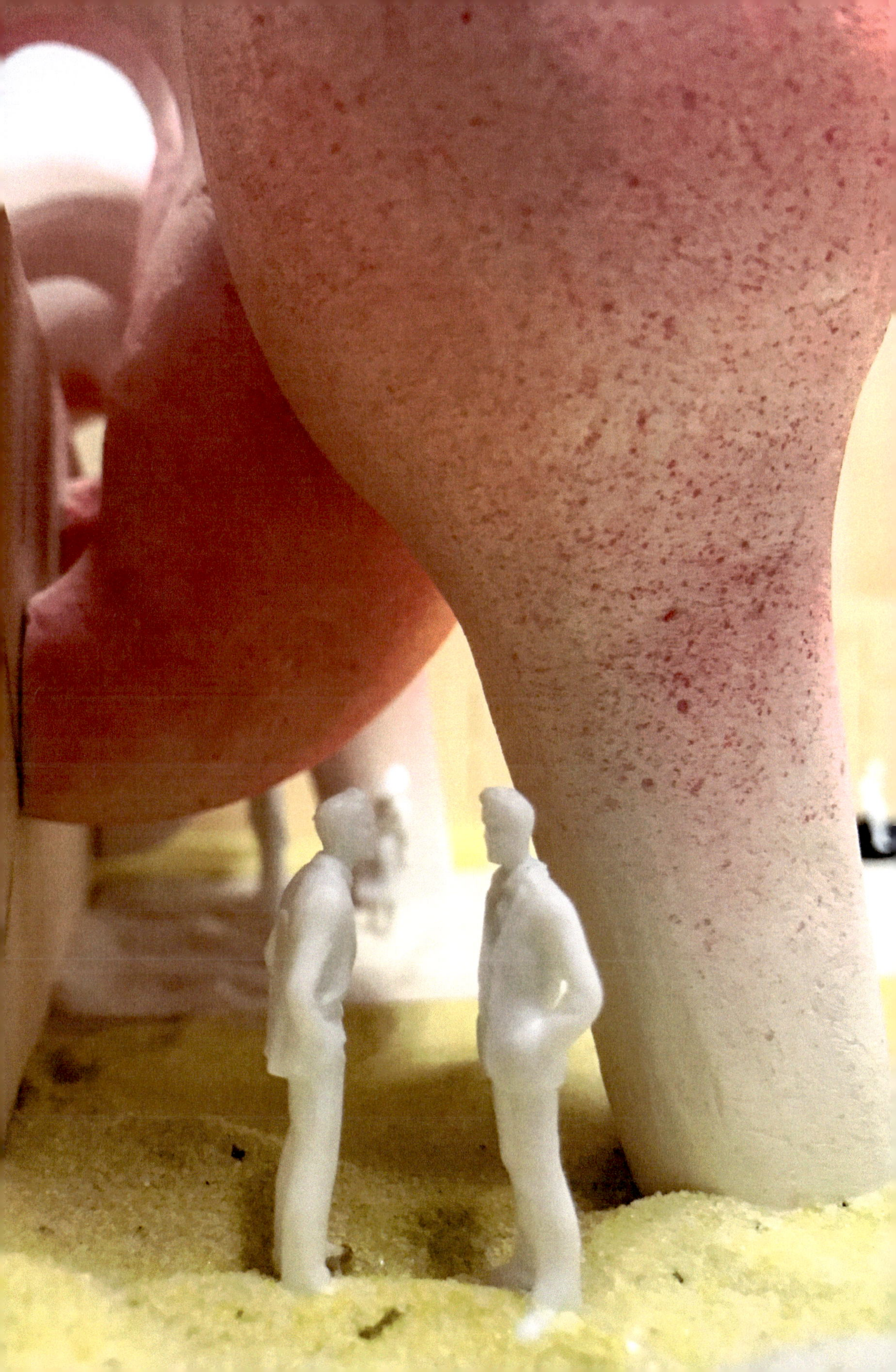

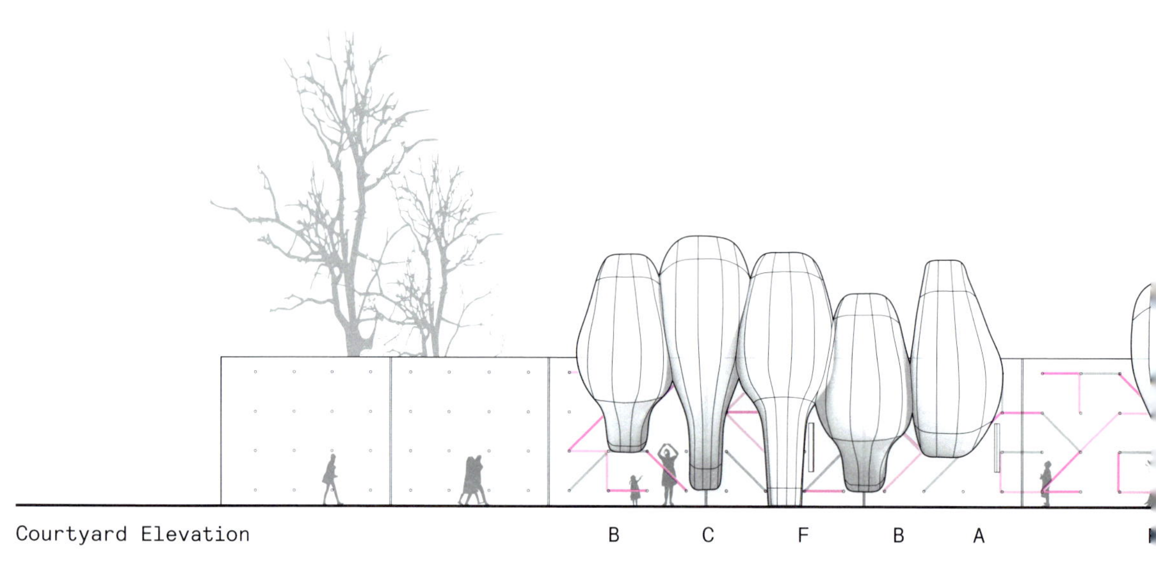

Courtyard Elevation

Street Elevation

One of our regrets about not seeing this built was that we were interested in experiencing the many characters of an inflatable form. Figured here as a strong set of individuals, they would also melt with deflation over the course of the week, becoming formless traces of their weekend Warm Up selves.

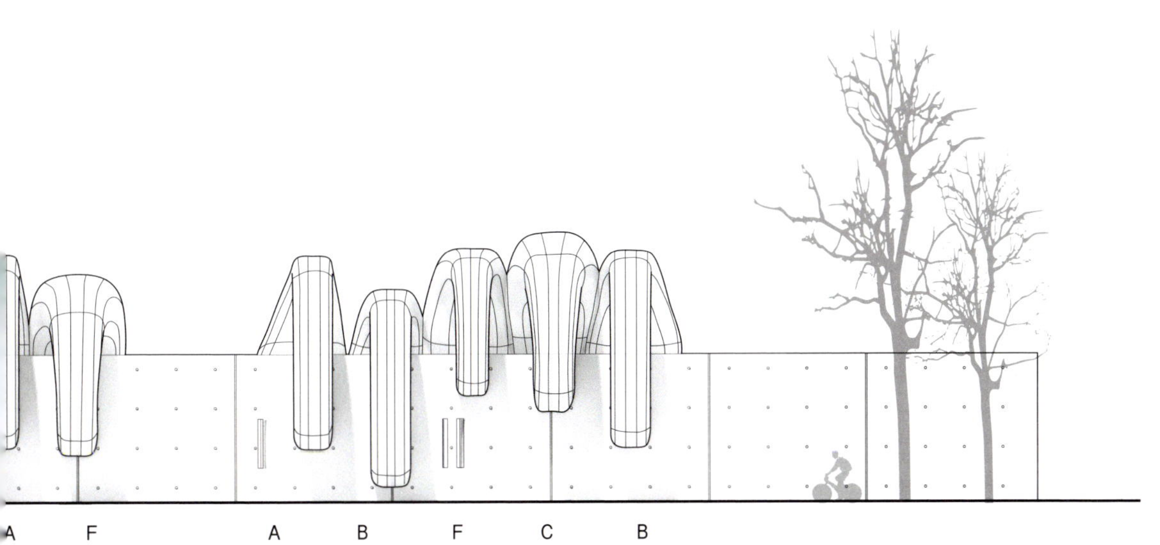

0 5' 10' 20'

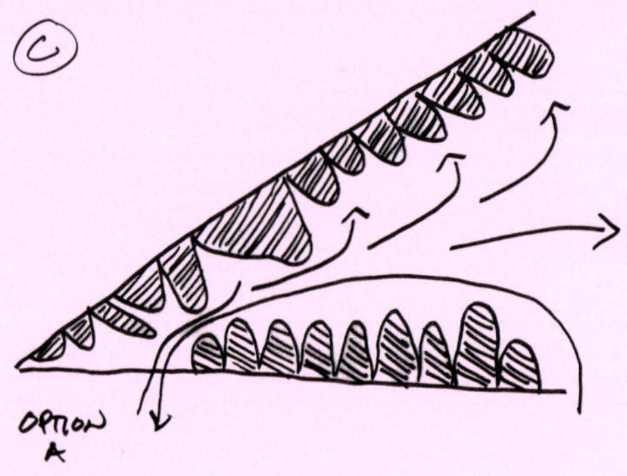
C
OPTION A

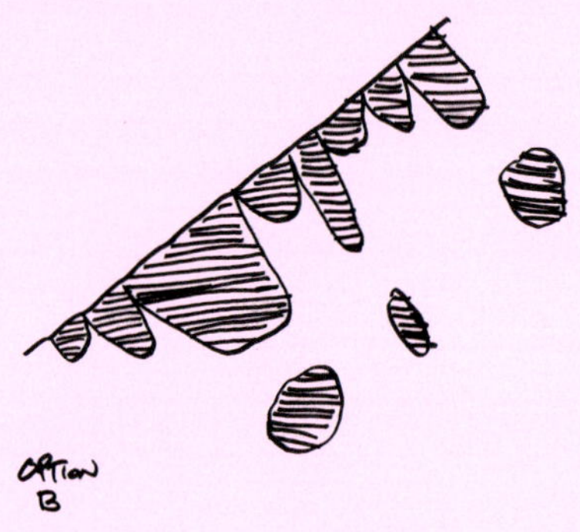
OPTION B

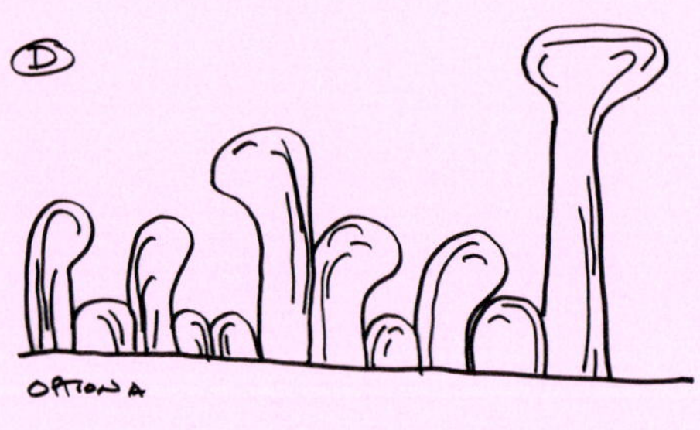
D
OPTION A

OPTION B

E
OPTION A

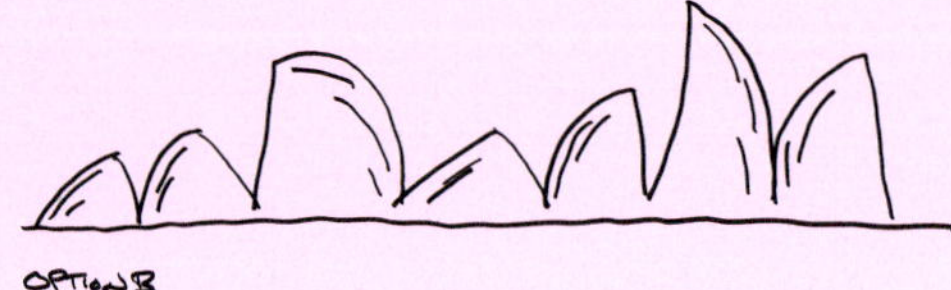
OPTION B

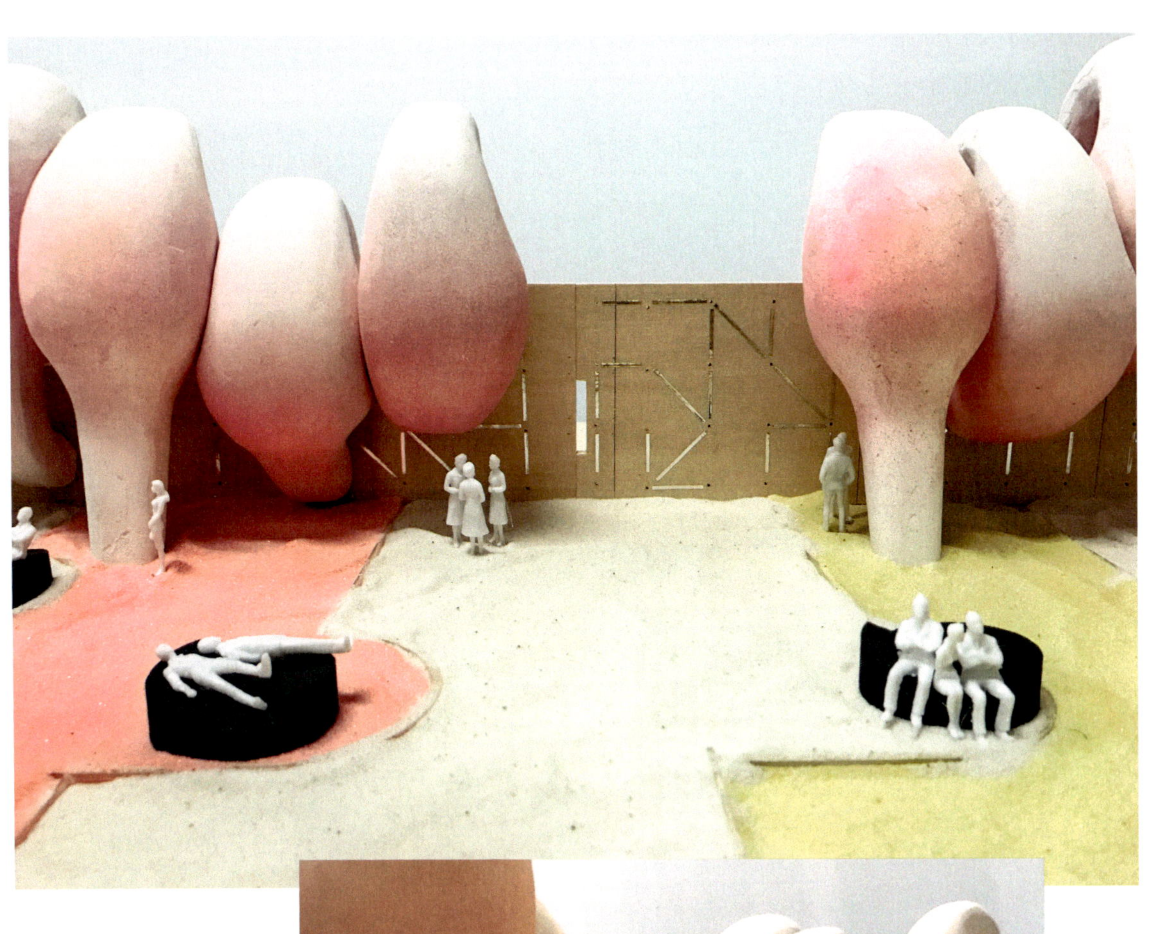

Think twice next time you want to use real sand in a model to describe a proposal for two truck-loads of sand in the courtyard of a museum. People get nervous.

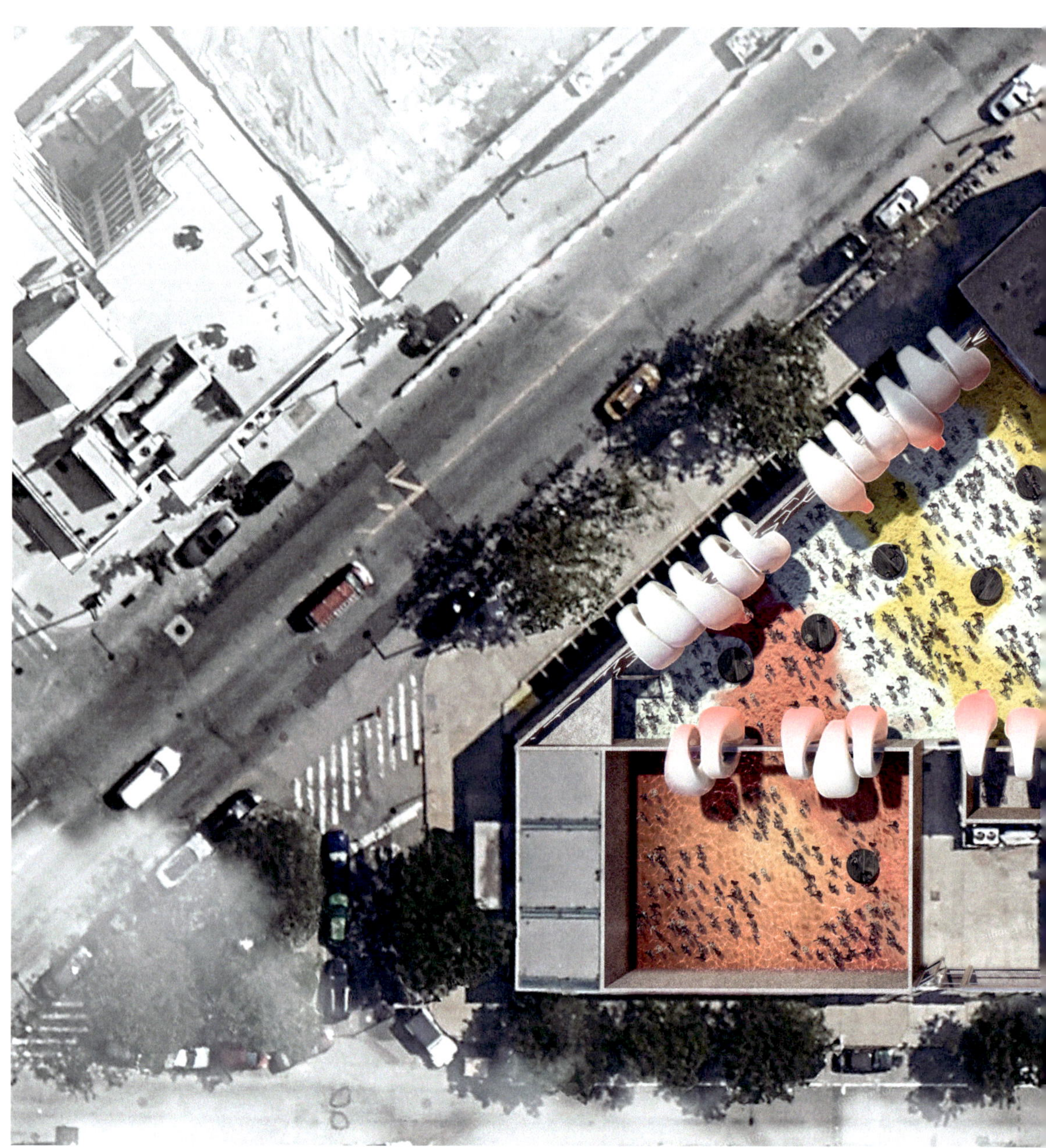

We were excited for the stripes of colored sand to become softened and mixed up over the course of the summer by daily activities. It was an experiment: maybe we would get areas of gradient or feathering or swirls of color... and likely there would have been patches that were more of a muddy mix.

MoM

Broken lines of light pulse on and off in different combinations in a kind of asemic writing, animating a script without a message.

Blow up the wall!, Video Still (2016)

A great deal in architecture may be language-like without being language. Some might say that the recent insistence that architecture is a language is only the last wave of a persistent verbal tide eroding vision, bedevilling our ability to see without language to guide our eyes.

—Robin Evans (1986)

Note

On tableaux

By tracing the limits of a territory, we delineate its frontier—the edge of what is known and, perhaps more significantly, the line from which everything else begins. The territory of known things is an island within a vast ocean of unseen, illegible depths. Limits tell us things; they (miraculously) bind opposing pairs, they expose fault lines, breakages, and points of failure in our thinking. Toni Morrison reminds us that failure "contains information that can lead to knowledge—even wisdom. Like art."

Take the very concept of a horizon: it is a frame, a boundary. At the same time, it is also the line from which everything else begins. When we look out across a vast landscape, the horizon is a line at infinity—as an image, sky and land collapse into a flat plane, the two separated by this imaginary line. This image, where incommensurable terms are assembled into a broad, flat frame, is a tableau, a vertical, shallow frame in which opposing and unlike things can be brought into proximity. As such, a tableau becomes a device for design in a manner akin to assembling parts against a background. A tableau approach is one of assembling, arranging, and organizing more than framing and enclosing.

Installation & Workshop, with Virginia Commonwealth University, Middle of Broad Studio, Richmond, VA (2013)

Monument Alley, MoB Workshop

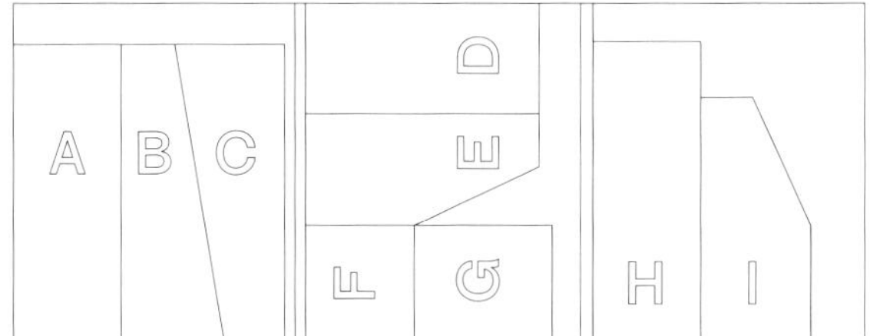

PARKING
ANY
TIME
NO PARKING

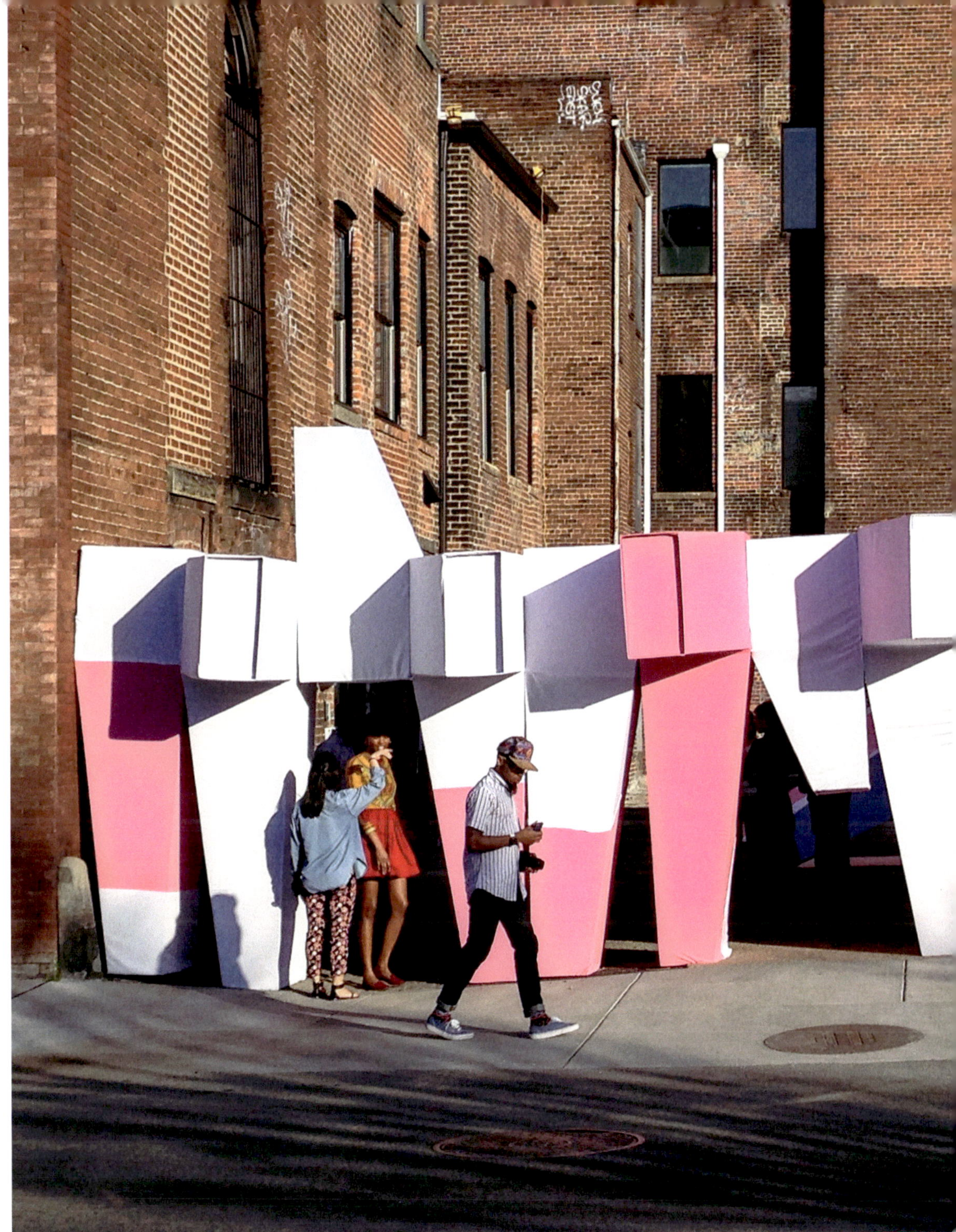

These objects were made in collaboration with graphic, interior, and fashion design students at VCU. We hit on an interdisciplinary opportunity when the fashion students suggested they could sew the graphics of the forms that had been modeled by the interior design students. Fabric has a vibrancy that is hard to replicate by other means.

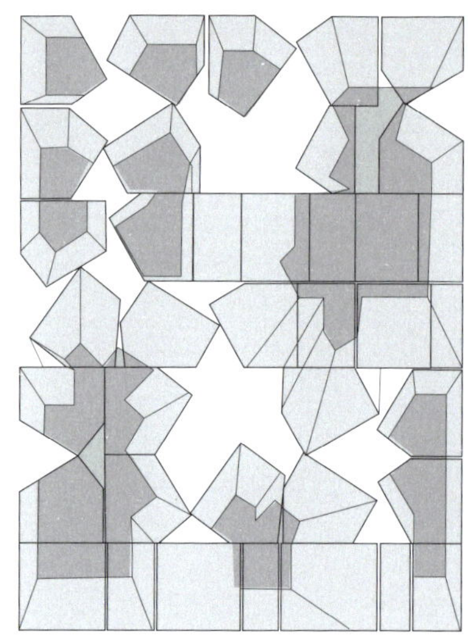

Pigeon Shed Urbanism (2012)

Transart Gallery (2013)

We were at 50 percent CD with this version and about to be fired because our client found this scheme stifling. The final design direction emerged out of a single intense meeting wherein she asked us to incorporate aspects of an earlier SCHSH project that she loved.

For consideration:
Categories, things, (not) making sense

Eija-Liisa Ahtila,
Love Is a Treasure
(2002)

Jorge Luis Borges,
"The Analytical
Language of John Wilkins"
(1942)

Hieronymus Bosch,
The Garden of Earthly Delights
(1490-1500)

Georg Cantor,
"On a Property of the
Collection of All
Real Algebraic Numbers"
(1874)

Christian Hubert,
"The Ruins of Representation"
(1981)

Donald Judd,
"Specific Objects"
(1964)

Lev Manovich,
"Database as Symbolic Form"
(1999)

Philip Ursprung, ed.,
*Herzog & de Meuron:
Natural History*
(2002)

Sarah Whiting,
"Bas-Relief Urbanism"
(2001)

John Whitney,
Matrix III
(1972)

Gio Ponti, *Villa Namazee*, View of the Internal Courtyard (1957-64)

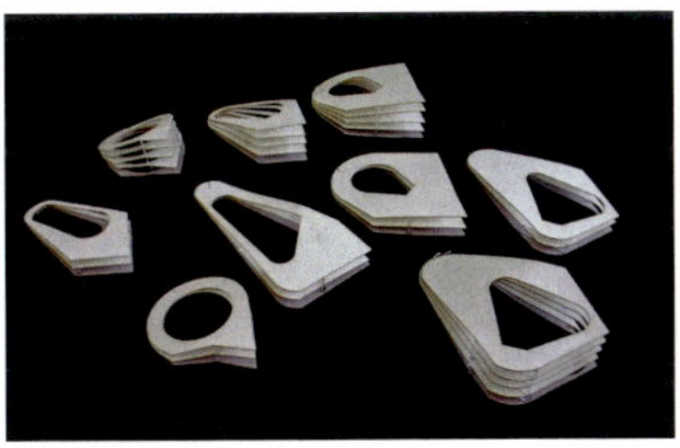

Taichung City Cultural Center
(2013)

Peter DeCamp Haines, *Artifacts*, Photo by Stewart Clements (1978-2023)

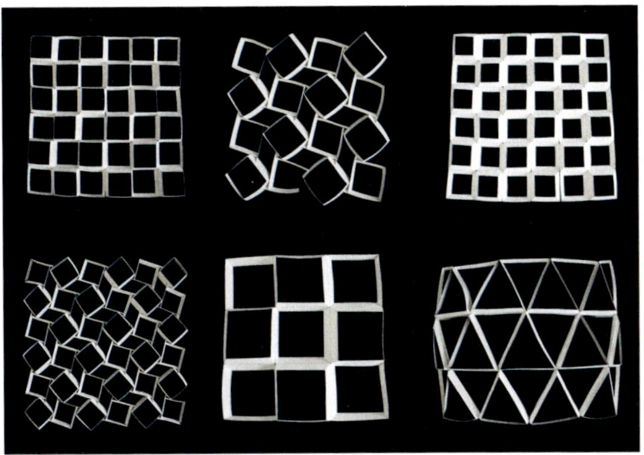

Shepherd School of Music Courtyard, Canopy Studies (2011)

Agricultural Urbanism (2011)

Arrange

loose
incidental
disperse
drift
diffuse
increment
informal
(re)assemble
(re)adjust
(de)compose
transit
(re)order
vicinity
uneven
variable
disintegration
move
distribute

How to practice architecture where intersecting forces continuously destabilize social and cultural relationships and reorder space? These positionally marginal places challenge the limitations of our inherited tools. Here, projects are as much ways of learning from and with(in) sites as anything else.

Untitled (ArtPrize) (2013)

Can we consider restoration and conservation operations of revealing instead of returning to a prior state? At the scale of material assemblies and site, can we adjust, mend, and uncover? At the scale of site and street, can we arrange and connect, align, or support?

What can the U.S. suburbs or rural context teach us about making architecture?

What of our personal experience is not reflected in our education and training? What tools for architecture and urbanism might be furnished by that experience?

What is ordinary to us that may be common or uncommon to others? What might result from cultivating an appreciation for the mundane?

We talk about types and typology. We can think of a type as less an ideal and more an idea articulated in architectural or urban form. By adjustment and arrangement, by removal and addition of material within an existing condition, can we work to reveal an idea that is possible in the building or site?

What is an approach that acknowledges the existing but works toward another stage? At the same time, how do we anticipate returning to the work and facing changed conditions?

Blanking (exhibition) (2018)

When I was teaching at Cooper Union in the first year or two of the fifties, someone told me how I could get on to the unfinished New Jersey Turnpike. I took three students and drove from somewhere in the Meadows to New Brunswick. It was a dark night and there were no lights or shoulder markers, lines, railings, or anything at all except the dark pavement moving through the landscape of the flats, rimmed by hills in the distance, but punctuated by stacks, towers, fumes, and colored lights. This drive was a revealing experience. The road and much of the landscape was artificial, and yet it couldn't be called a work of art. On the other hand, it did something for me that art had never done. At first I didn't know what it was, but its effect was to liberate me from many of the views I had had about art. It seemed that there had been a reality there which had not had any expression in art.

The experience on the road was something mapped out but not socially recognized.

—Tony Smith (1966)

Thinking about suburbs (and other places)

When we look at communities, how do we know what we know and why do we think about it the way that we do? In the case of cities, there is an expectation that they are dense and full of human and vehicular activity, that urban forms are continuous and unbroken (with intentional exceptions). Canonical schemas—think Pope Sixtus V's plan for Rome and Ildefons Cerdà's Barcelona plan—legitimize and naturalize these frames of reference.

But when we turn to the U.S. context, we meet these categories: urban, rural, suburban. The first two are somehow clear, a result of the dominance of Western/European concepts of the city and its absence. The third is less so, even as many of us readily reach for this descriptor in conversation. The U.S. Census Bureau and American Housing Survey give us some clues for how the term is used in policy, but the meaning of *suburb* is constructed as a negation—not core city but not rural—or as something perceived (survey respondents responding positively to "suburb" as a description of where they live). A working definition: a suburb is a municipality or continuously developed area without an urban core or substantial commercial district, with a large number of residents traveling 1–3 hours daily to their jobs ("bedroom communities" as opposed to places of business) and a history of significant population growth occurring in the period following WWII. Physically, they are characterized by large areas of land (at a scale of 1 mile) subdivided into lots as sites for individual residential buildings or larger commercial parcels, with more than half of the area dedicated to automobile parking. Greenery or "nature" appears episodically, often in traffic islands and parking strips—think concrete-ringed grass and hearty shrubs—and regularly enforces the logics of automobile circulation. Overall, the space feels horizontally extensive rather than vertically dense. There are more single-family homes than multi-family condominiums or apartments, and most dwelling units share typical or even exact features—perhaps mirrored—with their nearby neighbors; in these areas, houses are commercial products as well as unique places people call home.

In both form and experience, U.S. suburbs don't square with the Sixtus or Cerdà plans, models which prompt us to recognize a city as buildings subsumed into continuous fabric, where gaps read as omissions, punctuated by moments of object-monumentality. Suburbs give us something else. They give us a reference for working in places where the order can be described as casual, informal, incidental, not driven by an ideal form or forms, places less defined by order than by a spatial phenomenon happening in time. They are sites where, if you evaluate them against the traditional city, there is "nothing to see," and so they ask us to look harder, to look differently. This is the case with all sorts of urban communities: the postwar U.S. suburbs' containers for commercial turnover and their increasing lack of reference to any center located in physical space; the postindustrial city of Detroit as racialized target of organized abandonment; the expansive, growing megalopolis of Houston presenting an infrastructurally troubled blue city in a red state; and Marfa, the high desert water stop along the Union-Pacific Railroad that Donald Judd sought out for its remoteness, but whose proximity (60 miles) to the U.S.–Mexico border sets it within the special 100-mile zone wherein the federal government makes warrantless stops with impunity. Decidedly more is at play in these places than form and space. How can we consider this broader set of criteria, in a reframing of the architectural idea of context, when we work in these places?

Building Preservation, The Chinati Foundation, Marfa, TX (2022)

The John Chamberlain Building Restoration

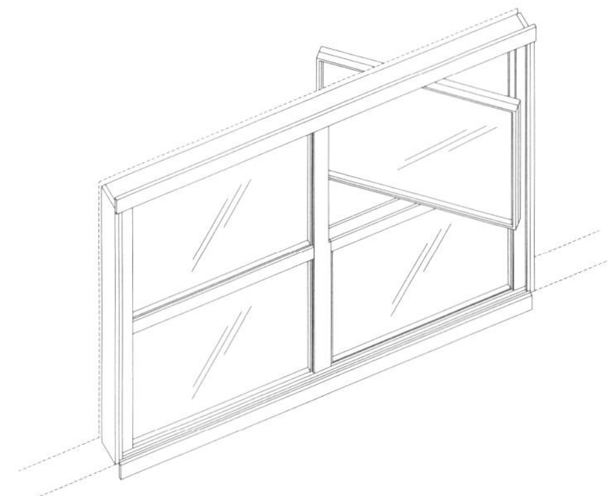

Exploded Perspective,
Scope of Renovation

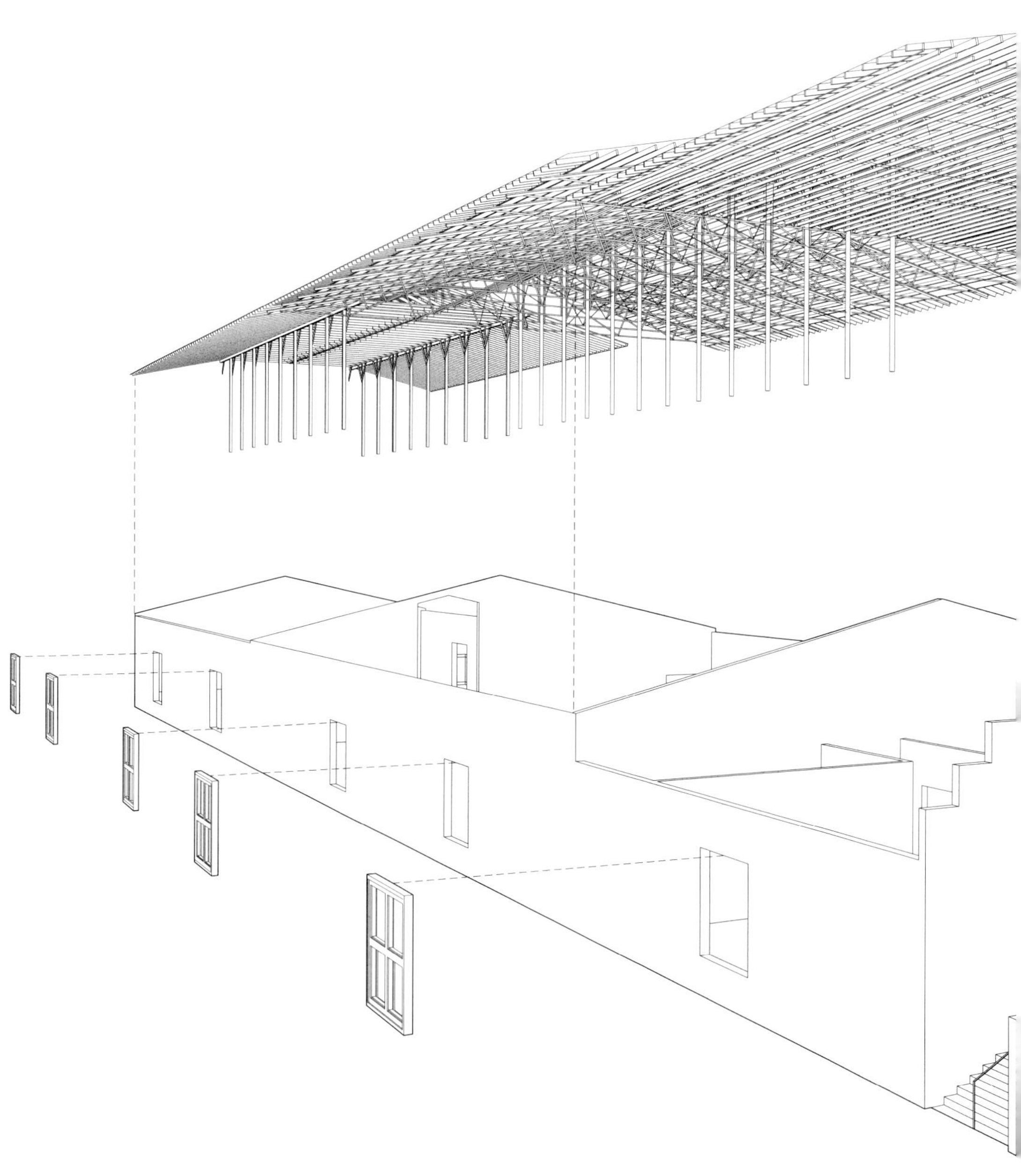

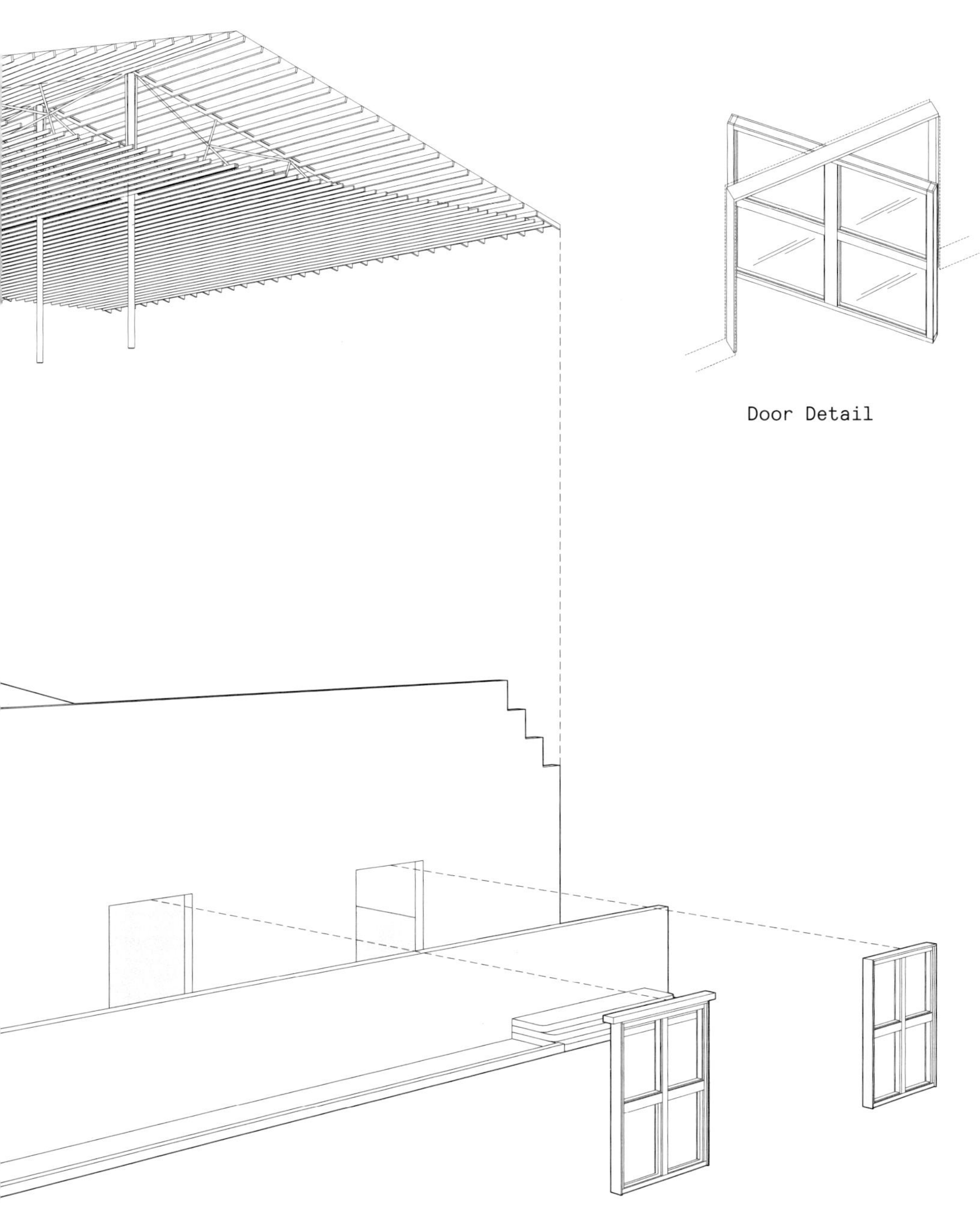

Door Detail

To restore the operation of the windows, steel (found in Judd's later sketches) was integrated into the window design. This was tested in mock-up and incorporated into the new doors.

Troy Schaum, *Blanked Windows at the John Chamberlain Building* (2021)

Adjusted: Surface, Structure, Opening

> The buildings were adjusted to the art as much as possible. New ones would have been better. Nevertheless, in reworking the old buildings, I turned them into architecture.
> —Donald Judd (1987)

In 2014, my architecture practice started the weighty task of planning the restoration of the John Chamberlain Building in Marfa, TX. In contrast to the detached clarity of his artwork, the decisions around Donald Judd's architecture can sometimes feel intuitive, responding to a variation of conditions, as if imagined moment by moment. From Judd's perspective, however, the "adjustments" and "reworkings" he enacted had transformed the vernacular building into architecture. Throughout our restoration process, we engaged with what these "adjustments" and "reworkings" might mean and investigated how they materialized, exploring the tension between his desire for typological ordering systems that certainly existed in his designs for new buildings and the found qualities of the vernacular warehouse buildings.

This tension emerged from two qualities associated with Judd's work. First are the formal interests of his art, which make themselves known in his architecture. Seemingly endless modes of spatial order effortlessly fall out of a syncopation between form, color, and geometry. Second is a practice of situating, restoring, and revealing the historic fabrics and landscapes of vernacular buildings. In the former wool and mohair warehouse that became the site for the installation of art by John Chamberlain, Judd left perhaps the most visible attempt to resolve the tensions between those two modes of his architectural work.

In Marfa, Judd created an urban assemblage out of a broad collection of buildings that he adjusted into architecture between 1972 and his death in 1994, with each individual project still in different states of realization. A process of simultaneously revealing and altering the building fabric to explore a space between the real and idealized history is at the core of Judd's practice of reworking. Looking at the buildings today, one clear way to excavate these methods is to see the building through the individual elements of surface, structure, and opening, each of which seems critical to Judd's overall vision. Many of the artist's architectural works in Marfa exhibit variations of these features, but it is the John Chamberlain Building that contains Judd's most complete articulation of all three. Following his reworkings through each of these fundamental warehouse components uncovers a negotiation that implicates both the given conditions of the building and the legacies of an idealized formal typology.

The extensive beige stucco surface, free of any real defining details, is the feature that produces overall continuity and unity for a building that is really an accumulation of buildings. The building we know today is formed from three distinct structures (west, middle, east) built in two distinct phases. At different points in history, its exterior stucco surface was covered in painted signs, various expressions of the terracotta block, and even an overscaled mural with a map of Texas. In remaking the facade of the building, Judd adjusted this complicated history away through patching, infill, stucco repair, and finally painting. While this crisp unity of the surface was one of the most striking features of the warehouse when it opened in 1983, when we became involved in the project, it had become interrupted with cracking joints, misshapen patches, and water-stained interior walls.

Work proceeded to repair the stucco and underlying terracotta block, reinforcing the most wind-battered corners of the facade with new mortar. The southwest corner of the building had subsided into the soil that was compacted by the local flooding along the nearby railroad tracks. That portion of the stucco wall required structural underpinning before repairs could be completed. Large sections of the original window openings in the masonry walls of the east building were infilled with a patchwork of wood frames disguised under the stucco finish. These sections needed to be repaired with terracotta block. And finally, the plaster and stucco around the whole building was refinished to the original pristine beige finish.

The basic structure of the building contains a conflict between two column layouts, the resolution of which Judd used to rework the organization of the entire building. There are two structural systems: The one in the west building is defined by a wood frame with a double row of supporting columns that creates a navelike organization. The middle and east buildings are supported on elegantly thin steel drill pipe fashioned into trusses. While the trusses are exposed in the expansive space of the middle building, they remain concealed in the east building behind the plaster ceiling of the entry gallery. It is this transition from a centered row of columns in the east to an off-center void in the west that establishes the main contradiction in the design of the plan. This asymmetrical axis of entry and movement is resolved through the introduction of the off-center entry and circulation axis that connects the entry in the east through to the central void of the "nave" in the west.

The lightweight quality of the structure, while strikingly elegant, was one of the primary liabilities when we encountered the building for the first time in 2014. Marfa's famous winds create uplift that, over time, lifts and drops the roof. Our intervention involved reinforcing the continuity and connection of the structural elements with diaphragms to brace the roof, which was anchored to the newly solidified walls. Our team, including the structural engineers from Simpson, Gumpertz & Heger, identified corroded flaws in the steel trusswork that had emerged after being painted over by Judd's original crew and developed a steel sleeving technique to repair them, while maintaining the trusses' delicate, light quality.

The last category of intervention was the iconic wood window openings. Judd's treatment of the openings presents a small laboratory of applications for a consistent formal device, the two-over-two wood frame, with a variety of different functional uses. The center pivot used as the entry door along the aforementioned off-center axis is the most well-known, but the majority of the windows are fixed in their squarish but symmetrical opposed openings. These windows feature one corner with a thinly wood-framed glass pane that was designed to rotate open to allow cross ventilation in an otherwise un-conditioned gallery. The far west wall has a two-over-two window that opens as two one-over-one sliding panels. Experiencing this variation of use with all of the openings fully operable is one of the delights of the space.

Decades of Marfa's harsh light had taken its toll on these windows. The wood had deteriorated to the point that repair of any part required complete replacement. The span of the mullions meant that the wood became sagged and would render many of the functional features inoperable. Working with Peter Stanley, former director of planning and preservation at the Chinati Foundation, we developed a prototype that introduced a hidden steel frame into the main frame of the window and operable corner panes. This steel, something that Judd had experimented with himself in prototypes and other tests, allows the window to weather longer and be repaired more easily. In visiting the building now, the open windows and doors demonstrate the role these iconic openings play in connecting the interior to the immediate landscape and environment.

As the adjustments and reworkings described here demonstrate, the John Chamberlain Building provides a unique space for understanding the underlying framework behind Judd's practice of architecture. In Marfa, the buildings he altered acknowledge a time-worn layering of elements that alternately reveal and cover, contrast or complement. In each instance, we can see how Judd repositioned the context around each installed artwork while maintaining a continuity between buildings as you experience them over time and in their place.

Reprint of "Adjusted: Surface, Structure, Opening" by Troy Schaum (2022)

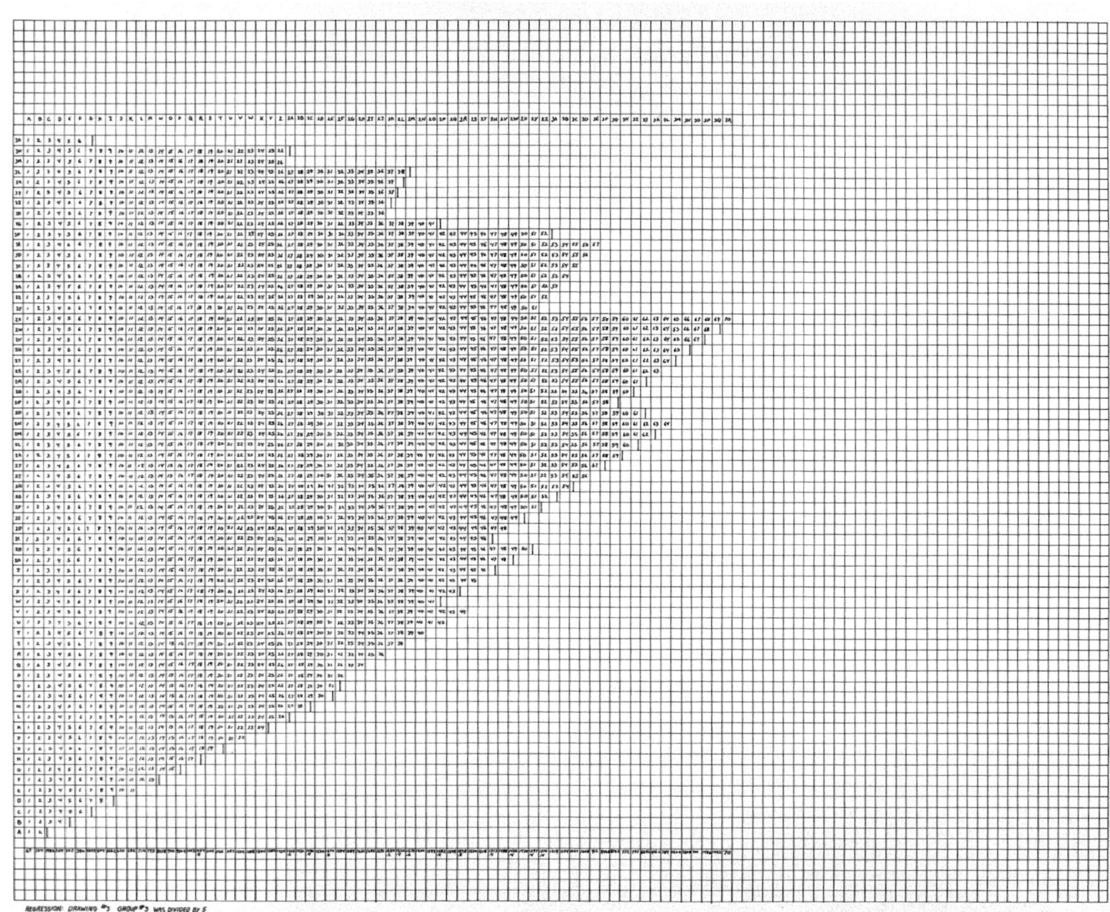

Charles Gaines, *Regression: Group #3 (4/7)* (1973-74)

Unlike Buckminster Fuller, I'm interested in collaborating with entropy.

—Robert Smithson (1971)

Sites as place and memory, Hejduk's Victims Project

Remote, liminal, at the edge. Uneven or diffuse. These are some words we use to describe certain built environments found outside the core cities, the major centers of capital. It's not a judgment, it's about articulating qualities of place that foreground the weathering of buildings/sites over time, at various scales, from their constituent and assembled materials and parts to their spatial and formal organization. These qualities are most apparent where a previously instated ideal form is frayed or grown over, disappearing into disinvestment but also into excess, including excess as *counter*-investment (see the radical acts of love we encountered in the Heidelberg Project and the neighborhood-based nonprofit Power House Productions). These qualities are connected to sites that are less seen, which sometimes means more things or different things are possible or necessary for survival.

"Bread for all, and roses too," a slogan popularized by Helen Todd, suffragist and workers' rights activist (1911).

Weathering describes material transformation (decay, patina), as well as the effects the fluctuation of investment and attention have on architecture and its patterns of inhabitation (seasonally occupied, maintained, vacant, tenanted). Some words for how we might meet these conditions follow directly from how we see them, leading us away from building toward adjusting, preparing, and arranging. These terms highlight design and form as moments of specific order within a continuum of change, as ways to move within stasis, regression, or even loss.

Looking into the canonical vault, we can retrieve John Hejduk's Victims Project as a reference. The version I am looking at is from 1986, in a book published by the Architectural Association, London. The cover folds out to the site plan; its title reads: "NEW SITE PLAN - SITE HAD FORMERLY CONTAINED TORTURE CHAMBERS DURING WWII." Site is both place and memory. A few pages farther, we come upon the introduction, which starts: "A place to be created over two 30-year periods. A growing incremental place—incremental time." We are thus brought quietly into the main body of the project. In that introduction, Hejduk outlines the process: the first steps include planting a grid of saplings (the first 30-year period brackets their maturation time), as well as laying down the main traces of the site ("tracings are like the hands of the blind / touching the surfaces of the face in order to understand / a sense of volume, depth, and penetration"). Formal rules provide a tangential aggregative logic that never closes upon itself, as well as a schedule for the sequential completion of individual buildings, which are drawn and dually named by program and protagonist. It is noted that the drawings and schedules only show a possible full outcome of the project; its actuality is to be decided by the citizens of Berlin: it could "be that all 67 structures can be built over two 30-year periods, the other possibility is that none of the structures is built. A third possibility being that some structures are built." Time, not form, determines the completion of the project, and poignantly: "A child of Berlin might be five years of age when construction on the site is commenced and could conceivably be 65 years of age when construction is completed."

Victims plays out in a collection of modes: sketches, drawings, prose, poetry, the naming of characters and qualities, the naming of programs, a construction schedule. As readers, we come to know its particularities and understand its logics, attuning ourselves to the project as process; interrelated parts are given value through their naming. Its architectural project is a corrective experience to the primacy of any one thing (e.g., image or form) as arbiter of meaning; we come away with a sensitivity and solemnity with which we might approach a site of our own interest, and an expanded sense of what to look for, who we might see, how to understand, what we can let go of.

And an example of an architectural response to grief.

Nigel Henderson, *Photograph showing construction site of flats designed by the Architect Denys Lasdun in the East End of London* (1952)

Diving into the Wreck

Exclusion is a quiet violence; it is insidious because, by its own logic, it is hard to detect. Conversations around disciplinarity appear to cohere the relevance and singularity of architecture insofar as they operate by defining boundaries and drawing limits under the dual claims of authority and ownership. And insofar as a few voices seek to represent a totality, such processes of identification are ones of exclusion: this particular centering of one thing does so by marginalizing others. Of course, not everything needs to be at the center, nor does everyone even want to be seen, but that is not a choice any one should make for another. Let's put aside for now any questions about whether claiming or arguing for architecture's relevance is even necessary or important discourse. Rather, let's look at the act of delineating boundaries and the defining of disciplines-territories. What comes to mind is a perimeter wall, a fortress wall even, where the wall is both symbol and reality. That wall is drawn to cohere an identity; it makes a claim about what is. This is done to ontological ends.

In 2017, Trump's U.S.-Mexico border wall was on our minds.

It has been some time that architecture has been preoccupied with its ontology. I remember when I first read Hans Hollein's polemic: "Everything is architecture." That bold explosion of the boundaries of architecture to encompass the world was so enthralling to me as a student, because it recast everything as something constructed, to be constructed. It projected all exigency—the potential of every reality—into my architectural imagination. It made architecture feel consequential, and to my yearning, idealistic heart, even hopeful.

But that no longer seems right. Everything is not architecture. There is so much more, but that doesn't have to make architecture less. It's not that questions (or proclamations like Hollein's) of ontology can't have a place, but for those who have trouble finding their own reflections in the received histories and any for whom a greater project of emancipation is part of their artistic striving, questions of ontology are not the most useful types of questions to be asking. What already belongs, what we have inherited, and what has already been written is simply not enough.

It is Adrienne Rich who named the "book of myths / in which / our names do not appear" in her 1972 poem "Diving into the Wreck." In it, she writes: "the thing I came for: / the wreck and not the story of the wreck / the thing itself and not the myth." We need, rather, guides to lead us outward, into the lived and real, but less known and less seen. For Rich, language is the material in which she fashions tools, constructs her place, and charts direction; she writes: "The words are purposes. / The words are maps." I too have come for the wreck, its unmapped reality... that potent, hulking, treasure of reality. If Rich has language, we have architecture. With its heterogeneous and ever-growing mix of concepts and practices, we can fashion our own maps and our own purposes to access, acknowledge, and move within the damage, the brokenness, and the beauty of the world in which we already live.

This is not to say these are "enough," but to recognize what we have at hand, and a reminder to use these concepts and practices to make what we don't yet have, to make what we need.

Reprint of "Diving into the Wreck" by Rosalyne Shieh (2017)

Quadtych (clockwise from upper left): Naho Kubota, *Transart Gallery* (2018); Lewis Baltz, *South Corner, Riccar America Company, 3184 Pullman, Costa Mesa* (1974); *Pinto Canyon Rock* (2013); Naho Kubota, *Transart Gallery* (2018)

Troy Schaum, *Marfa Landscape* (2013)

TS To start, I'd like to recall your remarks at a Judd event hosted at the Block. You turned to the crowd, pointed at the adobe brick, and said: "This is what we do, we fix the adobe. This is what we do." Then you summed up the whole energy of the Judd Foundation around the tangible, simple, and unassuming action of "fixing brick by brick by brick by..." I thought it was a memorable and insightful way to think about our efforts. There is a method for thinking about the role of a designer or an architect that follows that framework. That is the idea of the architect as a mason and the mason as an architect. There's a long conceptual debate on the intersections between architect and master builder. For instance, an Albertian model suggests an architect as the agent who draws, thinks, and perhaps writes about a project before building it. I don't think your father aligned himself with that model. For him, making is inherently the thinking of the project; the phases aren't separable. Looking at the way most architects and designers practice today, we make drawings and then somebody else makes the building. I think our efforts in Marfa are similar to the former model. I'm wondering if this distinction is meaningful to you and your work.

FJ I think the whole question is backwards. What if, instead of categorizing the efforts into different models, we think of them as just solving problems. Some are technological, some are design questions, and the rest are other things. These categories don't mean anything because it's still just solving problems. For instance, in cases like the Judd buildings, you're facing an actual wall that needs help and you have to figure out how to solve it. It's a given. The possible responses are pretty limited. Also, when you design something from scratch on paper, you're still given or have a context in which you're figuring things out. So they're not that different. And I don't think the distinction is as clear as you described, it's just problem-solving.

TS What are the parameters of problem-solving? In the case of Donald Judd, do you think the ethos of his artworks can be considered part of the parameters? Or was it so naturalized that it didn't have a considerable effect?

FJ No, no. Certainly, Don did things a certain way. And, if we work on one of the buildings that he inhabited, we're going to keep the building like that as much as possible. So, the work is very much a restoration and keeping things to what they were. That's very different from designing something from scratch or adding layers to something that doesn't exist yet.

TS As the art director of the Judd Foundation you're dealing with a vast range of production in different scales—from architecture to furniture to sculpture to prints to paintings. We work together only on the architecture portion, but I'm wondering if your dad's mode of engaging with different mediums is a reflection of this "problem-solving" attitude. I'm intrigued by this quote from him: "The buildings were adjusted to the art as much as possible. New ones would have been better. Nevertheless, in reworking the old buildings, I turned them into architecture." Contrary to his artworks made from scratch, he frames the adjustment of existing buildings as realigning existing conditions to match his concept of architecture. I wonder if the kind of adjusting he mentions resonates with your description of problem-solving and the kind of work that we're doing in Marfa. Is it different than the problem-solving you have to do when you're thinking about the furniture collection or other aspects of your dad's work? It seems messier than in other parts of his creative practice.

FJ Everything's different and the same at the same time. It's all very related, but each has different rules. However, within those rules, the problems are pretty similar. We can make new furniture. We can't make new art. So that's a distinction that is kept. When restoring buildings, we intervene in a more physical way than when we restore art, which we don't do ourselves and is very methodical and scientific. There are three sets of rules that are encircled by one set of rules. So it's just a question of different flavors of the same thing.

TS Do you mean the categories of architecture, furniture, and art as rules?

FJ Yes, like architecture, furniture, and art have their own rules, but they are within another, larger circle that is Don's rules. There are crossovers. For instance, the way the metal is bent in the furniture is so direct that you can understand exactly what the furniture is made out of. It's completely clear. There's no mystifying to the weight of the sheet or how the piece is made. It's very evident. And the same is true in the architecture and the art.

TS I agree that there are similar rules. I guess I'm trying to figure out if there is something different about the architecture that relates to Don's writing and thinking on the space between the real and an ideal; the idea that a work could or couldn't be a thing in itself.

FJ Well, he is not interested in the ideal.

TS Exactly. As we've been studying these buildings together, including some that you focus on, you notice something like the Block and its apparent symmetry. When you approach the Block and walk through the gate, you can feel and understand that symmetry. However, when we delve deeper into the project, we realize that the symmetry is somewhat illusory, due to the adjustments needed to respond to what was there already. So the symmetry that might exist with one of these pieces of furniture in this room doesn't exist in the buildings necessarily as a real thing. For me, this highlights an interesting distinction we're often trying to navigate in our work—the difference between an ideal set of rules and the reality of their application. I'm constantly learning from how your father approached this challenge, negotiating between the existing and what a building ought to be according to his subjectivity and set of rules.

FJ Negotiate. It's messier. Yeah, yeah, yeah. But you can see from his unbuilt design from scratch for the building at Bregenz that it's just like the furniture. The walls are the structure and are repeated, similar to how the rules of his furniture work. Don is not interested in narratives and stories. He wants to understand the world, and for him, art, architecture, and furniture are playful ways of understanding the world. But the rule is that the work has to be self-evident, it can't be hiding something. So in architecture works, he tries to make them more self-evident than they were originally. Like when he is lining up the walls at the Block, he's expressing: Okay, these walls are related.

TS Or when he's pulling plaster off a wall at the Architecture Office. Yeah. So you can see the actual structure of the wall versus some cladding.

FJ Well, even more to the point, he removed the renovations from the 1970s and didn't even bother to replace them. He just left it as it was, like, "That's good enough." So, it's not even an intentional exposure—it's just, "This is what it looks like, and here it is." Any architect worth his or her salt would be like, "Oh my God, we have to fix that."

TS The example of the Architecture Office that we're restoring currently is interesting. When we plan for a restoration, there's a certain level of precision and craftsmanship required. It's part of the foundation of the project, almost an inherent expectation. But ironically, that precision can feel at odds with the original intent of the project, as is the case at the Architecture Office.

I find it intriguing how we navigate within the rules—both the idea of rules and their practical application. We've read the texts and seen the extensive work you've done in publishing, but the rules aren't laid out explicitly; they're more of an implicit knowledge. What fascinates me about Don's project is the inherent integrity of the work, whether in architectural forms or other mediums. The work feels like a peer we engage with and learn from, despite the generational distance. Even though I never met your father, I feel as if I'm in dialogue with the work he produced. This is one way to understand the rules.

I wonder, considering your lifelong relationship with the project, how your experience—growing up not as the maker but as someone who experienced the work—shapes your approach to design. Does encountering the work through its spaces and experiences, rather than through sketches or geometric structures, change your perspective as a designer? I think it does. I can see that in your work—a sense of movement and an awareness of the subject's perception. This, I believe, echoes the challenges your father set up, but with a unique interpretation that is specific to your experience as you continue to work within the space of Marfa and his legacy.

FJ Yes, I learned it from the inside out. I learned about buildings before I studied buildings, not the other way around.

TS It's almost like a privilege you have. Don never had access to his work as just pure perception, but for you, and by extension your practice, the process begins with firsthand experience of walking through the spaces, understanding how they affect people, and observing how people interact with them. It's only after a retroactive analysis of the logic that the attempt to establish rules begins. I think there's something in this approach that influences your perception of design. It's a kind of subjectivity that's more embodied, more participatory. I see this in your own design practice in Monaco or LA. There seems to be a shift from your father's approach, where he conceptualized objects from a top-down perspective on a notepad, to this method, where you are fully embedded in the spaces. The Judd Foundation's offices are situated within the spaces we are drawing, making the work a continuous, lived experience rather than a detached process.

FJ I think the inspirations and mode of perception you're talking about come from everywhere, to a point that measuring them becomes unfathomable. I think everything of my experience is an influence on my work. Just like a bazillion drops forming a pond.

TS But do you, when you work on a project like the space in Monaco, do you see that as completely separate from this conversation?

FJ These influences linger in the background, but I don't have the same kind of restrictions as I do with Judd Foundation projects. When we're working together on Judd projects, the array of references becomes extremely strict in a way that my other projects aren't. For example, I was laughing because we were doing something about furniture on a separate project and then I realized, I was referencing a seat from a 1962 Maserati that I saw when I was 16. It's a reminder that everything finds its way back into our work. When we're dealing with Don's buildings, there aren't big subjects—it's about solving a million small problems. What do we do with this corner? How do we handle this window? It's all about the details, down to what a single square inch looks like. In this sense, the building becomes the primary reference point.

TS I'd like to revisit the idea of time. Maybe this is another "big subject," but it's a concept that frequently comes up and, in some ways, permanence is central to your father's work. The work could, in theory, just sit there, decay, and be left alone, and that would still be a valid version of the project. This idea isn't just something we learn from the work, but it's also deeply rooted in your father's intent. I find this tension fascinating—the tension between the artwork's physical presence and the ongoing project of preservation, which involves a kind of labor of care. This care is aimed at maintaining the work's permanence, which is a fluid concept. If most museum exhibitions last only three months, then 30 years of existence could be considered quite permanent. But when you compare that to the landscape surrounding the work, you realize that the idea of permanence in the context of nature is entirely different. How much of our work in preservation is focused on this concept of time and permanence?

FJ Well, time is perceptual, right? I mean, one part of physics says it doesn't exist at all. It's purely perceptual. If you're in New York, you know, and a week passes, you're aware of it. But if you go to Las Casas or Morales, they look exactly the same as they did 40 years ago. And you're facing mountains that have been there for millions of years. So your idea of time just, like, literally dissipates. Marfa is somewhere between New York and Las Casas.

What Don was doing in Marfa, regardless of the attention to permanence and ideals, was what he could do. He's not saying, Everybody should do what I'm doing. He's saying, Everybody should do what they can do in their space in their time.

TS I often think about what one person can do, and when I consider the scope of work in Marfa—how many projects and elements are involved—I'm struck by the scale. In Marfa, you can see the big set projects both at a scale of a town and then zoom in to the scale of individual works within a room. This layered scale is incredibly powerful; I haven't encountered another place quite like it. Marfa feels many times larger than any single project, almost like an urban environment in the sense of its collective nature, or as part of a broader landscape. Given this context, I'm curious about how you determine the limits of the project. I know there were more buildings when your father passed away, and you chose to focus on certain core elements. How do you decide what to include or exclude in order to understand and define the project Don envisioned? How do you set limits on what's necessary to grasp the essence of his work?

FJ You have to remember there was no plan at the beginning. It was all as we could do it, one thing after another as projects came up. For instance, if the economy had been really great in the '80s and all those buildings hadn't come up for sale, we wouldn't have them. There were many parameters involved that he could not control. There's an infinite number of possibilities. After he went to Australia in the '70s, he was like: "Oh my God, I should have gone to Australia. They have ranches that are 400 square miles." And when we had the place in Switzerland, he was like, "Well, at least it's a democracy. The United States is not so much!"

TS Why Marfa then? I first imagined your dad was trying to get farther and farther away from people, so he could think and work. But after understanding his work on the ranches and the landscape there I realized he was also trying to get closer and closer to some kind of wilderness. You don't necessarily see that landscape foregrounded in discourses around his work, but it seems essential.

FJ It's the whole reason for Marfa. Marfa itself was just where the school was and was very much secondary to the fact that you could get a ranch house in the middle of the mountains.

TS At the same time, there are a lot of other artists who work with landscape. What's interesting about your dad's relation to the landscape is that he wasn't doing work just for the sake of being in the vastness of landscape. The work was always situated in previously occupied ranches or spaces of inhabitation. He never performed a massive alteration to the existing landscape.

FJ He was totally uninterested in those kinds of phenomena and rather horrified by what other people were doing with bulldozers. The only earth work he considered doing was a wall, an adobe wall, one kilometer long near the Rio Grande. Which, I don't even know where you would do that, because it's not straight. Not to mess up the landscape was rule number one for him. It's a very limited supply. Landscape for him is not an abstraction, and his particular approach to the context sets his consistent and deliberate relationship to art, architecture, and landscape. It's an extreme environmentalism that other people might not share. He was not a fan of creating a crater; there's a perfectly good crater before, why mess it up?

TS What do you see as the future of the project of architecture in Marfa and preserving Don's work?

FJ It'll just keep going. It's like painting the Golden Gate Bridge. You start at one end and by the time you finish the other end, you start again.

Restoration & Planning, Marfa, TX (Ongoing)

Judd Foundation Planning & Building Restoration

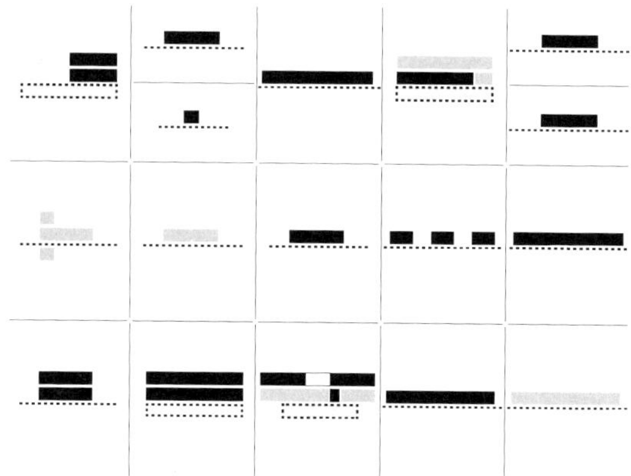

Marfa Plan Aerial View

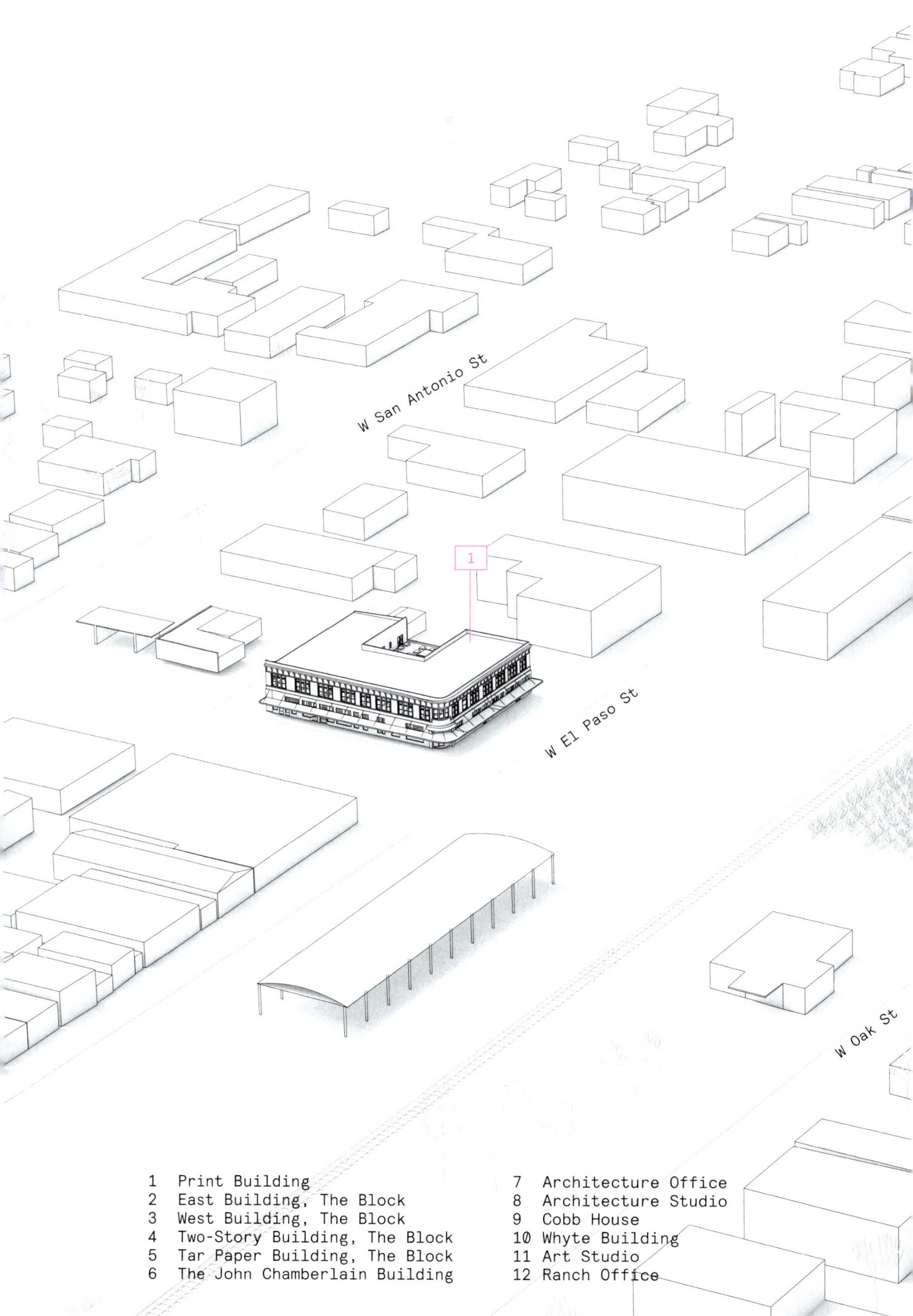

1 Print Building
2 East Building, The Block
3 West Building, The Block
4 Two-Story Building, The Block
5 Tar Paper Building, The Block
6 The John Chamberlain Building
7 Architecture Office
8 Architecture Studio
9 Cobb House
10 Whyte Building
11 Art Studio
12 Ranch Office

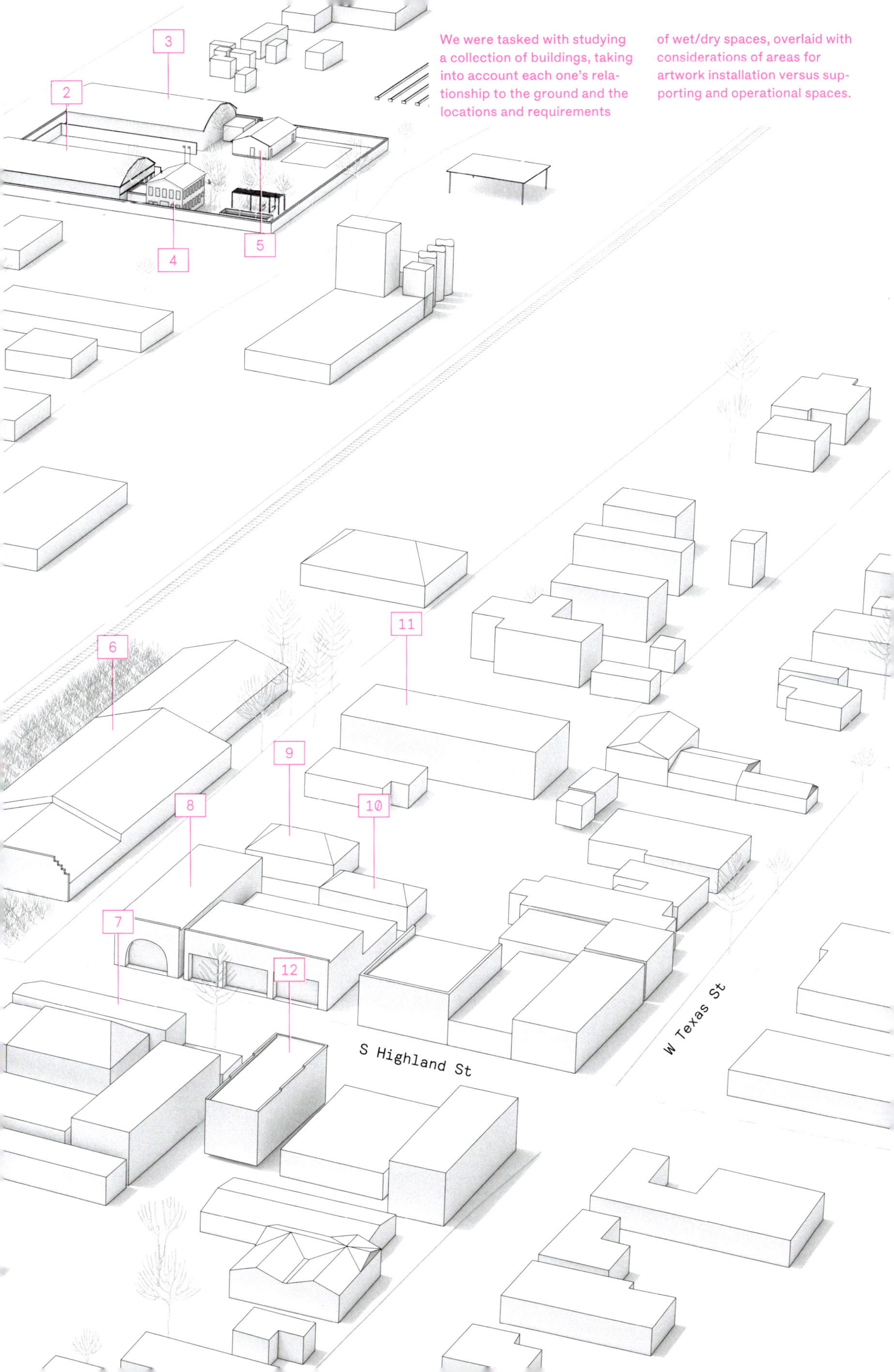

We were tasked with studying a collection of buildings, taking into account each one's relationship to the ground and the locations and requirements of wet/dry spaces, overlaid with considerations of areas for artwork installation versus supporting and operational spaces.

Exploded Perspective, Scope of Renovation

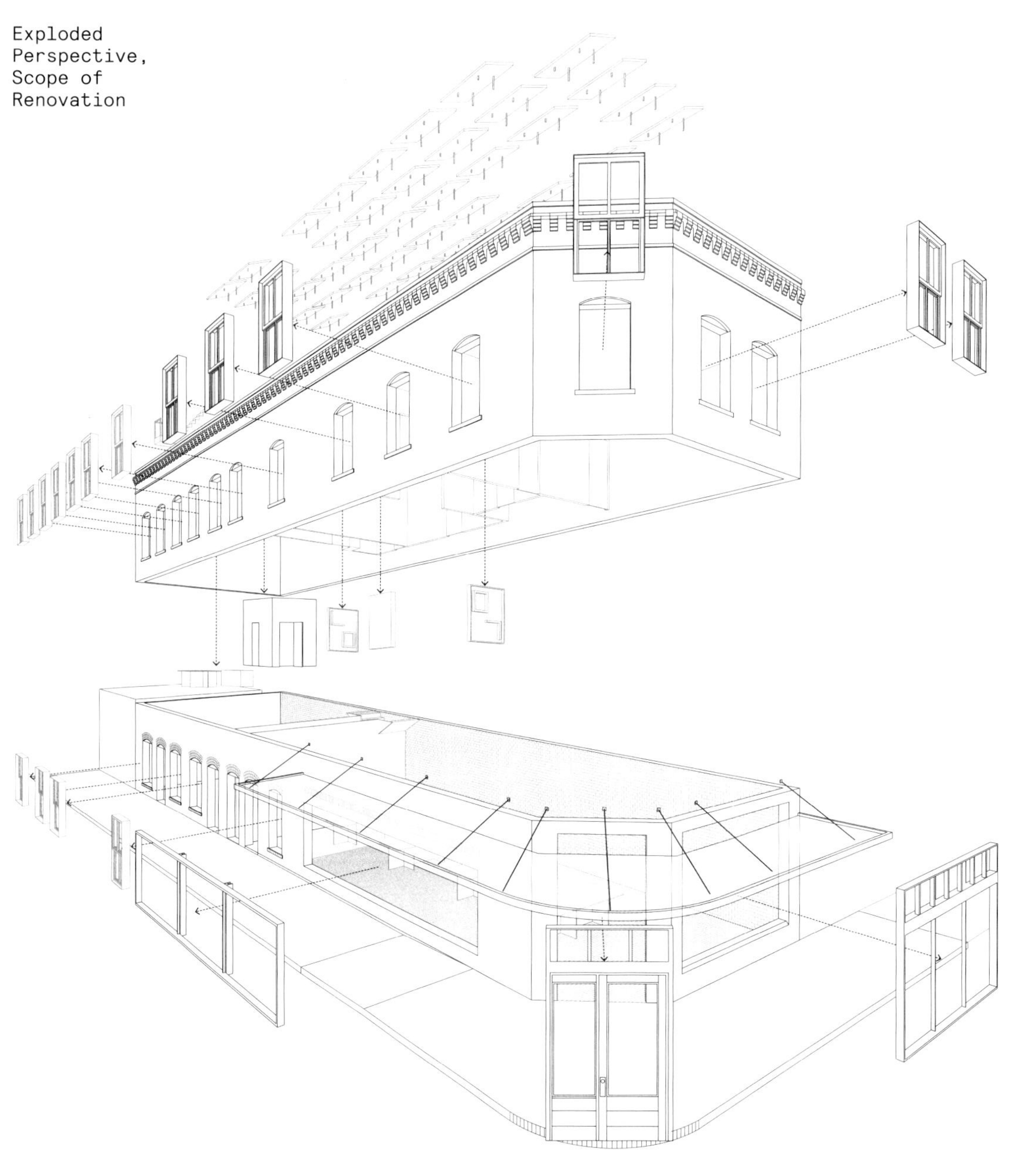

Architecture Office

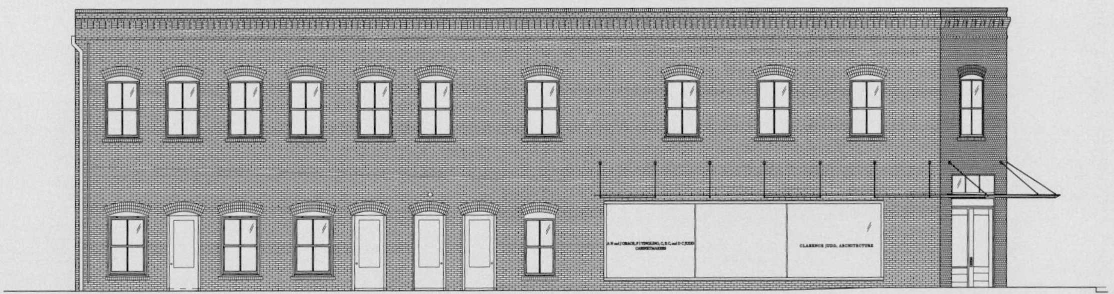

Elevation

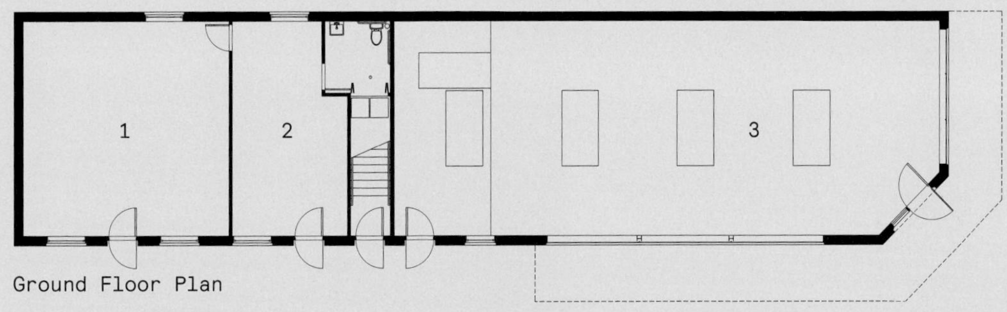

Ground Floor Plan

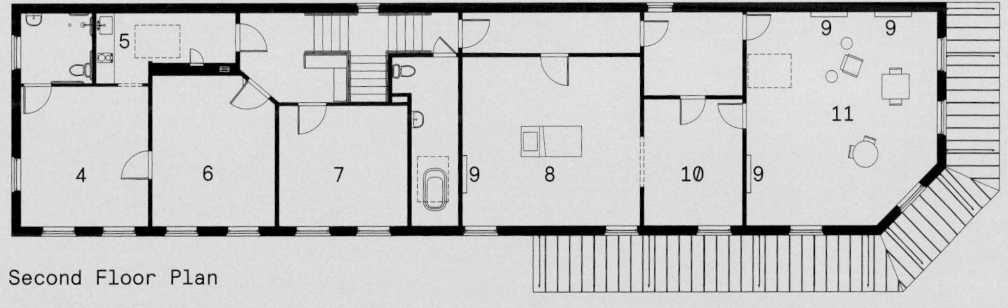

Second Floor Plan

Ground Floor

1 Project Room 1
2 Project Room 2
3 Judd Architecture Office

Second Floor

4 Dining
5 Kitchen
6 Bedroom 1
7 Bedroom 2
8 Bedroom 3

9 John Chamberlain Artwork
10 Sitting Room
11 Office

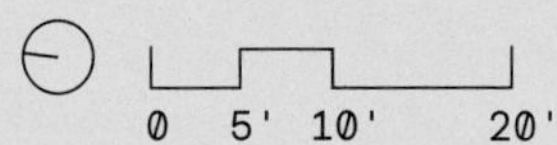

Window Header
Night Flushing Vent
Detail

0 2" 4"

This project was near completion when a fire swept through in June 2021, so in a way it's a project we did twice.

The joints on the Architecture Office were raked, the effect of which became more pronounced over the years. Judd also sandblasted the facade, visible on the right, which gave the bricks a unique texture.

Art Studio at
Las Casas

To be "trailered" to the remote ranch site, the 40ft-long steel beam had to be broken into 16ft lengths. The three pieces were then spliced together on site and inserted on new steel columns configured to match the existing details.

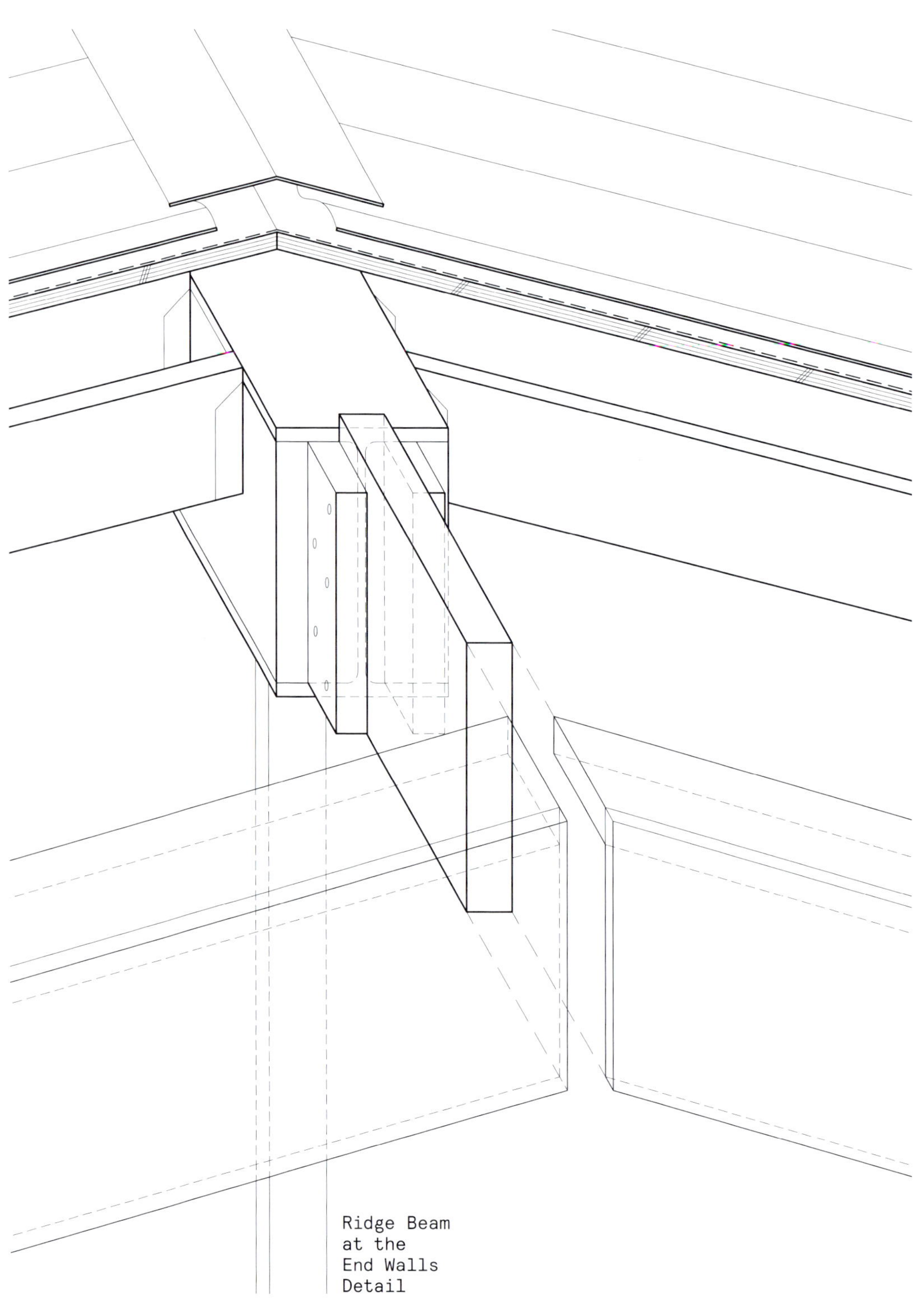

Ridge Beam
at the
End Walls
Detail

On-Site Adobe Reconstruction

To rebuild the collapsing wall, the adobero reconstituted adobe from the existing bricks to make new ones.

Untitled (Tainan Countryside) (2019)

I used to believe up until that point that there should be some radical separation between self and work—a separation that of course was theorized. I don't totally understand this anymore. I don't completely know why or how this is the case.

—Craig Owens (1983)

Using a combination of drawing, notes, and vignettes, draw from memory an early and significant "home" from your childhood or past. It can be your own home or another home you were familiar with. Represent it at three scales: as an interior space, in relation to an immediate exterior (e.g., entrance, driveway, corridor, main stair, front yard, lobby), in relation to neighbors (units in a multifamily building, the house next door).

Write and make notes on "home." This can be a definition, a description, or thoughts engaging the term.

Compose your drawings, sketches, and notes onto a single layout. Techniques may include orthographic drawing, perspective sketching, diagrams. Words should also be used and can be in the form of labels, memory fragments, longer narrative passages, etc.

On the Simmons Report

It must have been 1997 or 1998 when, as an architecture student looking to fulfill major requirements, I took Professor Robert Olgilvie's course, City Planning 118AC: The Urban Community. AC stands for "American Cultures," and it remains a requirement that all undergraduates must pass to graduate at UC Berkeley. I no longer have the syllabus, but I remember we read about teenagers in the suburbs of Los Angeles (Finnegan) and oral histories of immigrant and black Americans (Tataki). We were asked to think about what it means to be American (Martin Luther King Jr. and de Tocqueville) and the vital connection between people and place (Gans), we learned to appreciate the neighborhood as a living unit of community (Jacobs) and to recognize the community group as a site of political power (Castells).

What I read in that class crystallized a point of consciousness in me. It suggested I could connect my pursuit of knowledge, study, and research—all things you can learn about and work on, and work toward—to my personal experience. I was given permission to value the places I grew up in, as well as the places I didn't grow up in, that I carry with me always. I began to consider personal lives—mine but also those whom I count to be mine, however near or far they are to where I am now—within landscapes, buildings, environments; I began to see their position and relationships to social and cultural structures.

This class was significant for its content—it gave me access to a world I knew had always been there, but now had the eyes to see, the language to speak—and also because it was so determinedly emphasized within Cal's curriculum—you couldn't pass the finish line without it. How did the American Cultures program come to be?

In 1968 the Black Student Union and other student groups at San Francisco State formed the Third World Liberation Front to demand the histories of African Americans, Asian Americans, Chicanos and Chicanas, and Native Americans be taught in the university. Their efforts led to the creation of departments of Ethnic Studies at San Francisco State and UC Berkeley, and effectively organized a movement within the institution, carving avenues for continued agitation.

Twenty years later, the Faculty Senate at Berkeley was presented with the Simmons Report (1989), which endorsed the establishment of an American Cultures (AC) requirement, a curricular addition that would "enable students to develop a more informed understanding of the racial and cultural diversity of U.S. society." The report articulated a value of the university curriculum to be in a "living relationship with the students whom we educate." Two important points of emphasis were: the offerings should be comparative ("each racial or ethnic group should be studied in the larger context of American history, society, and culture... courses should substantially consider at least three of the five main racial/cultural groups in American society: African American, Indian American, Asian American, Chicano/Latino, and European American"); and they should be offered by departments across the university, distributing the intellectual labor of examining race ("We urge that race and ethnicity be a greater part of the domain of the broad range of disciplines (such as Social Welfare, Political Science, Economics, Business, English, Comparative Literature, Art History, and others) that interpret the American past and/or present").

The UC Berkeley Faculty Senate voted 227 to 194 to accept the report's recommendations. Summer seminars began in 1990; faculty across the university met to learn from each other and develop coursework that would meet the new requirements. Courses began in Fall 1991 and the first class to have completed the requirement graduated in 1995. By the time we showed up on campus in 1994, the majority of undergraduates present were subject to the requirement.

For a long time I thought about this experience from the perspective of being a student and the growth and edification this moment made possible for me, personally and academically. Now, in the roles of architect and educator, I am stunned by the difficult achievement of those generations of determined students (and their faculty allies). Two decades of student agitation and organization—pressure from below, essentially—led to a new and meaningful curriculum. In this expanded view, the student movements connect directly to the creation of new knowledges.

Nigel Henderson, *Construction work at the Hunstanton Secondary Modern School* (1953)

Ching Shieh, *Untitled (Fountain Valley, CA)* (2018)

Troy Schaum, *Jantar Mantar*, *Jaipur* (2004)

For consideration:
Other places, the personal, what exists

César Aira,
Ghosts
(2013)

Center for Land
Use Interpretation
(1994–)

Mati Diop,
Atlantics
(2019)

William Finnegan,
Cold New World
(1998)

Dolores Hayden,
"What Would a Non-Sexist
City Be Like?"
(1980)

Donald Judd,
"Guest Lecture at
University of Texas"
(1992)

Djibril Diop Mambéty,
Touki Bouki
(1973)

Colin Rowe and
John Hejduk,
"Lockhart, Texas"
(1957)

Alison and
Peter Smithson,
"The 'As Found' and
the 'Found'"
(1990)

Carolyn Kay Steedman,
Landscape for a Good Woman
(1987)

William Whyte,
*The Social Life
of Small Urban Spaces*
(1980)

Untitled (ArtPrize) (2013)

Fine

some
fall
gaps
adjacent
on
associate
another
together
near
here
there
orbit
pass
delay
suggest
attract
observe
detach
across
meanwhile

What shifts when we reframe crisis from a barrier that must be overcome to a territory of intensity within a matrix of stressors? Instead of trying to resolve, dissolve, or dissipate the knot, it can be tactically worked on, around, and within. Instead of ends, find places to start, directions in which to move, or small ways to continue.

Michele Abeles, *Arm, Plant, Bottles, Wood* (2011)

How do we hold unlike things together in relation, but without subsuming them under one order?

In a drawing or diagram, can different types of criteria that would otherwise hang together uneasily, coexist indifferently?

What about proximity without relationship? How does our perspective change when being nearby or being over (t)here is not less than being with?

How can we be purposeful with disjunctions and gaps? Is it possible to establish a space where the ad hoc and the non sequitur are at home, and to be a little nonsensical with how we work?

Can we let ourselves do what we want before we decide if it will be good or bad?

Instead of "Here is the best thing" or even "Here is a good thing," try: "This is something that can be done." What shifts? What are some things we can do? Who is here and what are they here to do? What can we do together?

Cy Twombly, *Untitled* (1970)

The limits of narrative and form

In *On Painting* (1435–36), Leon Battista Alberti writes about the *istoria* or narrative as it is associated with history painting: “The greatest work of the painter is the *istoria*. Bodies are part of the *istoria*, members are parts of the bodies, planes are parts of the members.” At center is the expressive figure: “the *istoria* will move the soul of the beholder when each man painted there clearly shows the movement of his own soul: we weep with the weeping, laugh with the laughing, and grieve with the grieving. These movements of the soul are made known by movements of the body.” Figures become individual actors in a multi-pointed composition, unfolding within a dramatic arc, amplified by their geometric formation, delineated and accentuated by light and atmosphere, within a system of representation that bridges color, figure, surface, and form. Idea is tethered to form and meaning is produced through composition.

This way of reading meaning in the interaction of figures is persistent. In 1922 El Lissitzky published a book for children, *About Two Squares*, where old and new world order are embodied in two squares of different colors and revolution is carried out through their interaction and the creation of new geometric projections.

This project of representation lives on in many architects’ preoccupation with form (our practice included); we take pleasure in it, believe in its utility… some will even fiercely defend it. The way Alberti writes about the power of individual figures in painting resonates with certain sensibilities: an appreciation of the plastic quality of architecture, where the form is almost alive, vivified by the eye and in movement, modulated by color and light. Perhaps it is almost as gripping as narrative because the ways we inherit (teach) it and keep it through language (discourse) are handed directly down to us from Alberti’s *istoria*.

What are ways to temper this impulse? Unintelligibility, glare and humidity, night and darkness, body, touch, smell, sleep, looking away or to the side, giving attention to what can be observed or felt, to the world as it is lived, to how it exists apart from something to be understood.

In the Round for Tempietto (2018)

File

Tempietto Exemplum

"What is gained from studying [Bramante's] Tempietto?"

To be honest, we don't often think about the Tempietto. The "role and use of precedent" is something that we grapple with, however. We bristle at the term *precedent*, mostly for its legal overtones, ones that seek to regulate and guide, that assume authority, and demand we answer or contend with received views or values. However, we have learned that when we react in this manner, our discomfort might be a kind of intelligence, and to follow such feelings of irritation by looking closely at their sources, potential meanings, and qualities. We can treat irritation as information, the examination of which may uncover levers to transform our thinking. And so, we have uncovered our annoyance as stemming from a perceived weight that we carry—that precedent is a weight laid upon us, one that demands we relate our work to an origin, to construct ourselves in terms of difference or similarity to exempla, to situate ourselves continually within a lineage. The irritation arises from the fact that we do in fact carry this weight; it is, at some level, a result of our own agency. Fine. We can be held accountable to our part in this.

to be met with curiosity

Without any claims to legitimacy, we offer a drawing of ours in dialogue with the Tempietto: a planimetric section, rendered as a pure figure, of an installation within an open-aired atrium above a traffic intersection in a postindustrial American city. Not unlike the Tempietto, it is centered within an urban, interstitial space. Unlike the Tempietto, each successive planimetric cut in our project reveals a figure that is distinct and surprising to us, for the plans here are results and not causes. Maybe like us, it's held by the center, but it's squirming.

The order of the Tempietto, its relation to projection, and to the means of representation may have given us an exemplum against which we can understand what we are doing. It might have given us the language to say all this. However, it may also be that the order of our project has given us the means to see that of the Tempietto.

Maybe it's a place from which to start rather than a place to end up.

Adapted from "Tempietto Exemplum" by Rosalyne Shieh and Troy Schaum (2018)

Commercial Adaptation Projects, Houston, TX (2016-22)

Houston Adaptations

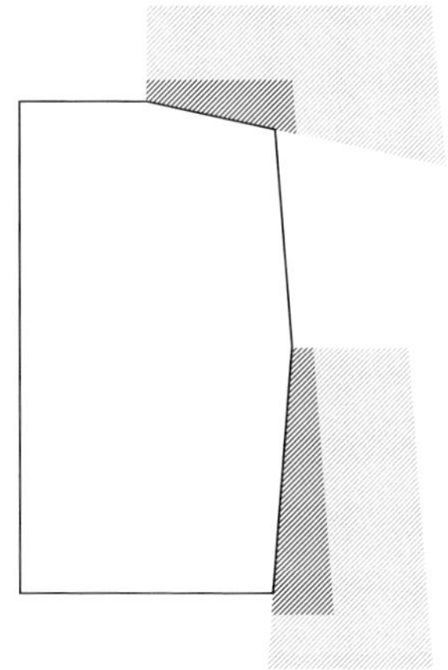

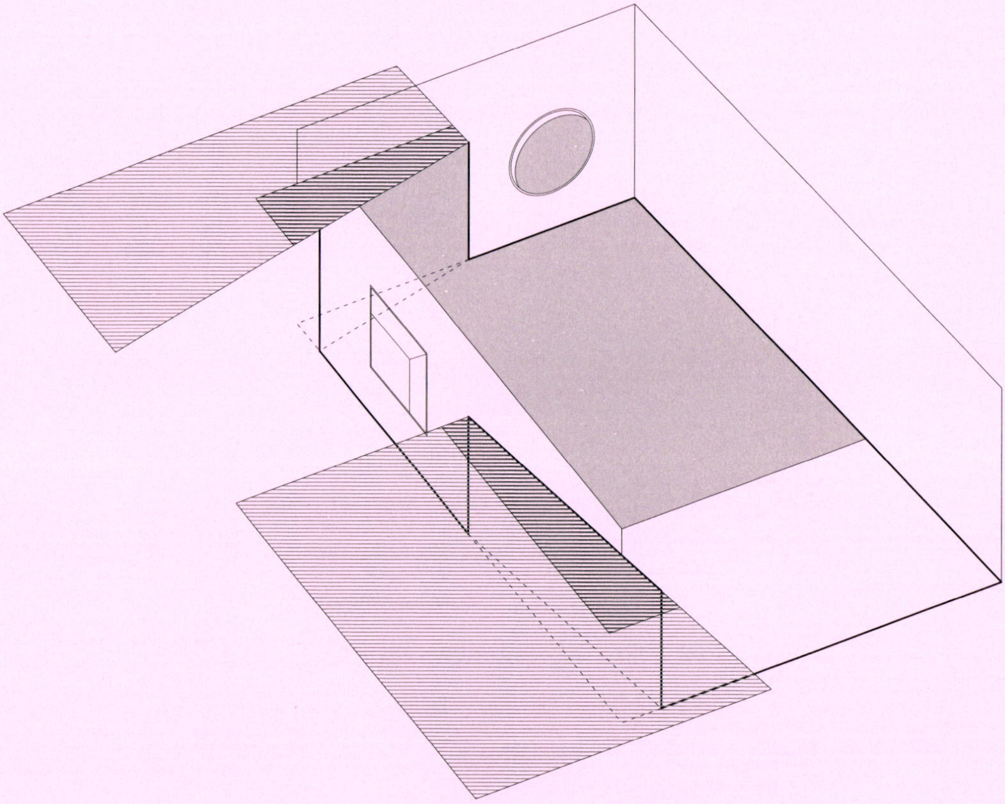

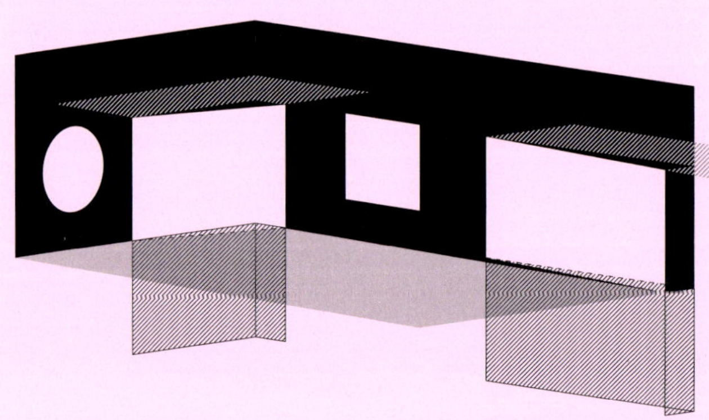

The strip mall is a ubiquitous type, a ready architectural stock.

BIRDS
BARBERSHOP

LOWELL STREET

BEYOGA
Teapresso Bar
Organic Coffee and Boba

Troy Schaum, *Exposed Ceiling* (2024)

Life's but a walking shadow, a poor player,
That struts and frets his hour upon the stage,
And then is heard no more. It is a tale
Told by an idiot, full of sound and fury,
Signifying nothing.

—William Shakespeare (1606)

On Ninagawa's *Macbeth*

Originally presented in 1980, Yukio Ninagawa's *Macbeth* resets Shakespeare's play in 16th-century Japan. In 2018, two years after Ninagawa's death, it was staged at Lincoln Center.

The slot of the proscenium has been lined with a dark wood frame and inset with solid doors that accordion to either side; beyond them are translucent sliding screens. The top of the frame is defined by a heavy beam that spans clear across the stage. It is decorated with gold accents: a row of long carved panels sandwiched between two rows of medallions—each one punctuated at the center with a small rosette—plaited in an overlapping pattern that runs from one side to the other, and bracketed at either end by T-shaped elements. The shape and placement of the ornamentation recalls wood joinery and the hardware of furniture; at the scale of a grand hall it has the effect of a cabinet altar writ large. The tropes of a domestic shrine typically used for ancestral plaques and figures of deities (*butsudan*) are transposed to the stage. This scale shift, small made big, has two effects: it equates the actors within the frame with deities and spirits, elevating or augmenting their status, and at the same time it miniaturizes them, constructing the audience as larger-than-life, omniscient viewers peering into a tableau vivant set within a diorama, where mere men play out their actions as if gods.

The performance opens with two wailing figures dressed in rags, hobbling down the center aisle. They open the doors, then settle down outside the frame, huddled on either side—where they stay for the duration. Sometimes they contort their bodies and issue noises in reaction to what is unfolding within the frame, but mostly they pass time without regard for onstage events, engaging in mundane activities: they nap, they eat, do handiwork, they sit quietly. Perhaps these two figures are time itself, avatars of duration.

Signifying nothing, their manifestation casts the center as the place where actions have consequences, where aesthetics and action are unified—the space of representation. Between these two figures and the stage can be traced the separation between duration and event, background and subject. These are two realities, one set within the other. From the inside looking out, there is nothing to see, no speaking roles, no names. This outside is not quite insistent, but the staging reminds us it is there, a part of the scene that is parsed not through legibility, but presence.

Édouard Manet, *A Bar at the Folies-Bergère* (1882)

The quality of light by which we scrutinize our lives has direct bearing upon the product which we live, and upon the changes which we hope to bring about.

—Audre Lorde

File
It's fine.

1. Seeing: *A Bar at the Folies-Bergère*, Édouard Manet (1882)

You've likely seen this painting. A woman stands behind a counter, her body facing forward, arms held away from her sides, hands resting on the marble bar. Reflected in the mirror behind her, a scene of 19th-century Parisian nightlife: people in hats and gloves gathered around and along tables in a vast space lit by glowing orbs; a single, colossal chandelier. At the top left, two delicate, green-clad feet perch on a trapeze. To the right of the frame, a customer stands silently. Is he waiting or has he been stopped in his tracks, frozen? The barmaid: the cast of her gaze falls short of us, landing somewhere in between and to the side, shifting our own gaze to the luminous skin that runs from her flushed chin to the bundle of flowers at her cleavage, encircled by a broad frame of white lace. This patch of flesh draws attention with an intensity usually reserved for the face.

Much could be said—has been said—about what we are looking at, but I'm curious... what it is that *she* sees? The way she is looking, seemingly at nothing, her eyes downcast. The distance at which she appears to hold herself may be a way of being present, even alert.

If direct looking is like a vector running from the eye to the object, here we can imagine that vector retracting and reversing direction, splitting and seeping down into her neck, torso, through her arms, and into her fingers, the force redistributing itself evenly throughout, pressing as gently and firmly in her fingertips as in the hollows of her eyes. "Looking at" softens and spreads into "standing within... and by." But the eyes are not closed and an unstudied gaze still sees. Eyes like glassy windows: maybe someone peers out—intently even—but the reflections keep us from seeing inside.

This way of seeing, or looking, has the appearance of passivity, a generalized visual focus, and attention to one's own body—which might manifest in the adoption of a posture, a pose, or deliberate patterns of movement. All of this is conducted while maintaining the possibility of observation, even vigilance, but attentiveness, or looking, is neither broadcast nor communicated. Looking is possible but cannot be assumed and calls no attention to itself. When you look without interest, the edges of your visual field—the periphery—is also where you become aware of your ears. Here, the visible and audible intermingle and are led outward to places near and far, to where sounds call. Where they meet, a sense of place, even presence, emerges.

This way of seeing may be familiar to those who know how to watch without drawing attention, who know that to maintain is a result of deliberate and constant labor, who have learned that failure to react is a tool for de-escalation, and for whom energy is precious and to be used only sparingly on the performance of outrage. The practice of survival furnishes tools for creating life, even art. Art is critical to survival: it produces openings in existing systems, making possible the movement necessary for life and change. In architecture, we are preoccupied with change. The breadth of our concerns ranges from the search for new forms and sensations to the rearrangement and provision of ways to live together more vibrantly.

2. Light

When I think of the qualities of light, I am thinking about warm and cool, diffuse and focused, dim and bright, and about the environment, figures, and objects: which surfaces reflect and which ones absorb—effects that are a product of their finish, texture, and material properties. Furthermore, I am thinking about whether certain arrangements give me a sense of enclosure, and whether some areas might recede into shadow. Light conspires with matter and texture to make vast and vibrant meadows, dusky hollows, and dark pockets, cool and still. Variation in light creates difference across the landscape; it can reveal openings and areas of refuge, both of which make movement possible. Light is not neutral. Take the harsh light of judgment: it casts the world into stark relief, reimaging it in black and white, leaving us with only a false choice. The tug of war that ensues is a struggle for domination by both sides: one cannot win without the other losing. But light can be adjusted and tuned in concert with an environment to set or maintain a mood, and if we can conjure it, the right mood may help us steer the turbulent straits between the narratives of loss and cynical opportunism, even return us from the escapism that characterizes so many responses to the difficulties of our times.

To circumvent the blockages that crisis can provoke, I invite us to move behind a protective mask without relinquishing our watchfulness and, in order to sustain the mood necessary to keep working, to tell ourselves: "It's fine." We can call this the *practice of fine*, characterized by indirect looking, the deferment of judgment, and the casting of just enough ameliorating light upon the world to mete out the ever-provisional assessment *it's fine*. A main tool of the practice of fine is to enact this light, a soothing light that holds. Being held is the sensation of place.

It's fine satisfies the need for judgment with a working estimation that allows one to keep moving until you figure out whether something is good or bad, ugly or beautiful, perhaps in an indefinite deferment. *It's fine* furnishes support for transitions, sustains continuance, and perpetuates movement, all of which are required for life. *It's fine* opens a space between encounter and judgment, or encounter and interpretation, long enough to see some of what is typically cast out under the light of judgment. It is not a rejection of aesthetics, but a rejection of the pairing of aesthetics and evaluation. What enters are questions of utility, pleasure, and choice—a rich and fruitful realm to be enjoyed, played within, and discovered. There is no catharsis or incorporation in an ethics of fine. In its light we can see difference without exclusion or comparison; because something is one thing, doesn't mean it can't be something else. Qualities can be identified without relation to another thing.

3. Movement: The Glance

> Wonder is the motivating force behind mobility in all its dimensions.
> —Luce Irigaray

In the practice of fine, we should look at how movement occurs, because movement is a mark of how change is made in a system. It starts with a slight widening and raising of the eyes, which pause and rest momentarily on someone or something before dropping and returning to a resting state. This gesture is the glance; it is how one approaches the other in this practice of looking. The glance offers a temporary opening that the other can step into; if not taken, the opening passes, retreating without rejection, restoring "a separation without a wound." This way of seeing might be described as an embodied, unstudied gaze, and it sees many things instead of one. It sees like an open palm offers touch, as if looking were a gesture.

The glance is not only a gesture for connection; it is also the means by which information is gathered, identifications are made, and things noted, named, and counted. This incidental looking is ambivalent to category or type, but it is not promiscuously so; it precedes the rules of decorum. For example, from where I am seated now, I can note:

—This corner, the line, that hollow.
—A door.
—Between the screen and the wall.
—Here, at the shadow's edge.
—Plates, stacked.

These things are seen and can therefore be counted, but in this counting, the final number is just the number where you stop. The finality has no significance. There may be actors but there are no protagonists. The sum of things named forms an open set, where number is an index of succession and process, tagging each item should you like to return to that spot in your archive of things seen. When you recognize something, whether in the same place or elsewhere, a new number is assigned, and across time, resonance and occlusion may occur. You can pick up again where you left off, adding new tags to old things, or parts of them, making combinations and handing out new numbers.

4. Object Lesson: Catalogues

There are clues in things. There is something at play in the world of things that is not planned, doesn't start with a story or a drawing, but can be observed, noted. To illustrate, here is a description of a place:

A galvanized metal roof spotted with intermittent squares of corrugated fiberglass. Beneath this, a bald slab of concrete and a loose array of circular drains. A few outlet cables hang down from fluorescent lamps rocking slightly on chains. Faint numbers in red or yellow are visible on the floor, marking spots to be found or assigned. It is rather unremarkable: a structure that provides cover and electricity. It can be used for parking, a market, or a playground. As a market, the roof shields carts from the hot tropical sun and dumping rain. These carts—no two are identical, but all are enough alike to form a single category—are arranged along aisles. Some have four wheels that lock into place, others have two wheels at one side, the other end propped on cinder blocks or ochre Klim drums filled with cement. On windy days, plastic bottles filled with water serve as weights to keep tarps from billowing upward. Stacks of old catalogues, taped together, are places to sit.

A-sá-lih—*simple, easy, ready, flat.* Of the many words Taiwan adapted from Japanese, a-sá-lih is used to describe a straightforward person; more likely to be invoked the further south you go, a-sá-lih also endearingly suggests an earthiness, even a touch of vulgarity. There is a sense of pride in being somewhat base. (Slippers and shorts are completely acceptable at a wedding banquet.) Once you start looking, this attitude is found everywhere in Taiwan's material culture. Taiwanese raised in the West are struck by how "ugly" Taiwan is, but I would suggest they look with "eyes that do not see." In place of an aesthetic that represents a culture is an attitude, a material ethics.

All material has value and food is a special type of material: I have watched a family member spend an hour picking through a large sack of shelled fresh beans, using a small knife to carefully excise the soft brown, slippery parts from each pale green, quarter-sized disc, and then washing the whole batch in cold water until each again felt waxy against the fingers, thus bringing hundreds of beans back from early decay. The result was a dish visibly transformed across every individual bean.

This attitude assumes fine and finds a way there. Fine is a positive quality, rather than one that falls short of being good. It is a making do rather than surviving, and *good enough* is synonymous with *good*.

Catalogues taped together to make a seat?

One might say: "Oh, how crappy."

But actually, it is neat and organized. Not trash. You can make it to the height you like. It's cheap. You might even arrange the catalogues by color. Put the one you like best on top. *It's fine* keeps us from seeing it as lowercase *d* design. It stops the fetishizing of the creativity of "poor people"; such fetishization is a false elevation, an insidious "tribute" that casts people of limited means as darling caricatures or pets unaware of how quaint their small and prosaic worlds are. *It's fine* is ambivalent about legibility; it incorporates the non-ideal in representation where a single occurrence is not an exception but a rule of once.

5. Object Lesson: Table

A table with inset sieves over tray slots, a vinyl protective cover, set with plastic bins and scales for sorting and weighing kelp:

Rosalyne Shieh, *Untitled (Penghu)* (2017)

6. It's fine.

> A bicycle shed is a building; Lincoln Cathedral is a piece of architecture.
> —Nikolaus Pevsner

It has been suggested that procrastination is less about avoidance and laziness and more a fear of not being able to meet one's own high standards and high expectations. Putting things off leaves less time to complete a project or task. When you finally get around to working, the body can be in a kind of crisis. Completion becomes a heroic act under the duress of time and mental stress; finishing, an act of surrender. Sitting back and shrugging your shoulders, you might "wisely" address yourself with self-mollifying words that point out the inevitability, the fate of the process. You might tell yourself: "It is what it is." Or: "At some point, you just have to stop." Maybe even: "Whatever." In effect, you are telling yourself: "It's fine." But this is not yet the practice of fine. You would apply the practice of fine to situations that are not of your own creation, and without a tone of resignation. Your voice might lilt, your head tilt, your shoulders even shrug as you turn to the next thing. What's more, the *practice* of fine would be mainly directed at processes outside your control as you walk toward them, maybe to court the unexpected or lead you to the surprising. In some cases, it may give you new capabilities for delight. The practice of fine could be described as a liberal application of the counterfactual, from the minor to the major, an assumption that becomes an ethos, willfully.

Celebrate every victory—even the possibility of victory is a victory. Every change is significant, not just phase changes or sea changes. Nothing goes uncounted, yet nothing needs to be counted. Enter a phase of radical recognition and the ability to detect an ever-finer grain of difference. Everything becomes immensely real through a perpetual awakening that needs no limit. This is about continually expanding into the reality that precedes recognition and representation. You may not understand, but understanding isn't necessary.

In the practice of fine, the self-serious ego is laughable and the strident tone of the manifesto is grating, even absurd. The alarmist is simply unhelpful. In the light of *fine*, we can lift our eyes and take a glance around. We see our surroundings as a unified field of color, brightness, and shadow, with a variable but continuous, gauzy texture; figures emerge: here, the silhouette of a cathedral; there, a bicycle shed; both bathed in the same soft light. In this place, Pevsner's declaration seems too loud, too brash, as if carried in by an overly modulated, stentorian voice from off stage, temporarily breaking the calm, but at most eliciting a pause and a giggle, or a shrug. It may slightly harsh our mellow, but draws little more than an eye roll—how we might react to certain overzealous conversationalists who so generously regale us with their explanations of our lives.

And maybe if the light is right, even that would be *fine*.

Reprint of "It's fine." by Rosalyne Shieh (2017)

Thomas Demand, *Embassy VII.a* (2007)

Rosalyne Shieh, *Untitled (Penghu)* (2017)

[A] table, a tabula, that enables thought to operate upon the entities of our world, to put them in order, to divide them into classes, to group them according to names that designate their similarities and their differences—the table upon which, since the beginning of time, language has intersected space.

—Michel Foucault (1966)

> Narrative is, at worst, packaging—and many films are already fairly arbitrary assemblies of emotional triggers, presented as attractive packages.
> —Rick Prelinger

In reading Prelinger's 2021 essay "Assembly over Algorithm," I'm thinking about the amount of attention we place on the construction of story in architecture. I'm particularly concerned with how we use narrative, but also the posing of problems and therefore solutions. By building systems of naming and reasoning, we (subconsciously, inadvertently) release the emotional pressure caused by material realities. This mindset and process operates at a remove from material reality, or in a way that does not feed into material change. The ability to release is useful and a way of caring for ourselves and connecting with each other (in architecture, it's also how we convince people), but how much of this work produces only temporary relief while allowing harmful realities to remain unchanged or even progress, furthering harm to ourselves, each other, and our environment? These last three things—us, others, the place we share—are in fact a single thing.

> Documentation, in fact, is itself compelling. It can be its own narrative. As we walk through a cemetery, the stones suggest stories...

How about loosening up our grip a bit? Assembling this book has been part of a long process of trying to do just that within our practice. What parts are useful? What ideas remain cacophonous despite an actualized project? Buildings in some way become facts of matter. But the questions within which they were developed and the questions or even doubts they cultivated live on. How do you share everything and not just conclusions? What are alternatives to the argument, the manifesto, the proof of concept? How do you share the ongoing and unresolved conversations? And also set out materials, instruments, products of practice as an offering? Can *suggestive* be an organizing principle?

> That we might locate narrative intelligence in the audience, rather than in the work itself.

What do we, as architects, want to do in making a book? I think we want to put it all down, use form and organization to make it not *not* make sense, designate some specific areas (ideas) within the larger field, and then open it to readers. Imagine how you might invite visitors into a building: some wayfinding, but no guided tours.

Park Slope Apartment (2016)

This exercise can be done in movement or at rest. Spend the duration of this exercise primarily in the state you choose. You will need a means of taking notes and a clock with a second hand or a digital timer.

Breathe and take a moment to be observant through your senses. When you are ready, start the timer or note the position of the second hand on the clock. At every half to one minute, number and note something seen, heard, felt, tasted, or smelled. You can use words or doodles or both. Keep it short and imagistic (e.g., a trace of sour odor; rumble of a car driving outside?; four cups, different colors; suddenly dim, cloud movement; mouth is oddly dry). You can move between your senses or stick primarily with whichever you like. It's okay if timing is approximate.

Find a comfortable pace and maintain it. If you are walking, pause to make notes before continuing on. There isn't a right way to do this, let go of anything that doesn't work for you. Simply sense and note, sense and note until you have 30–40 observations, or about 20 minutes.

Townhouses, Houston, TX (2016)

Quitman Townhomes

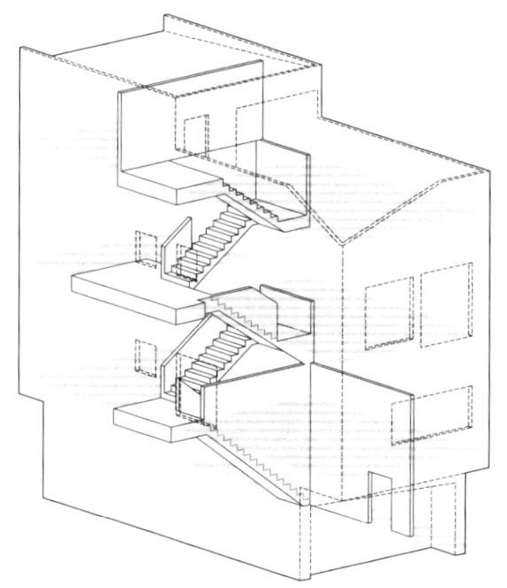

Sheared Section Perspective

This is the most affordable project we have ever built on a per-square-foot basis. Our training, before starting our own practice, engaged with projects that had ten times this budget. This is a typological experiment with a very limited spatial and material palette.

RS So, let me tell you something I always say to others: "Stan writes in a way where it feels like he wants the reader to understand." Having studied with you, I would extend my assessment to how you approach pinups, lectures, and desk crits—my experience was that you always communicated in a way where I felt you wanted us students to understand, sometimes rather complex and involved ideas or histories, and you were willing to do work along the way to fill things in or explain how others have formulated related questions, with the aim that we could figure out how to work, and therefore take part in the larger conversation... and do it on our own terms. Your way of communicating in teaching and writing suggested to me that I could be part of the conversation, that I could try. And I'm aware that after so many years, I'm still trying to do that—it's something I've carried with me.

I see it as an investment in the accessibility of ideas and the clarity and precision of language... but it is also something else—and this is central to what I've taken from you as a teacher and a writer—I see a kind of generosity, not one about giving or giving back (i.e., philanthropy or charity, which doesn't change the overall structure of power and might actually consolidate it), but something different. A generosity in form and clarity, a willingness to disclose, a transparency of your own position and relationships, an orientation to the person with whom you are talking that both acknowledges and respects their positionality. It's a pedagogy—teacher as guide, as one who shares and supports—that extends beyond the classroom. I know it's connected to or motivated by values, but I would go so far as to call it a political position. Does any of this resonate for you?

SA Well, I'm gratified to hear that, of course. I like to think I'm allergic to pretense, and I believe that it is possible—and preferable—to communicate complex ideas in simple, clear language. I've always thought that's the mark of true intelligence. On the other hand, I'm skeptical of (and try to avoid) jargon and obfuscation. I think the political aspect you're talking about is that you have to respect your audience—give them credit, and assume they are smart, open-minded, and willing to learn. I never dumb it down, no matter how challenging the ideas are, whether it's for students, colleagues, or clients. That said, I do take a certain pleasure in shop-talk—the exchange of technical expertise and ideas with other practitioners. I'm always amazed, for example, to eavesdrop on my musician and composer friends. I don't understand a word, but it's a pleasure to listen in on that kind of high-level exchange. I suppose it's also about knowing your audience.

As far as teaching goes, unless you are deeply cynical, you don't teach for as long as I have without learning from your students. That's perhaps another aspect of the political dimension you mention. It's not about a top-down power dynamic, it is a two-way exchange.

RS There's the aspect of how you communicate, but then there is also the craft of choosing words and making sentences. Can you talk a bit about how you think about language, its use?

SA It's a tricky question because I was educated in a period—the late '70s, and the 1980s—when architecture was in the midst of its fascination with language—what has been called the linguistic turn, when the field was working its way through ideas based on semiotics and structuralism, and later, say mid-1980s, poststructuralism. All based, at some level, on the idea of understanding architecture through the lens of language. So I would probably reframe the question in terms of writing as opposed to language. Because for me, when you put the word *language* on the table, I tend to default to that 1970s, postmodern idea of architecture as language, of understanding architecture itself as a representational system, rather than the use of verbal language. A lot of what I've done in my writing and as an architect is pushing back on that idea of architecture as a system of representation. Architecture will never communicate with the same degree of discursive transparency as language does. It has other, and for me richer possibilities, than simply being understood as one medium among other media.

In "Practice vs. Project," for example, I put forward a model of discursive practice versus material practice. I was pushing back on the idea that there's some theoretical template out there, an abstract set of ideas against which you measure design and building. I wanted to point out that writing is itself a practice, with its own protocols and techniques, and its own discipline. I suppose, to some degree, my target was somebody like Peter Eisenman. Peter is a really important figure who has contributed a lot to the discipline, but he's an example of someone who starts from theory and then tries to build the project around that preexisting theoretical template. And that's what I was being critical of.

And so in my writing, it was always very, very important to pay attention to the difference between discursive practices, which are about language and media and communication—language in its written form—and not try and turn the architectural project into a form of language, of media. In my mind, that opens up a whole set of possibilities that are at once broader and more open-ended, not constrained by language, and more unpredictable.

RS Is it important to write?

SA It's very important to write. Or at least it's important to me; I don't want to say that every architect needs to write. First of all, I would distinguish between the writing of an architect and the writing of a historian or a critic. For architects, there is more at stake, whereas the historian or critic can, and should, maintain a certain distance. It's a truism, but it's a true truism that when an architect writes about the work of another architect, or an example from history, they're always writing about their own work. At least for me that has been true.

And there are many different kinds of writing, each with different qualities and goals. In my case, there is speculative writing about urbanism; "Field Conditions" was, in part, a proposition about infrastructural urbanism, for instance. It is in cities where architecture's public and political dimensions become most clear, and where these questions become most urgent. But the field conditions piece was also about formal strategies—part-to-whole relationships, serial repetition, self-similarity. That aspect connects to art practices, and speaks to other working architects—these are formal problems we work through every day. Preston Scott Cohen likes to say that all architects are either adders or dividers—distinctive ways of thinking about the work, and how it is made, and what your formal preferences are. I've also written a lot about drawing and representation; that's a longstanding fascination. For my generation, reading Robin Evans was an effort to understand how the process of drawing operated within practice—Evans is writing from inside the discipline, writing not so much about what it means but how it works.

And more recently I've written quite a bit about the work of architect colleagues and friends. I don't want to call it critique, exactly. I would say that I have pretty much made it a rule that I will never write about something that doesn't in some way interest or engage me. I see my job not as passing judgment, but clarifying and laying out the issues and questions around a particular building, a project, a specific work, or a particular group of architects, and then letting the reader make up their own mind.

RS You bring up Robin Evans and I wonder what influence he's had on your writing, because I have a similar experience reading your work and reading Evans's. I start in a place and he brings me through the text, and I end up with a very different aspect of the thing that we started with.

SA Exactly. Evans was a historian, but he was trained as an architect. I've always argued that he could never have written and understood and analyzed those complex operations of descriptive geometry the way he did if he didn't know how to make the drawings. There are drawings in *The Projective Cast* where he's reconstructing these projective operations of Delorme, and I can't figure them out. They're incredibly complex. So even though he's a very careful historian, he's writing as an architect, and writing about the of discipline of architecture. And you're right, he would take the reader along on that journey; he had a very specific way of constructing sentences. It could get complex, but if his writing sometimes feels overelaborate, it is because he is going out of his way to make sure the reader understands. I try to avoid that sometimes baroque complexity, but I admire his clarity, and the way he brings the reader along, laying out the steps in his own thinking. In a sense, he allows the reader to retrace the intellectual journey that he took—I think all good writers do that.

RS It's interesting to hear you name these different kinds of writing that you do. If we think of the various modes of writing, it's not too much of a stretch to also consider the ways in which we communicate and share ideas in conversation, in discussion, in reviews, in desk crits... Spoken exchange does not often find a place in the written or visual record of architecture, and yet it is such a large part of the culture, and so influential to the formation of ideas.

SA It's curious, right? We don't talk about talking much, given how collaborative architecture is. Architecture happens in the conversations in the studio, the conversations with people you're working with, the conversations with clients, with builders, and so on. Yet none of that makes its way into the final presentation of the project. It's instead presented as something that emerged out of a vacuum.

RS That resonates with a thought I had about our conversation today—that it's a real, spoken exchange but we're guiding it to be heard, or read. There's an ethos about that, which is related to the reality of architectural practice, as not just a series of projects and a discursive activity, but also literally all the things we talk about with each other. So much information gets traded this way. One idea we had for this book was that we could write some of those exchanges down and share conversations that connect to influences, build out the context within which some of our ideas have been hatched and developed.

One example of that influence is that I was certainly inspired by *Points and Lines*, with its structure of projects set within ideas and essays, manifestos. It's a book that is both record and resource for a reader who wants to understand, enter, or be part of the conversation.

SA I appreciate what you're saying about *Points and Lines*; I had a similar approach later with *Situated Objects*. The way I thought about those books, the projects had a particular relationship to the writing that wasn't one-to-one, but parallel, maybe crossing over at certain moments. And the writing doesn't explicitly explain the projects, but it lays out and explores a certain number of issues and questions that the projects are exploring in a different way. Together, the writing and the projects form a kind of resource. It sounds like that's something you're trying to do with your book, and I'm very sympathetic to that.

Actually, the first thing that came to mind when you described the book project was your thesis at Princeton: the idea of not doing a project-based thesis, but a form of research-work and a manual. There's a history to that, the discipline of treatises and manuals and pattern books. At a certain point, the idea of the pattern book was looked down upon, as something formulaic, that would stifle imagination, and promote repetition. But I'd argue for the idea of a pattern book not as a definitive solution, but as a starting point, and one that represents the shared culture of the discipline, is a useful one.

I do sometimes ask, "Who reads these books?" I suppose you've asked yourself the same question. When I'm asked, my answer is always, "I hope that it's students."

RS Yes, of course. I think students read these books. They put them on their desks, they look for inspiration, they look for help. We certainly did. My intended audience is always students, in the broadest sense of that word, where being a student is characterized by an endless curiosity to the world around us, in physical and nonphysical ways, and their interrelations. These are also characteristics I value most in the architect, in seeing like an architect. One of the things we said pretty early on in the conception of the book is we want it to be helpful.

SA I like the idea of making the book into a resource and seeing it as a contribution to the discipline that will have its own didactic character, that students will use it rather than consume it. And I think it is important to lay out the context within which the projects emerge—the day-to-day exchanges in the studio, the back and forth with clients and builders. The work doesn't emerge out of a vacuum, and I think it's important for students (and the public) to understand that.

Beyond that, I have always understood architecture as a discipline in conversation with itself. That is to say, as a working architect, you're in conversation with the history of the discipline, with predecessors who've worked on similar issues, as well as with your peers—those with whom you form affiliations and connections. And that conversation is not necessarily always discursive. If you say that a particular project is in conversation with another project that means the conversation is nonverbal. It that takes place through visual and architectural means.

RS Right, there are all the conversations that wouldn't qualify as discursive. And then there are another set that aren't even about building, per se, but are being carried out, shared, sometimes shaping and influencing the work quite significantly.

This also brings up something else, and that is more generally those ideas, instincts, fixations even, that we have that, where they come from is harder to pin down. It can be a formal proclivity, a tendency to repeat. Not like a concept, more like a hunch, things we simply do or try—and not always with a clear vision. There is a logic of making that is unto itself, that doesn't necessarily start with a thought. For me this, as an experience, was something I encountered in that first studio you taught, 501, the introductory studio for MArch students.

SA Teaching first year studio at Princeton was honestly a steep learning curve, because before that, I'd only ever taught advanced studios. And I do think that first year is a different thing—it is more skills driven, and you're trying to bring the students into the disciplinary conversation, whereas with upper level studios, you assume that they're already part of that conversation.

RS That was a very contentious studio.

SA Your first studio? I'm only finding this out.

RS Yeah, my first studio. You asked us to begin with an image—any image—which we were to work on visually with marks, colors, through drawing, to produce or to work up a...

SA A diagram, right? I'm remembering this now.

RS Yes. Diagrams that would direct a series of interrelated site organizations, like program, movement, mass, and surface. We were really stumped. Even those of us that had studied architecture beforehand were used to working with a concept first, or understanding the site and responding to it. You were asking us to do things without asking what it meant, without regard for what was there—at least not initially—and it was very hard for us. We were really frustrated. I remember saying: "It's so arbitrary!"

SA Interesting.

RS But actually, that was what you were asking us to do. To be arbitrary. To take the pressure off the starting point. The exercise took our eyes away from looking directly at the thing, and instead, work with a mediating image to build a visual system that could accommodate intersecting performative and formal criteria, that could bring together discontinuous forms, surfaces, and networks, each type having its architectural implications.

I mean, sure, twenty years on and with lots of thinking since, I can articulate it this way now...

SA That studio probably happened fairly soon after I'd written "Practice vs. Project," and to some degree that essay and my ethos in studio came out of my experience with Rafael Moneo and the idea that as an architect, you approach every project, every commission as if it's something new, something individual. You don't try to slot that commission or that project into some larger theoretical narrative or arc. You produce the ideas out of the thing, out of the work, out of the process of working rather than having a preexisting template of ideas that you're trying to fit the work into.

It's curious to me that we tend to consider students more free, because sometimes I think students can be very rigid. They have this idea that they have to work out the project in their head, know where it's going, know what it means before they actually start to draw, when in fact it's exactly the opposite. You only discover things by working.

There's a line I borrow from John Cage. He said an experimental act is one where you don't know the outcome in advance. I wanted to instill a little bit of that uncertainty into the design process: you start down a road and you don't know where that road is going to take you. And of course it was John Cage who famously said, "Begin anywhere." The anxiety of beginning is an anxiety about ending up in the wrong place. So it's about giving up the preconceived idea of where you want to end up, and approaching the work more openly. That's what I was trying to get at in that studio.

My trust in process certainly comes from my own experience as an architect, and was probably also learned while working for Moneo. I remember him developing ideas early on in a project that I thought were really promising, and then he'd go off in another direction. It was the experience of starting down the road in one particular direction, then finding, through some detour, another solution that turns out to be more satisfying. But you could never have reached that other solution without going down a road that might end up being a dead end. That's what leads to paralysis—the fear of finding yourself at an impasse. But it's a lot better than not starting at all. With time you learn that design is iterative, and every time you make an iteration of a scheme or a project, you understand the project better. The idea that you go in a linear way from analysis to problem solving to a solution, in my experience, that's just not how design works. It's a very nonlinear process. It's interesting (and probably true) that that can make students nervous.

RS It made us really nervous, and a bit mad, but I learned so much from it. That first exercise was an unschooling for me, a beginning of a different way of thinking and working.

SA Speaking of working, I did want to maybe ask you a bit about your work. There's something in yours and Troy's work that is... it's funny, it goes back to your question about writing and clarity, and what you were saying about instinct. There's a lot of clarity in your work, and then there's always a twist. It's never the primary organizing gesture, not some large disruption, but rather a small but nonetheless significant inconsistency. But also it's like, I don't know, that classic thing of the defect woven into the carpet because it can't be perfect. Can you talk a little bit about that swerve, that gesture, that incompleteness?

RS That would assume that we are in control of it? [laughs] I don't know. Maybe my answer is a bit earnest: it is perhaps an orientation toward something you could call a formal awkwardness. I think often, for architects and designers, work is the outcome of a process where you generate a lot of stuff and then you choose, and then you generate a lot of stuff, and then you choose, and then you're like, "This one, in my gut... It feels a little weird. Maybe I like it."

SA Exactly.

RS And then, we ask ourselves, "Should we pursue this?" And we try to talk about it, and we give language to it as a way to try to engage it.

Troy and I have talked about this. To use a musical analogy, it's like a single off-key note or a short run that shifts a major-keyed piece temporarily into a minor key. It just shows up... and you run with it.

SA I like that idea that you choose the one that's a bit uncomfortable. It's that little swerve I mentioned. It is almost like it provides a way in for the viewer. It acknowledges that the object is not fully resolved, and in turn leaves it to the viewer to complete it in their own experience of the building.

RS Yes, a kind of incidental moment, where the project looks back at an observer.

SA I've always said that for me, success for an architect is not when people respond to your building exactly as you had thought they would or intended. It's when they do something unexpected with it. When they exercise their own creativity, and do not simply mirror the architect's ideas.

That's one of the fallacies, that somehow the architect embeds meaning in the building, and that meaning is then decoded by the people who perceive it and use it and visit it. The building has a life independent of the architect; any significant work of art is significant because it has a robust quality that allows for multiple interpretations, some of which may be the opposite of the author's intent. (This is way more true of architecture than it is of other art forms, by the way—with a piece of music or a painting or a sculpture, there's a much more immediate connection between the author and the audience.)

Let's say you build a library in Queens or somewhere, and there are local people for whom that building is a resource in their neighborhood. They may enjoy the light, they may enjoy the materials. They may think the space is interesting. They probably pay attention to convenience and the way it works. Those people are not going to situate it in terms of a disciplinary discourse and understand what the architectural references are. As architects, we have an obligation to make our building succeed on that level, probably our first obligation. But I don't think it's any contradiction that then an informed student or another architect colleague could go to that building and say, "Okay, yeah, I see. Here's what you're doing and that's why you're doing it. This is a reference to that, and this is an interesting solution to that particular way of making a roof or a stair or something." A successful building has to operate in both contexts, talk to different publics.

And then, everything I say about a building, you can multiply it by a hundred, and it applies to the city, right? Because the city is a collective entity and the city is also the place where you have the greatest diversity of publics. Any building that exists in an urban context has to engage these multiple audiences. Or in rural and exurban contexts. That was the argument in *Situated Objects*: the urban/rural divide is not as strict as we think it is. And many of the expectations that come with building in the city are now operating in these exurban sites. The shadow of the urban context is always there for me; the city today is everywhere and nowhere. And as much as we complain about the way the city has changed, there is still a certain robust culture of the city that I don't think we can ignore as architects, even if you're not working specifically in an urban context.

RS The way you talk and think about work, teaching, even just now, about whose experience we should consider, what I take away from it is a horizontalism. It provides a countermodel to something hierarchical or issuing from an origin point.

SA I like that I description. It's setting up something that expands, a field to the extent that you can have multiple variables interacting simultaneously, and the field is, of course, a horizontal phenomenon. It's not hierarchical. And that has to do with a collective understanding that goes back to the political project of architecture. Expanding the field has become a bit of a cliché, but I like the idea that you open the project up to multiple affiliations. It's not a closed, private thing. Nor is it the work of a single genius author.

RS Exactly. Understanding that a project is open to multiple processes begins to recognize the validity of many positionalities. Meaning is not locked within an object; rather, it is a situated and dynamic product of place, of personhood, of individual and collective experience, and of cultural specifics. Like how we talk about architecture—there is no "right way." I want to borrow something Trinh T. Minh-ha said in the context of film: "The relation of word to image is an infinite relation." There is always distance that cannot be collapsed, between architecture and what you might say about it. That space is so important. It's why I've always resisted using writing to tell you what the architecture is doing or how to see it. The architecture will show you itself.

Proposal for Pedestrian Bridge, Houston, TX (2018)

In the Round

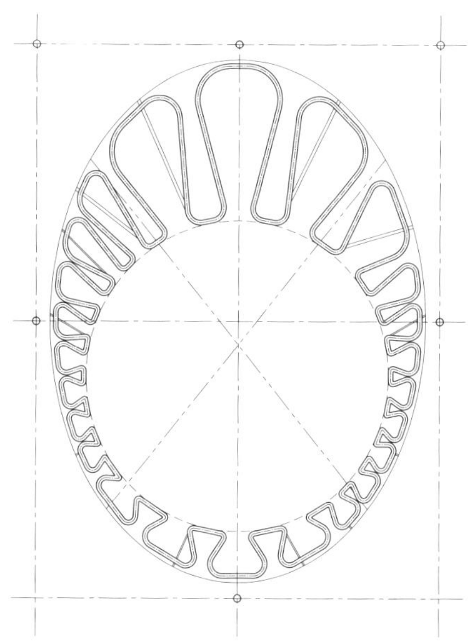

In the Round,
Full Rotation

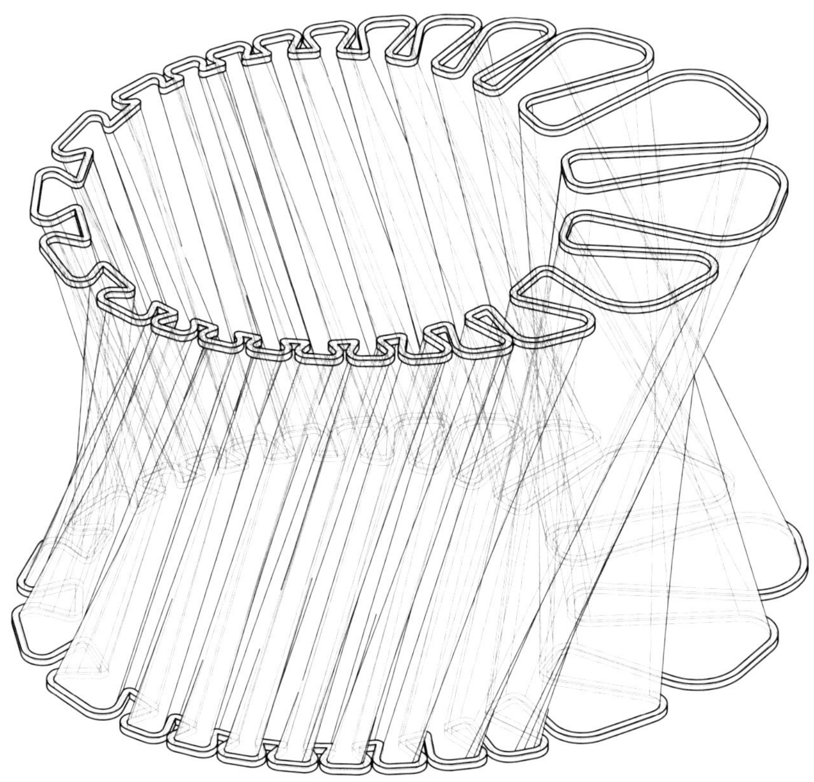

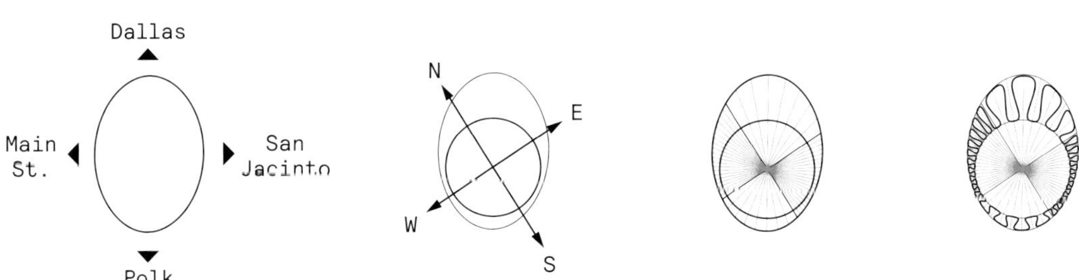

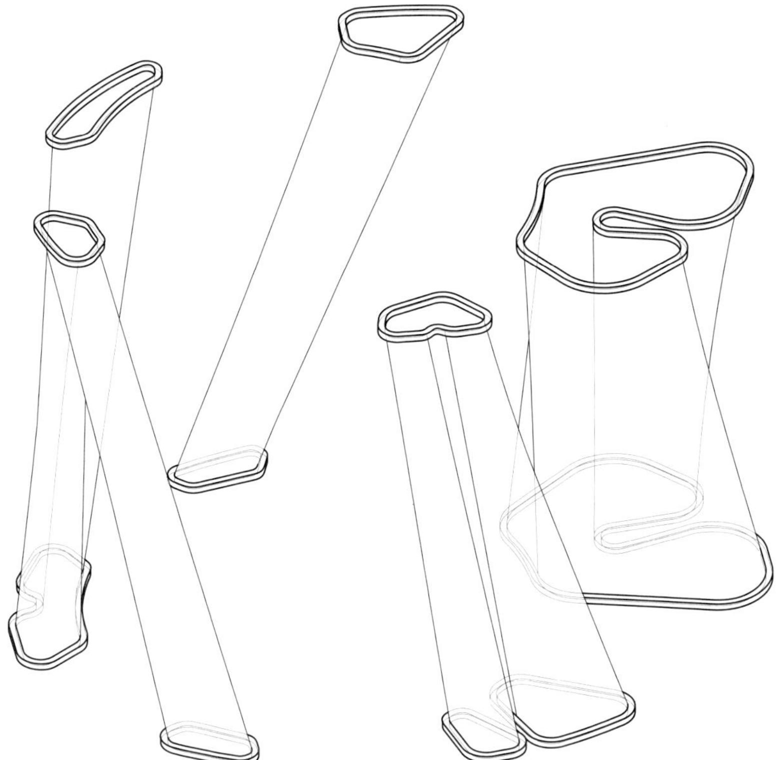

Circulation Drawing

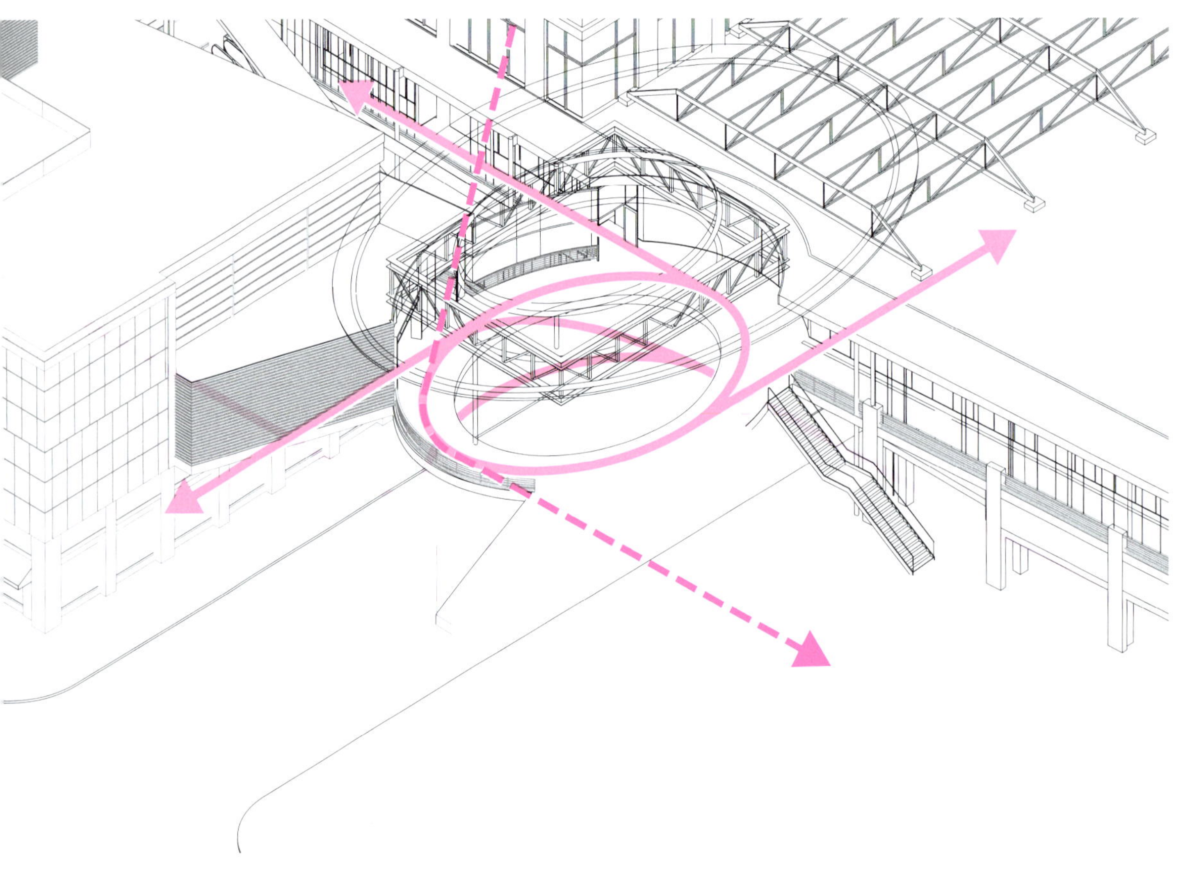

Longitudinal Section and Views

Detailed Plan

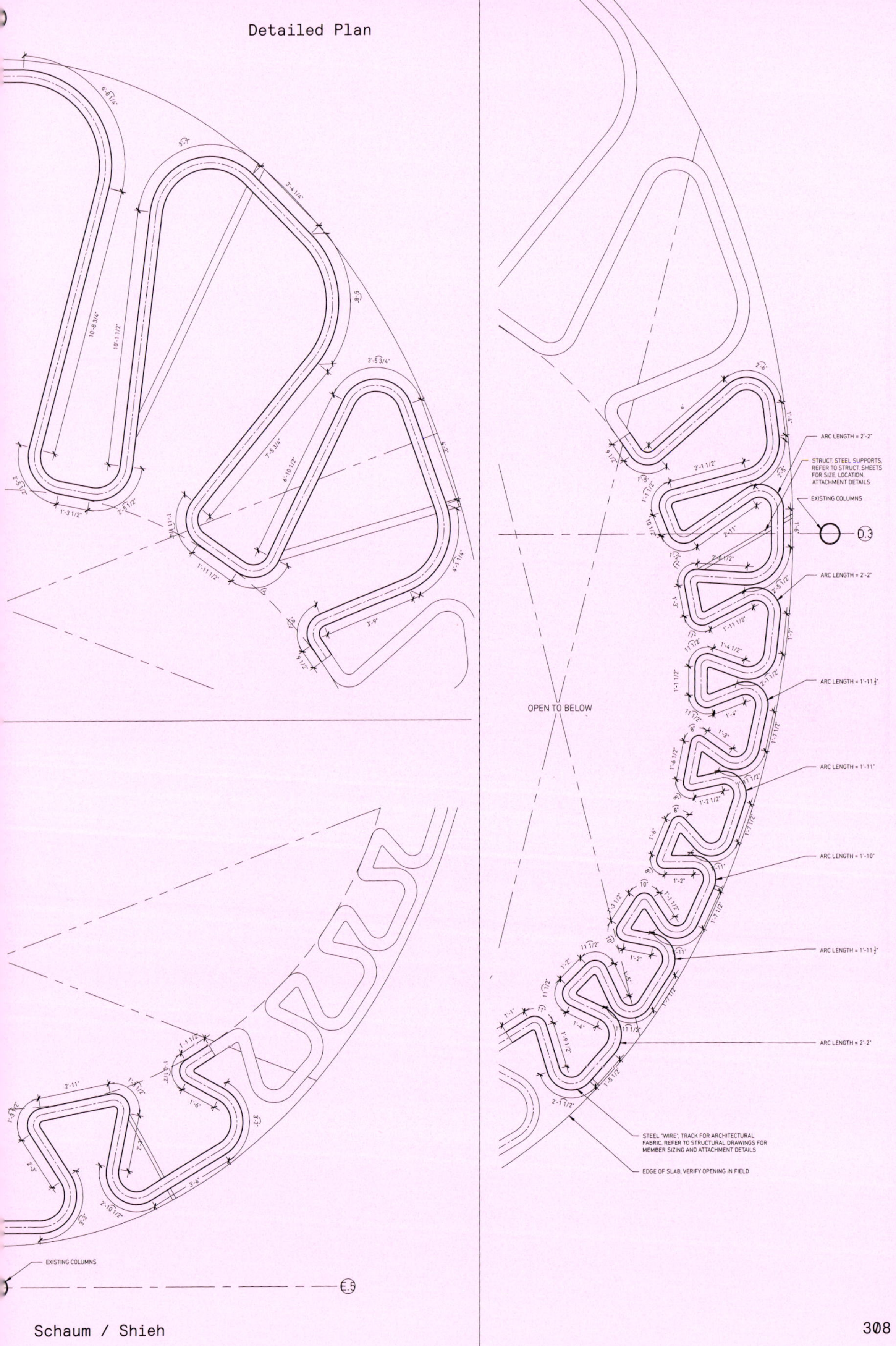

For consideration:

Nothing happens, excess, presence

Richard Artschwager, *Chair* (1966)

Chantal Akerman,
*Jeanne Dielman,
23 quai du Commerce,
1080 Bruxelles*
(1976)

Robert Altman,
Nashville
(1975)

Teju Cole,
“Object Lesson”
(2015)

Elizabeth Grosz,
“Chaos, Territory, Art”
(2005)

Alexandra Juhasz
and Alisa Lebow, eds.,
Beyond Story
(2021)

Ursula K. Le Guin,
“The Carrier Bag Theory
of Fiction”
(1986)

Liz Lerman and
John Borstel,
*Liz Lerman's Critical
Response Process*
(2003)

Boyd McDonald,
Cruising the Movies
(1985)

Susan Sontag,
“Against Interpretation”
(1964)

Tom Wolfe,
*The Kandy-Kolored
Tangerine-Flake
Streamline Baby*
(1965)

Rosalyne Shieh, *Untitled (Tainan)* (2019)

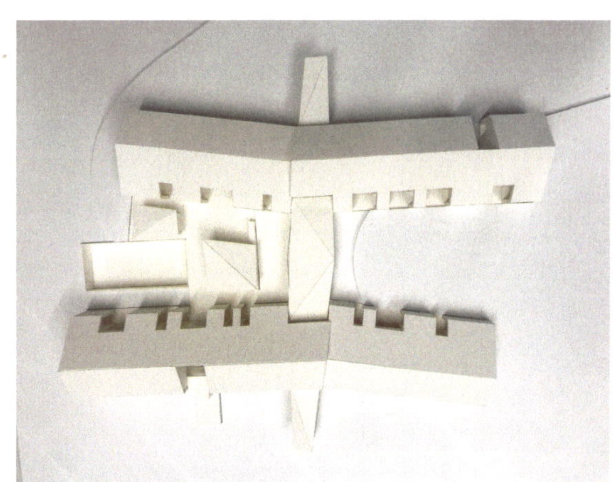

Treehill House (2020)

Wonder

Troy Schaum

> This paradox—with effort it becomes effortless—is precisely what makes history disappear in the moment of its enactment. The repetition of work is what makes the signs of work disappear. It is important that we think not only about what is repeated, but also about how the repetition of actions takes us in certain directions.
> —Sara Ahmed

How does one produce a theory of architectural practice? Architecture requires being alternately stubborn and flexible, capable of both speculation and grinding problem-solving. Its theoretical framework is hard to define, and acknowledging that every practice—and every practitioner—has their unique circumstances, I'd say that underpinning our work is a persistent engagement with wonder.

Wonder, of course, is both an operation and an emotion, a curiosity invoked to describe states from the sublime to the mundane. At one level, it is a notion of the everyday; we can wonder when the pot will boil or if the front door is on the correct facade. At another, it is the grand emotion of transcendent experience. It's the blue-sky possibilities of relentless optimism and also the yammering doubt at the prodigious bother of it all.

Wonder also manifests for me this way: I find myself "blanking" at times, staring into space for indefinite periods, my thoughts lost somewhere between the sky and the ground. I do it often enough that my wife has developed a technique for snapping me back to the present: she whispers dimension strings into my ear—"Six inches, five feet, two inches"—until I return to the present. Her light characterization of my pressing concerns doesn't always retrieve me, but it works often enough to be useful. I do sometimes think in measurements.

My blank trances are not unique to me, nor to architects. The process of design is a search for knowing what has not yet come to be through the prosaic tools offered to us in the present. This produces a speculative gap, bridged through representation and imagination. Perhaps the trance happens *because* a gap exists between the moment a project is initiated and its realization. Much of our practice at Schaum/Shieh lives suspended in that gap—what I'd call the territory of the architectural imagination—reaching in multiple directions and remaining in a state of wonder.

One challenge in defining the conditions of our work is that architecture is a practice that exists in the elusive temporality of the near future, that liminal space of continually becoming and rarely realizing. Both the episodic projects and the continuity of an office unfold over long stretches of time and are filled with recursive reflection. The span between the idea, the first click of the mouse or scribble of the ballpoint on a Post-it, and the realization of the idea in some completeness is utterly flexible. More often than not, completeness stays just beyond the horizon; our effort instead spent attending to whatever task seems critical at the moment. All the while, the broader motivation oscillates between the possibility of serving publics and communities and the potential for experimenting with the discipline's formal and compositional concerns.

Many of Schaum/Shieh's projects—maybe a ratio of 12:1—have remained in the space of unbuilt speculation (and that is before accounting for versions of each project that live for a week before being cast aside). Even in the designs that have made it through construction and enter into the built environment, the physicality exists as an approximation of the ambition that set off our exploration; the finished building is simultaneously more dense, immediate, and harder to access. And when (if) this version of the present does arrive, it is often fleeting: we hurry through a flurry of inspections, punch lists, photography, and openings, usually already immersed in the new relationship of the next project.

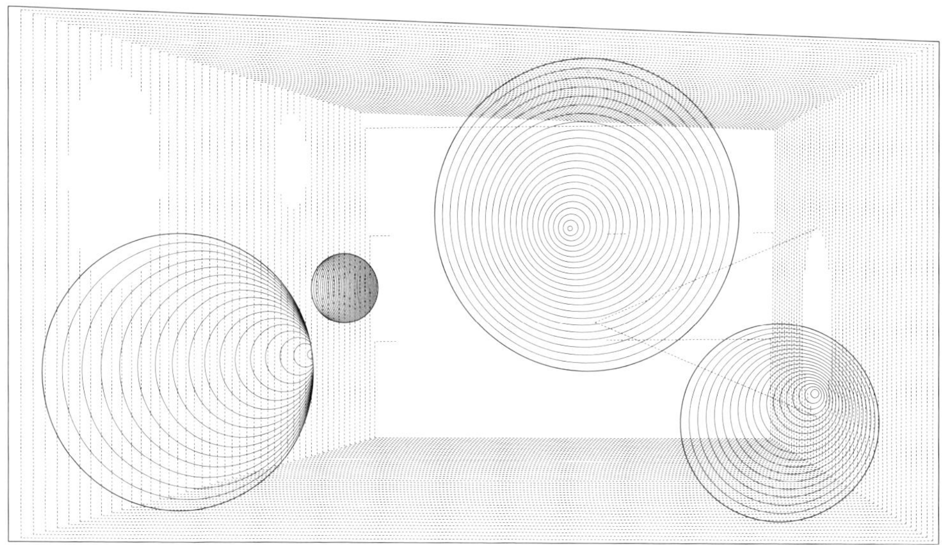

Iceberg & the Forest (2017)

Wonder is curious

In her book *Les causes de la mort*, the philosopher Anne Fagot-Largeault examines how the causes of death are understood and categorized within medicine, biology, and more broadly. She traces the breadth of minor concerns and many decisions a physician makes in caring for a patient. Physicians must attend to the regulation and manipulation of many small, sometimes irreconcilable variables of the patient's situation and the environment of specialties that support various treatments. In this engagement with moment-to-moment interrogation of the manifold variables of life, physicians work at what Fagot-Largeault describes as the "science of the particular." This kind of search, probing many facts as they change in real-time, is at odds with the demand to refine a practice toward a narrow bandwidth of discursive disciplinary questions. The sense of a total medical practice—attending to an exhaustive number of incidental facts—is an appropriate analog to the practice of architecture.

The first step is seeing and framing the particulars through representation. Making drawings and models by moving colored lines across black screens, markers over tracing paper, bending matte board, and gluing plastics. Each model represents a world in which we are probing the mechanics of place, space, and inhabitation. Decisions are often tied to the many minor concerns of the present that create the conditions to reflect on possible futures. This rhythm produces a kind of design that initially appears to emerge as the unintended result of the accumulation of incremental decisions. Yet, by reflecting on such particulars, a set of themes and structures emerge—what we like to think of as blanks—and those motivate thought.

A technique of investigation coalesces: through the repetition of particular queries, specific responses to the demands of each situation emerge. In some cases, ideas stick and begin to build small universes of their own. These blanks, malleable and fungible, start to carve a line that lets the work stay responsive to the moment while saving space for critical reflection. They linger in the studio, reappear in conversations, and demand reformulations in new contexts: in writing, in teaching, in a new project half a world away. In this sense, the project of this book on blanking becomes an archive of such sticky particulars.

Architecture, as we practice it, is a continual process of engaging particulars. Of course, architecture is not strictly defined as a profession of science but it is a mode of cultural expression. The most striking tension with the rationality of building science, the rupture that emerges, is that architecture's work is less an empirical search for truth and more a form of social and political reflection. Perhaps we could even describe the practice of architecture, leaning on Fagot-Largeault's formulation, as "art of the particular." It is remarkable how animated and wonder-filled all those particulars seem to become through persistent scrutiny.

Wonder is impulsive

> Sitting wide-eyed under a planetarium sky or furtively leafing through the *Weekly World News* in the checkout line, we wait for the rare and extraordinary to surprise our souls.
> —Lorraine Daston & Katharine Park

If I had to characterize the energy that propelled the investigations of this book, it would be one of relentless, optimistic engagement, that largest, most generous sense of gape-mouthed wonder. The work shares an ambition and a belief that design matters. The space between curiosity and experience has led us to three types of projects: projects we can get lost in, sites we can get lost in, and relationships we can get lost in.

In his interview with the *Paris Review,* novelist Javier Marías wrote: "A novel, any artistic artifact, accepts less than reality does. Things do happen, but sometimes if you put them in a novel they aren't believable. Life is a very bad novelist. It is chaotic and ludicrous." And like life, the process of initiating projects has been chaotic and ludicrous, perhaps tricky to narrate believably. Most of the work is initiated externally, as the condition of a commission, though White Oak Music Hall began with an email from ambitious music fans; the Shenandoah House, at a dinner of a friend of a friend; our work in Marfa, with a colleague's tour of the Chihuahuan Desert. Many other projects promised to start but then fizzled away because of a collaborator's ordinary financial problems or petty misrepresentations. The challenges of a site can be obvious or subtle initially, but site conditions will ultimately become a dominant force in the commission. In starting projects, wonder emerges as a precondition of engagement with a world that is too complex to archive or predict.

Every one of our projects responds to an internal question that takes shape in the relationship between technique and expression. The exploration of the parameters that organize the construction of a building requires a curiosity for composition. Because of the scope of our work, that curiosity is mediated through a near-infinite set of potential ordering structures for choreographing the attendant material and operational relationships. The range of possible futures suggested by the project's external conditions are filtered through the lens of technique and recursively interrogated—alternatives leading to more alternatives.

Collectively, the overwhelming power of this work is the phenomenon that numbers, when they become so large as to escape immediate comprehension, create a condition of formlessness and a loss of perspective akin to confronting natural wonders. Large, complex buildings have a scale that presents problems in multiples that sometimes exceed simple comprehension. Architecture deals with issues of scale, but it is in the problem of numbers that formlessness takes hold. In the face of that density of variability, our work has taken up contours of questions that we formulated as blanks.

Wonder is doubtful

In his 1985 *AA Files* review piece "Not to Be Used for Wrapping Purposes," architectural historian Robin Evans offered that architects often write defensively or offensively, using the words to create boundaries and project confidence while shielding their design content from direct scrutiny. This confident, self-assured expectation of practice does not reflect the chance and the provisional way in which projects and ideas unfold in our practice. The problems of the contemporary built environment remain complex enough that any position developed ahead of the engagement with the particular risks being derivative or naive. Just when you feel the design is all buttoned up, ideas meet material; material aligns with structure, and spaces sync, while slowly, a curious hesitation arises. Realizing we are still suspended in the gap, we wonder again about the details: if it is good or good enough, or even if it is too good or needs to be good at all to work. In this context, blanking becomes a strategy to balance this space of confidence and doubt.

Admitting this feels counter to the buffed sheen of contemporary architectural practice, which requires projecting a sense of confidence and consistency. But the expectation of polished clarity rarely matches up with the nimble spirit of our design production. Our process is closer to a series of questions: Is the opposite of your good idea also a good idea? How much agency does a building have? How much certitude should we convey? How can we engage with the doubt that our careful adjusting of the particulars has stirred up? Does that manifest as its own creative force?

In responding to a *New York Times* interviewer regarding the confidence and certainty in his creative process, musician Brian Eno suggests, "I would like to cultivate a charisma of uncertainty, a charisma of admitting that you're making it up as you go along." In that exchange, he articulates that the instability of uncertainty, manifesting as doubt, can become a definitive creative force. He is attempting to describe the messy irreducibility that belies nuanced creative work. So am I.

Taichung City Cultural Center (2013)

Wonder as a multiplier

In *Blanking*, we've tried to identify the many conceptual "blanks" or concerns that swirl around the discourses in which our practice materializes. Out of all the terms that made it into this book, perhaps *wonder* and its shifting definitions provide the most helpful framework for answering the question of what has propelled us since our first collaborations. The term's meanings, morphing between curiosity, amazement, and wariness, describe our perpetual predicament. If this book begins with Blanking and concludes with Wonder, then the succession of six chapters in between organizes our collective theoretical investigations into a layered reflection on our studio's process.

Geology describes work that looks at geological timescales and forms related to landscape and movement. The projects here were motivated by a curiosity about understanding places beyond the immediacy of the present. We explored how buildings, cities, and sites are enmeshed in processes that play out over long periods with effects that emerge as incremental yet dramatic shapers of space and our experiences of it. The projects here explore the relationship between the trajectories of movement over different timescales and shape an architecture that simultaneously negotiates building and landscape. The tension between the present immediacy of the act of building and the temporalities of phenomena that produce sites and cultures over time permeates our practice. Shenandoah House is both a landscape-inspired roof surface and a line in plan that stitches between two sets of outdoor gardens. The gardens are thresholds between the interior of the house and the broader mountain landscape. How does this way of seeing displace our agency in favor of the multitude of other human and nonhuman actors on the site?

Void looks at the status of precedent and place. The city form that characterizes the American suburbs that Rosalyne and I encountered as children in the '70s and '80s—communities built of asphalt, concrete, and little patches of lawn—left us with the impression that within seeming voids, some kind of charged residue can and has persistently molded our memories. Early in our collaboration, we had several opportunities to think about how to see and thoughtfully engage in emplacing work with and within voids. The void oscillated between foreground and background in these spaces, never settling. This instability made the representational speculations of Sponge Urbanism and the collaborations on Moran Street critical to formulating a way of seeing in the void.

Platform imagines a constructed space of cultural engagement. Especially in a city like Houston, characterized by an intensely dispersed cosmopolitan community, how do you create spaces for the public to appear? The buildings supporting that activity must mark space in the loosely defined urban fabrics and recede into the background to support emergent publics. This chapter looks at our blanking techniques that build frames for staging that kind of urban interface. Projects like White Oak Music Hall and its many stages, each oriented to a different environment, create spaces crowds can possess. Both WOMH and Houston Endowment operate volumetrically to structure space internally and embedded in the adjacent landscape.

Sets and the problem of the multiple reflect how we react to the contemporary status of the object in the disintegrating, unstable physical and cultural contexts of the exurban city. Many of our more formal and compositional blanks have considered the part-to-whole relationships in articulating an object in a field or a field in an object. In that context, the formulation of sets became a method for manipulating internal and external relationships. In developing the mathematical theory of finite and infinite sets, Georg Cantor demonstrated that there are countable and uncountable infinities, which prove the existence of varying-sized infinities. Such is the realization of managing the sets of objects and ideas in a design. One set of limitations counterintuitively conjures an infinite set of new possibilities, and the problem of limits becomes tied to the problem of infinity. Transart Gallery, negotiating the intersection of massing and facades logics, exemplifies this formulation of set-based composition; the set becomes a way to spatially engage the site beyond its context. That project took over five years, while other installations, studios, and competitions iterated similar formal ideas at different scales.

Arrange reflects on the particulars of maintaining and caring for cultural artifacts in precarious environments. Donald Judd developed an architectural craft of adjustment that tweaked historic sites just enough to articulate an ideal architectural order. Our work on the Architecture Office Building for the Judd Foundation and the John Chamberlain Building at the Chinati Foundation were conceived as total projects that situated art, architecture, and landscape together. The scope of preserving and extending Judd's work has created a characteristic of restraint that is a helpful counterpoint to our other, more formal work.

Fine explores the architecture of the everyday and our role in perpetuating it. We share a fascination with the prosaic artifacts of the contemporary city, those functional and malleable. A fundamental tension becomes hyper-apparent in these projects: designing vs. editing, the space between high craft's bespoke production and manipulating known solutions and materials. It is often true that when we set out to work in one mode, we do another. Townhomes, apartment interiors, strip malls, icehouses, and commercial shells demand an economy of means and flexibility with craft that continue to teach us how impactful, subtle, and uncanny the neighborhood remains.

Across each, and as a whole, the most critical function of this archive is an attempt to reflect on what the impulse to wonder can produce. A single summation of the diverse conditions of a practice in the making remains elusive. Wonder alone may not be enough to construct a theory of practice, but our entanglement with its problematics and potential continues to leave us in suspense.

Transart Gallery (2017)

Conversations

Exercises

Files

For consideration

Notes

Projects

Blanking

6–15 Andrea Branzi, *No-stop city: Archizoom associati* (HYX, 2006).
Garnette Cadogan, "'The Ground Is All Memoranda': Walking as Register, Responsibility, and Re-enchantment," lecture at Harvard University Graduate School of Design, Department of Landscape Architecture, April 16, 2024.
Jay Cephas, Igor Marjanović, and Ana Miljački, "The Common Wind of Worldlessness: In Conversation with Fred Moten and Stefano Harney," *Journal of Architectural Education* 76 (2022): 43–50.
Ruth Wilson Gilmore and Léopold Lambert, "Making Abolition Geography in California's Central Valley with Ruth Wilson Gilmore," *The Funambulist* 21 (2019).
Philip Glass and Ira Glass, "Glass on Glass," St. Ann's Warehouse, April 28, 2009.
Avery Gordon, *Ghostly Matters: Haunting and the Sociological Imagination* (University of Minnesota Press, 2008).
francine j. harris, conversation at MacDowell, summer 2017, and over text, October 2024.
Audre Lorde, "The Uses of Anger: Women Responding to Racism," *Sister Outsider: Essays and Speeches* (Crossing Press, 1984).
Adrienne Rich, "Diving into the Wreck," *Diving into the Wreck: Poems 1971–1972* (Norton, 1973).
Eve Kosofsky Sedgwick, "Queer and Now," *Tendencies* (Routledge, 1994).
Robert Venturi, Denise Scott Brown, and Steven Izenour, *Learning from Las Vegas* (MIT Press, 1972).

9 Rosalyne Shieh, *Untitled (Chàp-it hūn)*, 2017. © Rosalyne Shieh.

10 Catie Newell, *Untitled (13178 Moran Street, Detroit, MI)*, 2009. © Catie Newell.

15 Tucker Douglas, *Icehouse at Raven Tower*, 2015. © Schaum/Shieh.

Geology

18 Robert Rauschenberg, *22 The Lily White*, ca. 1950. © 2024 Robert Rauschenberg Foundation/Licensed by VAGA at Artists Rights Society (ARS), NY.

20 Troy Schaum, *Jodhpur Quarry*, 2022. © Troy Schaum.
Anne Marie D'Arcy, *Untitled*, 2016. © Anne Marie D'Arcy.

21 Rosalyne Shieh, *Untitled (Penghu)*, 2017. © Rosalyne Shieh.
Rosalyne Shieh, *Untitled (Penghu)*, 2017. © Rosalyne Shieh.

22 Troy Schaum, *Kaohsiung Silos*, 2011. © Troy Schaum.
William Carlos Williams, "To a Solitary Disciple," *Others: An Anthology of the New Verse* (Knopf, 1916).

23 Mary Oliver, "Wild Geese," *New and Select Poems, Volume One* (Beacon Press, 2004).

24 **About Face**, see full credits page 329

25–31 Conversation between Sarah Whiting and Troy Schaum was recorded on August 8, 2024 in Cambridge, MA.

32–39 **Kaohsiung Maritime Cultural & Pop Music Center**
This project adapts the site of old port infrastructures as a center for civic cultural programs. Organized on a spatial field of 50m spherical cells, the building forms grow out of a thickened landscape that links various elements of the project and serves as a substrate from which figural pieces of the project emerge. The line between the city is the principal organizing element and loops to integrate major programs and anchors the project on the Old Hamaseng Rail Line bike path.
Client: Kaohsiung City Government
Collaborators: Albert Pope, Buro Happold Engineers, LYA Architects/Planners
Design team: Matthew Austin, Erin Baer, Andrew Daley, Eléna English, Marti Gottsch, David Huang, Ali Naghdali, Jessica Tankard
Location: Kaohsiung, Taiwan
Program: Maritime museum and performing arts center
Renderings: David Huang
Status: Competition proposal, completed 2010

40 **Taiwan Research**
A series of projects (Agricultural Urbanism, Island Transect, Pigeon Shed Urbanism, Slider Towers) that study how place, precedent, and speculation operate simultaneously as architectural propositions and conceptual frames. Each project invents within a found site to imagine what is possible given those conditions. The emphasis is on proposals for urbanism that operate at the scale of the individual building.
Client: Research, speculative
Location: Taiwan
Status: 2009–present
Research team: Ryan Botts, Gail Chen, Yu-An (Andy) Chen, Michelle Luming Lee, Rachel Mulder, Sasha Plotsnikova, Alex Yuen
Support: Sandy & Dr. Chris Yen, Bob Cheng
Aldo Rossi, *The Architecture of the City* (MIT Press, 1982): 29.

41 Bernard Tschumi, *The Manhattan Transcripts* (Academy Editions, 1994).

42 **Island Transect (Taiwan Research)**, see full credits above

43 Gregory Bateson, *Steps to an Ecology of Mind* (Chandler, 1972): 465.

44–59 **Shenandoah House**
This house, situated in the Allegheny Mountains of western Virginia, is a residence for a couple with a planned future life as a writers' retreat. It sits on a slope with views on two sides. Elemental forms alternate uphill and downhill along a spine in self-similar pairs, differentiated by the sinuous roof line. It's a single house as well as a series of indoor and outdoor rooms woven together.
Client: Withheld
Collaborators: Blue Ridge Green Construction, Truesdell Engineering
Design team: Giorgio Angelini, Andrea Brennan, Tucker Douglas, Ane González Lara, Claire Wagner
Location: Lexington, VA, USA
Program: Private residence and writers' retreat
Status: Completed 2023
Photo credits: (45, 52–59) Naho Kubota, © Schaum/Shieh. (50, 51 top) Adam Rosen, © Schaum/Shieh. All other photos, © Schaum/Shieh.

60 Troy Schaum, *Site Visit (Houston, TX),* 2020. © Troy Schaum.

62 **Taipei Performing Arts Center**
Multi-stage performing arts center situated atop one of Taipei's busiest night markets. The sculptural volumes of the different theater types float in the horizontal mass of the shared canopy enclosure. Layers of public space rise from the street-level market to the lobby and finally to the occupiable green roof.
Client: Taipei City Government
Collaborators: Chris Leong
Location: Taipei, Taiwan
Program: Performing arts center
Status: Competition proposal, completed 2008
Urbox
A hotel built from a system of shipping containers. The containers have been adapted and combined into a series of structural elements sized to individual rooms and aggregated to accommodate larger gathering spaces.
Client: Private Developer
Collaborators: Tina Manis
Design team: Tsvetelina Zdraveva
Location: Dubai, UAE
Program: Resort hotel
Status: Unbuilt proposal, 2015
Troy Schaum, *Jai Prakash*, 2004. © Troy Schaum.

63 Carol Bove, *From the Sun to Zurich*, 2016, stainless steel and urethane paint, 93 ¾ × 199 ⅛ × 87 ⅛ in (238.1 × 505.8 × 221.3 cm). © Carol Bove Studio LLC. Photo: Dan Bradica
Rosalyne Shieh, *Untitled (Penghu)*, 2017. © Rosalyne Shieh.
Taichung City Cultural Center
Organized in five masses and five large voids, sectional differences create unique connective spaces between the library and museum, which come together in a unique hybrid program and cultural center for the city. Each void has a characteristic atmosphere that organizes the complex and supports various shared programs.
Client: Taichung City Government

Collaborators: Albert Pope
Design team: Ryan Botts, Eunike, Nathan Keibler, Anneli Rice, Ian Searcy, Tsvetelina Zdraveva
Location: Taichung, Taiwan
Program: Central library and art museum
Status: Competition proposal, completed 2013

Void

66 Catie Newell, *Untitled* (*Detroit, MI*), 2009. © Catie Newell.
Peter Smithson, in response to John Summerson, "The Case for a Theory of Modern Architecture," lecture at Royal Institute of British Architects, May 21, 1957.

68 Catie Newell, *Untitled* (*Detroit, MI*), 2009. © Catie Newell.
Fumihiko Maki, *Investigations in Collective Form* (School of Architecture, Washington University, 1964).

69 Rafael Moneo, "On Typology," *Oppositions* 13 (MIT Press, 1978): 38.

70–79 **Sponge Urbanism**
Conceived as a "minor" plan, Sponge Urbanism transforms the platted organization of Detroit into a multidirectional one that interrelates a lower density of building with an expanded field of land use. Extending the practices that residents already use to manage their transforming landscape and urban conditions, the plan is an open document that can be adapted in pieces by individual actors. Drawing techniques and diagrams combine to construct a view that, while impossible, makes visible the sponge-like order.
Client: Research
Location: Detroit, MI, USA
Program: Design research and speculative urbanism
Status: Completed 2010–17

80 John Hejduk, detail of *The Nine Square Problem: conceptual drawings with notes between 1963 and 1985.* John Hejduk fonds, Canadian Centre for Architecture. © CCA.
Grace Lee Boggs, "Seeds of Change," *Bill Moyers Journal* (June 17, 2007).

81 Ian Buchanan, "Binary," *Oxford Dictionary of Critical Thinking*, 2nd ed. (Oxford University Press, 2018).
Elaine Scarry, "Building and Breath: Beauty and the Pact of Aliveness," keynote lecture at Aesthetic Activism Conference, Yale University School of Architecture, New Haven, CT, October 13–15, 2016.

82 Aerial view of the neighborhood on the northeast side of Detroit, Michigan.
Henri Bergson, *Creative Evolution* (Macmillan, 1922): 298.

83–85 Rosalyne Shieh and Troy Schaum, "Sponge Urbanism," *Architecture is All Over*, Esther Choi and Marrikka Trotter, eds. (Columbia University Press, 2017): 136–148. (Essay revised 2024.)
David Runk, "Detroit Looks at Downsizing to Save City," *Washington Times* (March 9, 2010).
Albert Pope, "The Primacy of Space," *Ladders* (Princeton Architectural Press & Rice University School of Architecture, 1996): 1–13.

86–95 **13178 Moran Street**
This project is a prototype of Sponge Urbanism. Located in a single-family house on Detroit's northeast side, a sleeve form cuts diagonally from the roof to the opposite side of the first floor, adding two new faces to the building and a cross-orientation to the house. This stair/room is designed to be used as a theater or small auditorium, focusing both inside and outside audiences toward the screen, supporting small public programming and speculating on alternative uses for domestic housing stock.
Client: Funded research
Collaborators: 13178 Moran Street was a part of an installation by Five Fellows: Full Scale, in collaboration with Ellie Abrons, Adam Fure, Meredith Miller, Thom Moran, and Catie Newell
Design team: Sam Burner, Joe Proper, Pauline Shammami, Maria Sviridova
Location: Detroit, MI, USA
Program: Installation in an existing house
Status: Completed 2010

Photo credits: (87) Catie Newell, *Untitled*, 2010. © Catie Newell. All other photos, © Schaum/Shieh.
Support: University of Michigan Taubman College of Architecture & Urban Planning

96 Frank Gohlke, *Landscape (K-mart), St. Paul, Minnesota*, 1974. © Estate of Frank Gohlke.
Marco Torres/Houston Press, *Untitled*, 2016. © Marco Torres.
Benoît Rossel, "Interview with Eric Baudelaire," *BOMB* (Summer 2017): 46.

97 *New Topographics*, LACMA, 2009.

98 Rosalyne Shieh, *Untitled (Kaohsiung)*, 2018. © Rosalyne Shieh.
Robert Venturi, Denise Scott Brown, and Steven Izenour, *Learning from Las Vegas*.

100 Étienne-Jules Marey, *Du mouvement dans les fonctions de la vie, leçons faites au Collège de France* (Bibliothèque Nationale de France, 1968): 116, fig.18.
Troy Schaum, *White Oak Music Hall Amphitheater*, 2016. © Troy Schaum.

101 Wim Wenders, *Two Cars and a Woman Waiting*, 1983. © The Museum of Fine Arts, Houston, Gift of Nina and Michael Zilkha.
Louis I. Kahn, *Traffic Study Project*, 1952. © Louis I. Kahn Collection, The University of Pennsylvania and the Pennsylvania Historical and Museum Commission.

102 Wally Santana/Associated Press, "*Taiwan lawmakers brawl over trade agreement with China*," 2010. © Associated Press, all rights reserved.
Joe Deal, *Untitled View (Albuquerque)*, 1974. © The Estate of Joe Deal, courtesy Robert Mann Gallery.

103 Unknown, *Eiffel Tower, Top-Down View* (n.d.).
Wim Wenders, *Drive-In, Marfa, Texas*, 1983. © Wim Wenders, courtesy of Wenders Images.

Platform

106 Christian Unverzagt, *Untitled (13178 Moran Street)*, 2010. © Christian Unverzagt.

108 Peter Molick, *Raven Tower*, 2016. © Peter Molick.
Kian Goh, Anastasia Loukaitou-Sideris, and Vinit Mukhija, "Introduction," *Just Urban Design: The Struggle for a Public City* (MIT Press, 2022).

109 Jane Jacobs, *The Death and Life of Great American Cities* (Random House, 1961).

110–123 **White Oak Music Hall**
White Oak Music Hall is a cluster of music venues in Houston consisting of The White Oak Music Hall, The Lawn, and Raven Tower. The project is a seven-acre assemblage of new and adapted buildings, open-air structures, landscaped areas, and paved and decked surfaces along both sides of the Little White Oak Bayou. Pieced together from one large main site and a collection of smaller lots, the project is feathered into the neighborhood, making an open campus of loosely cohered urban infill.
Client: White Oak Music Hall
Collaborators: 5 Engineering, M-Corp Engineering, KCI Technologies, Jaffe Holden Acoustics, SRL International, Lighting Associate, Inc., Gin Design Group, Generations AV
Design team: Giorgio Angelini, Tucker Douglas, Ane González Lara, Nathan Keibler, Anika Schwarzwald, Ian Searcy, Anastasia Yee
Location: Houston, TX, USA
Program: Amphitheater and multi-stage music hall
Status: Completed 2017
Photo credits: (111–113, 118, 120–123) Peter Molick, © Schaum/Shieh. (121 bottom) © Julian Bajsel.

124 Troy Schaum, *Arare-Koboshi at Katsura Imperial Villa*, 2024. © Troy Schaum.

125–131 Conversation between Garnette Cadogan (in Cambridge, MA) and Rosalyne Shieh (in Kaohsiung, Taiwan) was recorded on July 17, 2024 over Zoom.

132–141 **Houston Endowment Headquarters**
This scheme for a community-based nonprofit has three sides facing the park and one oriented toward the city, situating the institution as an anchor for the neighborhood and developing a plan for the park that reflects community goals. At the ground level,

engagement spaces extend into the landscape; on its upper floors, terraces breathe in light and air through pockets of shade. An active atrium—built from paths of movement—is the heart of the project, creating transparency and visual connection, and supporting the interaction and gathering of visitors and staff.
Client: Houston Endowment
Collaborators: HKS, Andrea Cochran Landscape Architecture
Design team: Andrea Brennan, Zhiyi Chen, Ekin Erar
Location: Houston, TX, USA
Program: Institutional and cultural center
Status: Invited competition proposal, completed 2019
Video: Lost and Found Films: David Usui, Ben Wu
Renders: Motiv: Pawel Podwojewski

142 Joe Deal, *Corona del Mar*, 1978. © The Estate of Joe Deal, courtesy Robert Mann Gallery.

143 Michael Sorkin, ed., *Variations on a Theme Park: The New American City and the End of Public Space* (Noonday Press, 1992).
Teresa Caldeira, "Variations on a Theme Park," *Journal of Architectural Education* 48:1 (1994): 65–67.

144 Catie Newell, *Grounds for Detroit,* 2012. © Catie Newell.

145 Jane Jacobs, *The Death and Life of Great American Cities*.
Assata Shakur, *Assata: An Autobiography* (Lawrence Hill Press, 1987).

146 Troy Schaum, *Patrones y conductas by Elia Arce at Transart Gallery,* 2018. © Troy Schaum.
Oliver Wendell Holmes Jr. quoted in Jacobs, *The Death and Life of Great American Cities*: 2.

148 Arthur Leipzig, *Chalk Games*, 1950. © The Estate of Arthur Leipzig, courtesy of Howard Greenberg Gallery, New York.
Taichung City Cultural Center, see full credits page 325

149 Eleanor Antin, *Death of Petronius*, 2001. © Eleanor Antin.
In the Round, see full credits page 333
Island Transect (Taiwan Research), see full credits page 325

Sets

152 Ray Yoshida, *Unreasonable Lineage*, 1975. Felt-tip pen and crayon on paper, cut out and collaged on paper, 18 ½ × 24 inches. Collection of the Madison Museum of Contemporary Art. The Bill McClain Collection of Chicago Imagism. © Raymond K. Yoshida Living Trust, courtesy of Madison Museum of Contemporary Art, Wisconsin.

154 Robert Morris, Green Gallery Exhibition, New York, 1964–65, Installation View, *Untitled (Table)* 1964, *Untitled (Corner Beam)* 1964, *Untitled (Floor Beam)* 1964, *Untitled (Corner Piece)* 1964, *Untitled (Cloud)* 1962. Painted plywood. © 2024 The Estate of Robert Morris / Artists Rights Society (ARS), New York. Photo: © 2024 Estate of Rudy Burckhardt / Artists Rights Society (ARS), New York.
Leo Steinberg, *Other Criteria* (University of Chicago, 1972).

155 Steinberg, ibid.

156–171 **Transart Foundation for Art & Anthropology**
The Transart Foundation for Art & Anthropology is a multifaceted platform for an artist and independent curator. The building houses exhibitions and performances, and is a forum for community dialogues about the role of art in our lives. The project is designed around a 3,000sf gallery and library. The large gallery spaces are punctuated by a circulation core that integrates a library and a reading/writing room.
Client: Transart Foundation: Surpik Angelini
Collaborators: Zia Engineering, Lighting Associates, Inc., Welch Construction
Design team: Giorgio Angelini, Tucker Douglas, Ane González Lara, Nathan Keibler, Kevin Lin, Anika Schwarzwald, Ian Searcy, Anastasia Yee, Hazal Yücel, Yixin Zhou
Location: Houston, TX, USA
Program: Residence and private gallery
Status: Completed 2018

Photo credits: (157, 164–171) Naho Kubota, © Schaum/Shieh. All other photos, © Schaum/Shieh.

172 **Beyond the Totems**
Beyond the Totems is a response to a call to think about the relationship between the "sharing economy" and urban space in Manhattan. Our contribution sought to emphasize the physicality of what that exchange suggests.
Client: Storefront for Art and Architecture
Design team: Tucker Douglas, Ane González Lara, Ameilia Hazinski
Location: New York, NY, USA
Program: Exhibition, installation
Status: Completed 2016
Donald Judd, "Specific Objects," *Arts Yearbook* 8 (1965).

174–179 **About Face**
About Face is both an architectural object and a vessel for small gatherings. It is a sleeve cut through a domestic space, originally conceived for a house in Detroit, and transformed into a freestanding exhibition object in Venice, Italy. Twenty-one structurally integrated, fiber-reinforced resin panels make up the structure, which is both stair and room. About Face posits a strategy to reorient an existing house and transform the adjacent vacant lot.
Client: La Biennale di Venezia, 13th International Architecture Exhibition
Collaborators: About Face was part of *Grounds For Detroit,* an installation and exhibition curated and constructed jointly by: Alibi Studio (Catie Newell), EADO (Ellie Abrons), MILLIGRAM-office (James Graham, Meredith Miller), SIFT Studio (Adam Fure), and Thing Thing (Simon Anton, Eiji Jimbo, Thom Moran, Rachel Mulder)
Design team: Giorgio Angelini, Sharif Anous, Helena Kang, Landry Root, Jenny Tolfa
Location: Venice, Italy
Program: Invited exhibition, funded research
Status: Completed 2012
Support: University of Michigan Taubman College of Architecture & Urban Planning and the Rice School of Architecture
Photo credits: (175–176, 177 bottom, 178–179) © Catie Newell. All other photos, © Schaum/Shieh.

180 **Slider Towers (Taiwan Research)**, see full credits page 325

181–183 Troy Schaum, "Finite Sets," 2015 ACSA Fall Conference. (Essay revised 2024.)
Robert Smithson, "Entropy and the New Monuments," *Robert Smithson: Collected Writings*, Jack Flam, ed. (University of California Press, 1996): 11.
Donald Judd, "Specific Objects."
Donald Judd, Video Interview by Christopher Felver, Marfa, TX (June 1994).

184–193 **Blow up the wall!**
In Blow up the wall!, the concrete walls of the courtyard at MoMA PS1 become support, ground, and horizon. Large, inflated figures—this urban garden's "native creatures"—hang and sway gently on the wall's edge, making a striking outward image, while creating small spaces that line the courtyard. A running cipher of linear lights and bands of colored sand that mix over time come together in an interactive environment that changes throughout the summer.
Client: Museum of Modern Arts (MoMA) PS1 Young Architects Program
Collaborators: Silman Engineering, FTL Design Engineering Studio, Arup Acoustics and Audiovisual, LMNOP Landscape Design
Design team: Steven Collard, Tucker Douglas, Drew Heller, Ibrahim Salman, Xiangcheng Xing, Hazal Yucel, Minhui Zhou, Yixin Zhou
Video Players: Ilya Rakhlin, Lara Hansmann, Patricia Kunkel, Ilya Rakhlin, Huidi Xiang
Location: Long Island City, Queens, NY, USA
Program: Installation
Status: Invited competition, concept completed and exhibited 2017

194 **Blow up the wall!**, see full credits above
Robin Evans, "Translations from Drawing to Building," *AA Files* 12 (Summer 1986): 3–18.

195 Toni Morrison, "No Place for Self-Pity, No Room for Fear," *The Nation* (March 23, 2015).

196–201 **Monument Alley, MoB Workshop**
Made during a one-week workshop and charette with interior and set-design students at Virginia Commonwealth University, this temporary urban installation of fabric-clad

cardboard structures was designed to transform between facade and field and to be a disruptive response to nearby Monument Alley. The workshop was timed to coincide with a public festival along the symbolic artery.
Client: Richmond First Fridays Events
Collaborators: Many students and faculty of Middle of Broad, MoB Job Project
Location: Virginia Commonwealth University, Richmond, VA, USA
Program: Installation, workshop
Status: Completed 2013
Photo credits: © Troy Schaum.

202 **Pigeon Shed Urbanism (Taiwan Research)**, see full credits page 325
Transart Gallery, see full credits page 328

203 Gio Ponti, *Villa Namazee*, 1957–64, view of the internal courtyard. © Hamed Khosravi / Tehran Projects.
Taichung City Cultural Center, see full credits page 325

204 Peter DeCamp Haines, *Artifacts*, 1978–2023, photo by Stewart Clements. A collection of pieces by Peter DeCamp Haines exhibited in the Boston Sculptors Gallery exhibition *Archaic Echoes* in October 2023. © Peter DeCamp Haines.

205 **Shepherd School of Music Courtyards**
In this project, the two courtyards are taken as a pair of contrasting environments: one is outdoors and casual, the other is interior, flexible, and suitable for quiet entertainment and formal events. The interior courtyard is enclosed by a glass canopy that diffuses light during the day and opens up to the night sky.
Client: Shepherd School of Music, Rice University
Design team: Sean Kizy, Brian Lee, Jason Pierce, Alex Yuen
Location: Shepherd School of Music, Rice University, Houston, TX
Program: Concept design for covered event spaces
Status: Completed 2011
Agricultural Urbanism (Taiwan Research), see full credits page 325

Arrange

208 **Untitled (ArtPrize)**
This project plays off the rhythm of recessed exhibition windows at the former City Museum of Grand Rapids. A minimum palette of fluorescent lights, paint, and acoustic panels construct a virtual wedge and cast a haze of color in the room.
Client: ArtPrize
Design team: Brad de Vries
Location: Grand Rapids, MI, USA
Program: Invited exhibition
Status: Completed 2013

210 **Blanking**
An invited exhibition of Schaum/Shieh's work.
Client: University of New Mexico School of Architecture & Planning
Design team: Ane González Lara
Location: University of New Mexico Architecture Gallery, Albuquerque, NM, USA
Program: Invited exhibition
Status: Completed 2018
Tony Smith and Samuel J. Wagstaff Jr., "Talking with Tony Smith," *Artforum* (December 1966).

212–221 **The John Chamberlain Building Restoration**
The John Chamberlain Building at the Chinati Foundation in Marfa, TX, was a former wool and mohair warehouse that Donald Judd adapted in 1983 to house 23 large-scale John Chamberlain sculptures for public viewing. Our work consisted of restoring the structure, including Donald Judd's architectural interventions. The roof and skylights were completely replaced, trusses reinforced, stucco and plaster restored, and Judd's original designs for the building's pivot doors, fixed windows, adobe perimeter walls, and sotol garden were restored to their original intent. New ADA ramps and handrails made the building accessible while keeping the building's character.
Client: The Chinati Foundation
Collaborators: SGH Engineering, JC Stoddard Construction, Jim Martinez (landscape)
Design team: Giorgio Angelini, Andrea Brennan, Zhiyi Chen, Tucker Douglas
Location: Marfa, TX, USA

Program: Restoration, art museum
Status: Completed 2022
Photo credits: (213, 218, 220–221) Alex Marks, © The Chinati Foundation. (219) Alex Marks, © The Chinati Foundation / Estate of John Chamberlain / 2025 Fairweather & Fairweather LTD / Artists Rights Society (ARS), New York.

222 Troy Schaum, *Blanked Windows at the John Chamberlain Building*, 2021. © Troy Schaum.

223–225 Troy Schaum, "Adjusted: Surface, Structure, Opening," *Chinati Foundation Newsletter* 27 (October 2022).
Donald Judd, "Statement for the Chinati Foundation," *Donald Judd Writings*, Flavin Judd and Caitlin Murray, eds. (Judd Foundation & David Zwirner Books, 2016): 485.

226 Charles Gaines, *Regression: Group #3 (4/7)*, 1973–74. © Virginia Museum of Fine Arts, Richmond. Adolph D. and Wilkins C. Williams Fund, 2022.2.4.
Robert Smithson and Gregoire Müller, "... The Earth, Subject to Cataclysms, Is a Cruel Master," *Arts Magazine* (September 1971).

227 John Hejduk, *Victims: A Work* (AA Files, 1986).

228 Nigel Henderson, *Photograph showing construction site of flats designed by the Architect Denys Lasdun in the East End of London*, 1952. © Nigel Henderson Estate / Tate Museum.

229 Rosalyne Shieh, "Diving into the Wreck," *Paprika!* Yale School of Architecture (September 7, 2017).
"Diving into the Wreck" originally appeared in an issue of *Paprika!* with the theme "Foundations." Editors Anna Rose Canzano, Emily Hsee, Gray Golding, and Julia Medina sought pieces that have "as [their] project the proposition of radically new foundational texts/rules/etc. for architecture and architectural education."
Adrienne Rich, *Diving into the Wreck: Poems 1971–1972*.

230 Naho Kubota, *Transart Gallery*, 2018. © Naho Kubota.
Naho Kubota, *Transart Gallery*, 2018. © Naho Kubota.

231 Lewis Baltz, *South Corner, Riccar America Company, 3184 Pullman, Costa Mesa*, from the portfolio *The New Industrial Parks near Irvine, California*, 1974. Collection SFMOMA, Gift of Carol Campbell Wenaas. © Estate of Lewis Baltz.
Pinto Canyon Rock, 2013. © Schaum/Shieh.

232 Troy Schaum, *Marfa Landscape*, 2013. © Troy Schaum.

233–237 Conversation between Flavin Judd and Troy Schaum was recorded on September 18, 2024 in New York, NY.

238–249 **Judd Foundation Planning & Building Restoration**
Work with the Judd Foundation is ongoing to assist in cataloging, assessing, and planning to preserve the Foundation's historic buildings in Marfa, TX.
Client: Judd Foundation
Collaborators: SGH Engineering, KCI Engineering, CEG Engineering, GK Engineering, Jim Martinez, Transsolar, Silman, Image Permanence Institute, Higgins Quasebarth & Partners, Method Construction, High Desert Concepts, Sam & Belle, Alpha Masonry
Design team: Andrea Brennan, Zhiyi Chen, Tucker Douglas, Ekin Erar, Ane González Lara, Joseph Hsu, Anneli Rice, Ian Searcy, Tsvetelina Zdraveva
Location: Marfa, TX, USA
Program: Restoration, art museum, cultural center
Status: In progress
Photo credits: (244–245 left and center) Rowdy Dugan, © Judd Foundation. (247) Matthew Millman, © Judd Foundation, Donald Judd Art © Judd Foundation / Artists Rights Society (ARS), New York. (248) Jessica Lutz, © Judd Foundation. (249) Alex Marks, © Judd Foundation. All other photos, © Schaum/Shieh.

250 Rosalyne Shieh, *Untitled (Tainan countryside)*, 2019. © Rosalyne Shieh.
Craig Owens, *Craig Owens: Portrait of a Young Critic* (Badlands Unlimited, 2018): 19–20.

252–253 William S. Simmons, Chair, "Report of the Special Committee on Education and Ethnicity," University of California at Berkeley (March 28, 1989).

254 Nigel Henderson, *Construction work at the Hunstanton Secondary Modern School*, 1953. © Nigel Henderson Estate.
Ching Shieh, *Untitled (Fountain Valley, CA)*, 2018. © Ching Shieh.
Troy Schaum, *Jantar Mantar, Jaipur*, 2004. © Troy Schaum.

255 **Untitled (ArtPrize)**, see full credits page 208

Fine

258 Michele Abeles, *Arm, Plant, Bottles, Wood*, 2011. © Michele Abeles and 47 Canal, New York.

260 Cy Twombly, *Untitled*, 1970. © Cy Twombly Foundation.
Ruth Wilson Gilmore and Léopold Lambert, "Making Abolition Geography in California's Central Valley with Ruth Wilson Gilmore."

261 Leon Battista Alberti, *On Painting* (Yale University Press, 1956).
El Lissitzky, *About Two Squares* (Skify, 1922).

262 **In the Round**, see full credits page 333

263 *Tempietto Exemplum*, Yale School of Architecture, April 12–May 14, 2008.
"Tempietto Exemplum" and the facing-page drawing were prepared for an exhibition curated by Spencer Fried and Amanda Iglesias.

264–271 **Houston Adaptations**
Circle & Square
This small, freestanding retail space was designed to punctuate a mall on a busy corner in northwest Houston. The structure is a basic extrusion with alternating facades of stucco and masonry. Storefront with steel plate canopies slice into the two primary facades at acute angles. The large circle and square openings frame the streetscape beyond.
Client: Re:Vive Development
Collaborators: LH2 Architecture (Architect of Record), Santee Engineering, Power Industry, CobbFendley
Design team: Andrea Brennan, Ekin Erar
Location: Houston, TX, USA
Program: Commercial
Status: Completed 2020
Photo credits: (265, 267) Andrea Brennan, © Schaum/Shieh.
20th Street Market
This project transforms a small 1950s strip mall in Houston's Heights neighborhood. The former washateria was remodeled with new columns, planters, and facade materials to update the existing, delicately modern colonnade. This remodel acts as one piece of a larger set of infill projects for this client across the city, testing formal responses to the exurban fabric.
Client: Radom Capital
Collaborators: Zia Engineering, Boxx Group
Design team: Tucker Douglas, Ane González Lara
Location: Houston, TX, USA
Program: Commercial retail restaurant
Status: Completed 2016
Photo credits: (268–269) Peter Molick, © Schaum/Shieh.
Lowell Street Box
Lowell Street Box is an adaptive reuse of existing warehouse buildings. Pitched-roof buildings were renovated, re-skinned, and connected by a new 3,000sf building clad in corten steel.
Client: Radom Capital
Collaborators: Zia Structural Engineering, Boxx Group, LAI Lighting
Design team: Andrea Brennan, Tucker Douglas, Hazal Yücel
Location: Houston, TX, USA
Program: Commercial
Status: Completed 2018
Photo credits: (270–271) Peter Molick, © Schaum/Shieh.

272 Troy Schaum, *Exposed Ceiling,* 2024. © Troy Schaum.

273 *Ninagawa Macbeth*, William Shakespeare, translated by Yushi Odashima, directed by Yukio Ninagawa, Lincoln Center, New York, NY (July 18–25, 2018).

274 Édouard Manet, *A Bar at the Folies-Bergère*, 1882. The Courtauld, London (Samuel Courtauld Trust). Photo © The Courtauld / Bridgeman Images.

275–280 Rosalyne Shieh, "It's fine.," *Log* 41 (2017): 161–168.
Audre Lorde, "Poetry is not a luxury," *Sister Outsider* (Crossing Press, 2007): 36–39.
Luce Irigaray, "Wonder: A Reading of Descartes. The Passions of the Soul," *An Ethics of Sexual Difference* (Cornell University Press, 1993).
Nikolaus Pevsner, *An Outline of European Architecture* (Scribner, 1948): 19.

279 Rosalyne Shieh, *Untitled (Penghu)*, 2017. © Rosalyne Shieh.

281 Thomas Demand, *Embassy VII.a*, 2007. © Thomas Demand, VG Bild-Kunst, Bonn, courtesy of the artist and Matthew Marks Gallery; Sprüth Magers; Esther Schipper, Berlin/Paris/Seoul; Taka Ishii Gallery.

282 Rosalyne Shieh, *Untitled (Penghu)*, 2017. © Rosalyne Shieh.
Michel Foucault, *The Order of Things* (Vintage Books, 1994): xix.

283 Rick Prelinger, "Assembly over Algorithm: Resisting Overnarrativization," *World Records Journal* 5 (2021): Article 4.

284 **Park Slope Apartment**
Renovation of a two-bed, two-bath apartment in Park Slope.
Client: Private
Design team: Ane González Lara, Tsvetelina Zdraveva
Location: Brooklyn, NY, USA
Program: Residential remodel
Status: Completed 2016
Photo credit: © Rosalyne Shieh

286–293 **Quitman Townhomes**
Built for a small development company, this project works within the increasingly prevalent townhouse typology. This four-unit set produces mid-market housing along the extended light-rail system. Each unit is a simple variant of the initial type.
Client: Revolution Homes
Collaborators: LSC Engineering, Revolution Homes Construction
Design team: Tucker Douglas
Location: Houston, TX, USA
Program: Residential
Status: Completed 2016
Photo credits: (287, 290–293) Peter Molick, © Schaum/Shieh. (289) © Leonid Furmansky.

294–301 Conversation between Stan Allen and Rosalyne Shieh was recorded on September 27, 2024 in New York, NY.

302–309 **In the Round**
In the Round is a large-scale urban installation constructed from perforated fabric stretched and twisted between two ornate profiles and suspended over a major intersection in downtown Houston. The overall form is a rippled cuff with contrasting interior and exterior surfaces. Viewers on the ground level are presented with In the Round's inner facade, while viewers on the elevated walkway engage with its exterior facade.
Client: Midway Development
Collaborators: Zia Engineering
Design team: Zhiyi Chen, Tucker Douglas, Ekin Erar
Location: Houston, TX, USA
Program: Public infrastructure
Status: Concept design 2016

310 Richard Artschwager, *Chair*, 1966. © The Estate of Richard Artschwager, courtesy of David Nolan Gallery.

311 Rosalyne Shieh, *Untitled (Tainan)*, 2019. © Rosalyne Shieh.
Treehill House
Single-family home and guesthouse on a sloping meadow. The house is organized in two bent bars that define an open courtyard at each end, framing adjacent views of a forest and pond.

Client: Jonathan & Carrie Brinsden
Design team: Andrea Brennan, Zhiyi Chen, Sheila Mednick, Claire Wagner
Location: Hempstead, TX, USA
Program: Residential
Status: Completed 2020

Wonder

312–318 Sara Ahmed, "Orientations: Toward a Queer Phenomenology," *GLQ: A Journal of Lesbian and Gay Studies* 12:4 (2006): 543–574.
Anne Fagot-Largeault, *Les causes de la mort* (Librairie Philosophique Vrin, 2002).
Sarah Fay, "Javier Marías, The Art of Fiction No. 190," *The Paris Review* 179 (2006).
David Marchese, "Brian Eno Reveals the Hidden Purpose of All Art," *New York Times* (November 13, 2022).

314 **Iceberg & the Forest**
Conceived for a yearly event organized by the Van Alen and Flatiron Partnership, the Iceberg & the Forest provides a moment for pause in the otherwise relentless rhythm of the season. A landscape made from a volume of laminated plywood and the trees carved out of it, the Iceberg & the Forest leverages the 25-degree angle of the Flatiron Building to construct an orbit between a singular luminous object and a field of trees.
Client: Van Alen Institute
Design team: Andrea Brennan, Tucker Douglas, Hazal Yücel, Yixin Zhou
Location: New York, NY, USA
Program: Public installation
Status: Competition proposal, completed 2017

316 **Taichung City Cultural Center**, see full credits page 325

319 *Transart Gallery*, 2017. © Schaum/Shieh.

knowledgments

Any building contains within its history a multitude of unseen authors, unheard conversations and counsel, paths diverted or not taken. This factor only becomes multiplied across an architectural practice. That is to say, the contents of this book have been made possible by the many people who have worked alongside, supported, stimulated, and propelled us over these last 15 years. We have included many of them within the story of each project team, but we wanted to highlight some here, as well. Our practice's initial shape was informed by early collaborators who became long-term friends: Ellie Abrons, Adam Fure, James Graham, Jaffer Kolb, Meredith Miller, Thom Moran, Catie Newell, and Albert Pope. Over the years, key members have sustained the Schaum/Shieh studio with their skill and creativity: Giorgio Angelini, Andrea Brennan, Tucker Douglas, Ane González Lara, Anika Schwarzwald, and Ian Searcy. The projects in this book would not have been possible without clients who understand that architecture is as much about discovery as delivery: Jonathan & Carrie Brinsden, Bryan Danna, Anna Deans, Will Garwood, Richard Griggs, Jagi Katial, Melissa McDonnell Luján, Jenny Moore, Judy Nyquist, Steve Radom, Johnny So, Peter Stanley, Will Thomas; we are also grateful to collaborators who continue to defy categorization and work with us in many spheres: Michele Abeles, Surpik Angelini, Carol Bove, William Dull, James Faubion, Flavin Judd, and Rainer Judd. We have shared space with architects and artists who fortified us with their creativity and companionship: David Obuchowski, Mike Szivos, David Usui, and Ben Wu. Thank you to Guy Nordenson for introducing us to another side of Marfa. Naho Kubota, Peter Molick, Jack Murphy, Maria Nicanor, Danielle Rago, and Honora Shea have helped our work meet the world. Sunil Bald, Stephen Cassell, Paul Lewis, and Ana Miljački have, with generosity and warmth, shared their intelligence and guidance in navigating this hybrid pursuit of building and teaching. We are grateful for the support provided by our institutional homes—MIT School of Architecture & Planning, Rice School of Architecture, and University of Michigan Taubman College of Architecture & Urban Planning—with particular acknowledgment to their respective fellowship programs that support the development of architects as teachers and researchers. Thank you to the early supporters of our design research in Taiwan, for taking a chance and making no demands: Sandy & Dr. Chris Yen and Bob Cheng. We sincerely appreciate Julie Cirelli, Renata Graw, Pouya Khadem, Sophie Kullmann, Emily Nemens, and Lucas Reif, who made this book a reality.

Troy Schaum
Among many mentors, I'm particularly grateful to Jim Jennings, an architect who taught me too much to account for here. Sarah Whiting has pushed me to search a little farther through each exchange over many years. My talented coworkers across many early stops in my career were a gift, especially Paul Burgin, David Campos, Ross Hummel, Michael Lin, Jason Long, Ziad Shehab, Shohei Shigematsu, and David Thompson. Friends who shaped my creative formation were Brian Bello, Adam Frampton, Emily Hodgdon, Lizzie Hodges, James Lowder, MaryAnn Medina, Seth Orgain, Clay Petsche, Hunter Pittman, Aaron Ragan, Brian Tabolt, and especially Caroline O'Donnell. At Rice, I've been fortunate to teach alongside Amna Ansari, Georgina Baronian, Shantel Blakely, Tei Carpenter, John Casbarian, Michelle Chang, Scott Colman, Farès El-Dahdah, Dawn Finley, Eva Franch i Gilabert, Reto Geiser, Carlos Jiménez, Lars Lerup, Ajay Manthripragada, Igor Marjanović, Albert Pope, Sam Stewart-Halevy, Maggie Tsang, Brittany Utting, Jesús Vassallo, and Ron Witte. My family, Bob, Kitty, Julie, and Mercedes, always kept me moving. My gratitude is without limits to Gökçe Günel, who never seems to lose her cool.

Rosalyne Shieh
For thinking and growing with me in the space where life meets work, thank you Ellie Abrons, Erika Anderson, Sunil Bald, Christi Byrd, Garnette Cadogan, Stephen Cassell, Oscar Cuevas, Elizabeth Frey, francine j. harris, Luce Lincoln, Jimmy Lowder, Meredith Miller, Romi Morrison, Hira Nabi, Catie Newell, and Jimmy Robert. For conversations about architecture, with affinity, thank you to my Bartlett cohort: Tahl Kaminer, Sotos Varsamis, and Cordula Zeidler. For making Houston home, thank you Kathrin Brunner, Albert Pope, and Amanda Pope. For modeling pedagogy as invitation, thank you Stan Allen, Liz Grosz, and Kathleen James-Chakraborty. For your buoyancy and shine, thank you Jaffer Kolb and Ryan Moritz. For friendship in youth and beyond, thank you Annie Choi, Daniel Reginald Kim, Marc McQuade, and Cricket Raspet. For showing me how a place remembers (even when I do not), thank you Iàn--a a-ko͘ (謝金燕), Êng-hn̂g--a a-ko͘ (黃銀園), Bi-iông (戴美容), Hok-seng--a a-chek (陳福生), Ki-lîn--a a-chek (陳麒麟), Huan-chi Tseng (曾煥基), Kailin Hou (侯凱琳), Ông Lāu-su (王昭華), HsiChen Liu (劉希真), Âng Ek Sim, and Cheng-Luen Hsueh. I am grateful to Macdowell and to the Fulbright Program for the gift of time and creative community. And for everything, my love and appreciation go to Ching Shieh, Connie Shieh, Perry Shieh, and little Sula Rage.

Colophon

Title:
Blanking

Subtitle:
An Annotated Archive
of Projects and Thoughts
on Architecture

Authors:
Troy Schaum
Rosalyne Shieh

Editor:
Emily Nemens

Associate Editor:
Pouya Khadem

Editorial Assistants:
Anna Davenport
Joseph Hsu
Vinati Kokal

Proofreader:
Aimee Selby

Graphic Design:
Normal (Renata Graw
and Lucas Reif)
with the support of
Kim Upstill, Austin
Watson, and Paul Zdon

Image processing, printing,
and binding:
DZA Druckerei zu Altenburg
GmbH, Germany

Published with support from:
MIT School of Architecture
& Planning, Rice University,
Creative Ventures Fund

Published by Park Books AG
Niederdorfstrasse 54
8001 Zurich
Switzerland
www.park-books.com
T +41 44 262 16 62
E info@park-books.com

Product Safety
Responsible person according to EU
regulation 2023/988 (GPSR):
GVA Gemeinsame Verlagsauslieferung
Göttingen GmbH & Co. KG
P.O. Box 2021
37010 Göttingen, Germany
T +49 551 384 200 0
E info@gva-verlage.de

Park Books is being supported
by the Federal Office of
Culture with a general subsidy
for the years 2026–2028.

ISBN 978-3-03860-400-6

On the cover: Transart, see full credits
page 328. All photos © Schaum/Shieh.